THE
GOOD FIGHT

Other Books by Ralph Nader

In Pursuit of Justice

Crashing the Party: Taking on the Corporate Government in an Age of Surrender

No Contest: Corporate Lawyers and the Perversion of Justice in America (with Wesley J. Smith)

Unsafe at Any Speed

THE
GOOD FIGHT

DECLARE YOUR INDEPENDENCE &
CLOSE THE DEMOCRACY GAP

RALPH NADER

1❂ ReganBooks
Celebrating Ten Bestselling Years
An Imprint of HarperCollins*Publishers*

HarperCollins books may be purchased for educational, business, or sales promotional use. For information please write: Special Markets Department, HarperCollins Publishers Inc., 10 East 53rd Street, New York, NY 10022.

FIRST EDITION

Designer: Publications Development Company of Texas

Printed on acid-free paper

Library of Congress Cataloging-in-Publication Data

ISBN 0-06-075604-7

04 05 06 PDC/RRD 10 9 8 7 6 5 4 3 2 1

To the American people, who deserve better

ACKNOWLEDGMENTS

Thanks are due to the reporters, editors, and producers of the mass media who report so many abuses of corporate and institutional power that they neglect to make aggregating connections and then proceed to overlook those who try to do so. Recognition is also due the Independent media people who do not overlook patterns, connections, and citizen activity directed to change conditions for the better. I take all these reports seriously and thank them for their finest moments that render this book an understatement.

Further acknowledgments are extended to my agent Jay Acton, my editor, the so-steady Bridie Clark, and to Marcia Carroll, Alan Hirsch, Peter Maybarduk, Tarek Milleron, Claire Nader, Laura Nader, John Richard, Robert Weissman, Terri Weissman, and Elizabeth Wood. They know their contributions to this work and my gratitude for their efforts.

This book is not about my current political campaign. It is a book about the prevalence of abuses of concentrated power in our country that transcend any election cycle.

CONTENTS

INTRODUCTION

"**F**reedom is participation in power," said the Roman orator Cicero. By this deep definition, freedom is in short supply for tens of millions of Americans, a scarcity with serious consequences. This absence of freedom breeds apathy. Average citizens do not fight for change, even about the conditions and causes that mean the most to them. Our lack of civic motivation is the greatest problem facing the country today.

Our beloved country is being taken apart by large multinational commercial powers. Over two thousand years ago, in ancient Athens, a fledgling democracy challenged the longstanding plutocracy, using politics as its instrument. The struggle between these two forms of government—one tending to place more power with the people and the other concentrating power in a few self-perpetuating hands—has been going on ever since under various guises and disguises. Democracy, whether representative or more direct, brings out the best in people because it gives them more freedom, more voice, more lawful order, and more opportunity to advance their visions of a just society.

In our country, however, there is a gap that needs to be closed—the democracy gap. It is often said that "power abhors a vacuum." When people do not claim power, the greedy step in to fill the void. Every day that capable citizens abstain from civic engagement allows our society and world to tolerate harm and to decay incrementally. The converse is also true. The tiny, cumulative efforts to build a more just society are comparable to the sources for a great river. The Mississippi River starts with a few raindrops in northern Minnesota. These raindrops merge into rivulets and then into brooks and then into streams and rivers that all swell into America's priceless and mighty river. Similarly, our efforts—small and large, daily and cumulative—spread the more noble sentiments of our humanity toward one another. But it isn't happening nearly enough to stem the downward slide of justice in our society.

Historic struggles for justice inform today's efforts to address contemporary injustices, and counter today's assault on fairness, decency, health, safety, and economic well-being. The media has been properly criticized for its massive tilt toward commercialism and entertainment, for reportorial staff cutbacks, remarkable redundancy, and neglect of citizen activities. Nonetheless, even with these and many other deficiencies of the ever-concentrated fourth estate, people are presented with more information about problems in their communities and nation than ever before. The vast amount of information available via the Internet complements and expands on reporting by the media. These should be additional motivating factors—but still, despite the increased flow of information about the problems facing our society, citizens are not organizing to take corrective action. Why?

Of course, many individuals and groups do strive to improve society, but they cannot accomplish the dramatic progress of earlier activists because of the overall state of American politics. The occasional civic victory is nearly always defensive—preserving past gains or defeating bad amendments and nominations. If "Truth in Advertising" laws were applied to the Washington agencies, departments, and many congressional offices, the doors to these institutions would be adorned with "for sale" signs. Doors once open to civic community and nonprofit organizations pledged to press the needs of the people are now barricaded.

There are dozens of reasons for the lockouts, including: the Niagara of campaign cash flowing into both parties from the same business interests; the routine bipartisan appointment of corporate emissaries to high government posts (as with Federal Reserve Chairman Alan Greenspan and heads of the Departments of Treasury, Defense, and so on); the declining influence of trade unions; the expanding influence of global corporations able to take jobs abroad; the relentless hyper-organization of trade association lobbies and corporate law firms; the convergence of the two major parties on corporate power, contracts, subsidies, and reduced regulatory law and order; and the widening corporatization of media, religious institutions, and many universities.

As Republican author and corporate governance leader Robert Monks puts it, "The United States is a Corporatist State. This means that individuals are largely excluded both in the political and corporate spheres." Indeed, the subjugation of civic values to commercial values represents one of the worst crises of our times.

Our country and its principles are abandoned by the very economic powers that control our destiny. Autocratic global corporations are deep into strategic planning. They openly and confidently strive to control our jobs; our environment; our political and educational institutions; our food, drugs, and other consumptions; our savings; our childhoods; our culture; even our genetic futures. Toward these ends, they incessantly move to control our elections and our governmental institutions. They lobby to limit our access to the courts and regulatory agencies, and block methods of law enforcement and exposure that would hold them modestly accountable for their more egregious wrongdoings. Is it not time for real people to plan for their own futures together?

The balance struck between democracy and plutocracy, between fair and unfair tax and budget priorities, between investor rights and corporate managers, between "a government of the people, by the people and for the people," in Lincoln's immortal words, and a government of the Exxons, by the General Motors; and for the DuPonts, determines the quality of our society. It is not coincidental that many centuries ago all the world's great religions cautioned their adherents not to give too much power and position to mercantile interests. So too, our greatest presidents issued warning after warning about "moneyed interests." Franklin Delano Roosevelt emphasized this in a message to Congress, "The liberty of a democracy is not safe if the people tolerate the growth of private power to a point where it becomes stronger than the democratic state itself. That in its essence is fascism: ownership of the government by an individual, by a group or any controlling private power." We would do well to heed this age-old wisdom as we ponder why our corporate and political leaders assume more and more control over our lives and futures.

This loss of control is felt ever more deeply. A *Business Week* poll in the year 2000 found 72 percent of the people believing that corporations had too much control over their lives. This was before exposure of the ongoing corporate crime wave that has looted or drained trillions of dollars from hardworking people. Society, like a fish, rots from the head down. Our leaders have been delivering for themselves and their circles, not for the people they allegedly serve. In return, too many people have been too trusting of, or resigned to, their leaders' mass media rhetoric. Our static political system often leads our elected officials to do the opposite of what they say. Double talk.

With limited choices, people find it difficult to demand more from their leaders, or to have effective modes of measuring their performance beyond the blizzard of soothing words directed at them. This feeling of powerlessness, however, can be diminished. Powerless people often aggravate their situation by giving up on themselves. They don't believe they're really capable of doing anything about the injustices affecting their families, their neighborhoods, and their communities. This makes them all the more susceptible to manipulation and flattery by unscrupulous power-brokers and their political proxies. This vulnerability results from the absence of an absorbed information base to provide a shield against artful propaganda and deception.

In one context or another, we are all powerless. The society is simply too complex. Contemplating participation in power in most contexts—environmental, political, social, economic, technological—invites anxiety. Yet, to throw up one's hands in defeat guarantees anguish and deprivation. Individual obligations absorb daily time and attention, of course, but ignoring our civic obligations, our public citizen duties, profoundly affects our daily lives as well. Most people have developed their own rationalization for not entering civil society as an engaged citizen, such as lack of time or know-how, or concern about slander or retaliation.

Growing up in a small New England town, with a pristine "town meeting" form of government, I witnessed the contrast between the few active residents and the many on the sidelines. My parents would bring me and my siblings to the often boisterous town meetings to see democracy in action. Town meetings were the town legislature. Some in the community did their homework and took their concerns to the local selectmen. They stood up and proposed, argued, questioned. They refused to take no for an answer. Others in the audience (and those who stayed home) seemed ambivalent. On the one hand, they were rooting for their stand-tall neighbors; on the other hand, they felt a little embarrassed to witness the pounding taken by the town officials.

The town activists, not the passive spectators, were the ones considered the mavericks. I recall once, the day after a town meeting, a couple of residents on Main Street pointed to one of the regular activists and said, "there goes old Mr. Franz." It was almost as if our community had the town citizen, the town drunk, and the town fool as unusual spectacles. But again and again, I observed the active citizens keeping our collective rights muscular by using them. More often than not, they improved conditions or thwarted misguided moves by town selectmen or the local business titans. And yet there were too few active citizens; many of them became discouraged and sometimes dropped out. A lack of a critical mass of involved citizens on any issue, whatever the scale, contributes to the "see, you can't get anything done," "what's the use," "que sera, sera" syndrome which feeds on its own futility.

So, then, what builds civic motivation? A sense of the heroic progress against great odds achieved by our forebears helps. Think what stamina and inner strength drove abolitionists against slavery, women seeking the right to vote, workers demanding trade unions to counter the callous bosses of industry, dirt-poor farmers of the late 1800s who, taking on the major railroads and banks, used their heads, hearts, and feet to launch the populist-progressive reform movement. These efforts advanced our country immeasurably. They were efforts by ordinary people doing extraordinary things without electricity, motor vehicles, telephones, faxes, or e-mail. They mobilized person-to-person. That history certainly motivated and excited me as a youngster.

There are other prospective sources to stimulate civic get-up-and-go. One such source could be called the "empty-stomach" feeling. Imagine how you'll feel years from now when your nine-year-old granddaughter or grandson looks at you with that searching eye and asks what were you doing when some environmental or social travesty was happening and could have been stopped. How will it feel to admit that you were busy watching television sitcoms?

And civic motivation can start with our personal experience, from which we derive the public philosophies that nourish and animate our consciences. It can start with family upbringing, or a jolting event.

My civic motivation resulted from a combination of observation and experience. The loss of classmates in highway crashes and the sight of bloody collisions and dying agony were seared in my memory. As a student, I hitchhiked thousands of miles. A number of times the driver and I were among the first arrivals at the scene of a highway mishap. That sparked my civic motivation. When I learned about the many simple ways the auto companies could have built vehicles to protect motorists from serious injuries, but chose not to, I knew what I had to do: Go after the giant auto manufacturers, led by GM with its technologically stagnant and unsafe cars.

By writing, testifying, mobilizing, and networking on Capitol Hill in the 1960s, I helped pass two laws that established a federal role in highway and motor vehicle safety. Even with irregular implementation of these laws, more than a million lives have been saved, millions of injuries prevented or reduced in severity, and tens of billions of dollars not wasted. I and many others exhibited the optimism of those years by advancing numerous other protections and remedies for people as consumers, workers, and inhabitants of toxic environments. We found members of Congress and key committee chairs in both the House and Senate who went to Washington to represent *people,* not corporations. They held inquiring public hearings on consumer injury and fraud, air and water pollution, workplace and household hazards, and secrecy in the government. Legislation followed investigation and debate, leading to safety and health standards at the workplace, shopping areas, and playgrounds. Lyndon Johnson, Richard Nixon, and Jimmy Carter signed these laws, and made uplifting statements about these legislative victories.

Those were years when the streets were alive with demonstrations and rallies. More than a few of the young were alert to the possibilities for making change, and not merely on campus. They taught one another about the many harmful and censorious conditions that their courses ignored. They aroused their elders on wars, civil rights, poverty, the environment, and stifling bureaucracies. Those were the years when so many of the national and local citizen organizations were founded or enlarged—groups that no longer can do what they once did to better America.

What the citizenry should expect of their governments depends in no small part on how much people know about their governments—their duties, their commitments, and who has unworthy or craven influence over them. The late Tony Mazzocchi, founder of the Labor Party, who traveled the country even when he was well into his seventies and who spoke with countless blue-collar workers about a worker's agenda, once bewailed: "Why do so many workers vote for politicians who turn around and vote against workers?" Well, there is no substitute for voters doing their homework, studying records, and seeing through the dense mists of fabricated political advertisements, shams, and evasions. Without such civic engagement, and without candidates for office who faithfully represent their constituents, our broken politics cannot be repaired.

Whether we think in terms of justice under law or equal protection of the laws, it is untenable that artificial entities called corporations are given most of the constitutional rights of real humans while aggregating powers, privileges, and immunities that individuals, no matter how wealthy, could never come close to attaining. The primacy of civic values, rooted in our Declaration of Independence and the Constitution, must become our common objective for the common good. When state governments started chartering corporations in the early 1800s, these relatively small business entities were not supposed to be our masters. No one contemplated the emergence of gigantic global conglomerates using governments and trade agreements for their narrow ends. Corporations were seen as our servants under the vigilant rule of law. That's a vision we need to re-create. The people must stand tall so as to reclaim their sovereignty over big business.

Strengthening the blessings of liberty and the benefits of justice invites us all to these challenges, both inside the electoral arenas and outside in the civic action arenas. What follows is an exploration of what independent thinking, rising expectations, a spreading community spirit, and renewed citizen action can do for us and posterity.

FAILURE OF ISMS AND THOSE LEFT BEHIND

My father had a pithy way to make a potent point. He described the two basic economic systems as follows: "Socialism is government ownership of the means of production, while capitalism is the business ownership of the means of government."

A small business restaurateur, he felt an aversion to concentrated power—whatever its garb. To him, limitless greed for wealth and power was the downfall of any system. He would often say that "capitalism is the freest economic way if only we can control it."

Controlling what is now corporate capitalism in all its varieties and contradictions is the task of organized civic values, law and order, quality competition, shareholder power over executives, consumer information, judicial remedies, and environmentally benign technologies. These checks, along with self-restraint by businesses (out of what used to be called "enlightened self-interest"), are needed to keep capitalism in its proper place so that a democratic culture can flourish toward the greater purposes of life for present and future generations. We have an ongoing debt to the Earth far grander and more expansive than any myopic corporate calculus. For the necessary independence that furthers civic values—democratic processes, civic voice, health, safety, a decent standard of living, peace, and yes, truth and beauty—we need to start with the Earth, its peoples, its flora, and its fauna.

By most measures, the Earth is not doing well. It is stalked too much by war and anarchy, by the exercise of concentrated, corrupt powers, poverty, disease, illiteracy, and environmental devastation. Dictators and domestic family violence, state and stateless terrorism further afflict the anxious mosaic of ordinary life. Giant corporations roam the Earth, pitting societies against one another in search of the lowest costs from serf labor and other exactions from authoritarian regimes while pulling down standards of living in more democratic countries. This downward drift is accelerated by transnational, autocratic systems of commercial governance known as the World Trade Organization (WTO), the North American Free Trade Agreement (NAFTA), and the African Growth and Opportunity Act (AGOA).

Three billion people try to survive on one or two dollars a day, hardly enough to deal with hunger pangs and chronic debilitation from bacteria, viruses, and toxins found in their putrid water, their air, food, and soil. With the failures of state-imposed communism and bureaucratic socialism, the large multinational corporation, supported by the International Monetary Fund (IMF) and the World Bank, becomes the remaining visible vehicle of economic growth and development.

One gauge of the global corporate model is whether it is diminishing, ignoring, or increasing the severity of the most obvious problems in the world.

Environment?

Fossil fuel and nuclear industries, petrochemical and mining companies, forest-cutting and pesticide firms, dragnet ocean fishing corporations, biotechnology (and soon nanotechnology companies whose speed of deployment is far ahead of their science) fail to behave as good stewards of the Earth.

Tyranny?

The global corporation has no problem dealing with dictators, in return for lucrative contracts, concessions over raw materials, and free reign to exploit people (in exchange for customary kickbacks).

Lethal Arms Trafficking?

These modern "merchants of mayhem" privately export deadly weapons to odious regimes with our taxpayer subsidies totaling billions of dollars a year. These sales fuel an arms race that increases the demand for more arms sales, corrupting more officials, starving nonmilitary budgets, and spreading poverty.

Disease?

That is what the tobacco industry and its addictive product create: the spread of cancer, heart, and respiratory sickness. Big tobacco finds new ways to addict its victims earlier and faster with seductive promotions and advertisements directed to tens of millions of youngsters in South America, Africa, and Asia. One out of four of these young people will die prematurely from tobacco-related disease. Inhumane indifference also characterizes the attitude of the heavily tax and research-subsidized pharmaceutical industry, which is so focused on profits that it barely spends research dollars on infectious diseases like malaria or tuberculosis. Drug company executives know that vaccines rarely produce big profits. Just big life savings. Drug companies prefer to sell drugs that are taken daily, or the lifestyle drugs that purport to reduce obesity or enhance potency.

Hunger?

The giant grain exporters like Cargill are expert at reducing spoilage from rodents, fungi, and pests that take a huge toll in third-world granaries. Yet, the Cargills rarely lend a hand there. Processed food giants promote products plump with sugar and fat and erode more nutritious indigenous diets in developing countries. Deceptively promoted soft drinks replace natural fruit drinks. Studies are already showing the harmful effects of diets that turn tongues against brains through seductive associations with modernity in flashy advertisements. Mother's milk is a threat to infant formula sales, so modernity ads instill fear and anxiety in maternal circles. Mothers respond. Infant formula then sells, costs poor families too much, is diluted for more volume with contaminated village water, and infant fatality rates surge. UNICEF in 1991 estimated 1.5 million deaths a year from this sequence and still the western infant formula giants continue to take their profits to the bank.

Capital and Credit?

Less-developed countries are full of potential entrepreneurs who lack credit to start local businesses. Multinational banks and other finance companies turn a deaf ear to them. They prefer to finance giant projects, like dams and pipelines, with suitable government guarantees or subsidized loans from the Export-Import Bank. The appropriate technologies for community needs, so well described by E. F. Schumacher in his pioneering book *Small Is Beautiful,* published in 1973, are not bankable in the West. Small credit needs for production and distribution are off the radar screen for the likes of Citigroup. Such banks prefer to start a credit card economy in a country like China to stretch the debt of the upper scale consumers and collect high interest rates. But the big loan money goes to third-world governments, as in

Africa and South America, where the spiral of refinancing, accumulated interest, and over-extension of credit worsens instability and drains public domestic investment.

Absent robust democracy in these countries, the creative destruction by these corporations is usually a one-way street, contrary to Joseph Schumpeter's thesis that such displacement is a mode of progress for developed nations. Recently, the *Multinational Monitor* magazine, which I founded years ago, devoted an issue to "Grotesque Inequalities—Corporate Globalization and the Global Gap Between Rich and Poor." Editor Robert Weissman's introductory words resonate:

> There is something profoundly wrong with a world in which the 400 highest income earners in the United States make as much money in a year as the entire population of 20 African nations—more than 300 million people.
>
> Global inequalities persist at staggering levels. The richest 10 percent of the world's population is roughly 117 times higher than the poorest 10 percent. . . . This is a huge jump from the ratio in 1980 when the income of the richest 10 percent was about 79 times higher than the poorest 10 percent.
>
> Exclude fast-growing China from the equation, and the disparities are even more shocking. The income ratio from the richest 10 percent to the poorest 10 percent rose from 90 : 1 in 1980 to 154 : 1 in 1999.

Corporate globalization was not supposed to exacerbate the gross inequalities that already exist in dictatorial and oligarchic countries. But why should we be surprised? Without democratic restraints and the rule of law, without the freedom for countervailing forces to flourish (such as free elections, agrarian cooperatives, land reform, and trade unions), global companies tend to reinforce authoritarian structures and trample the creative yearnings of civil society.

Weissman highlights the human tragedies behind the statistics of inequalities:

- A mother in one of the bottom ten countries on Save the Children's "Mother's Index" faces a 600 times higher risk of dying in pregnancy or childbirth than those in the top ten.
- Annual additional cost of achieving basic education for all: $6 billion. Annual amount spent on cosmetics in the United States: [over] $8 billion.
- Annual additional cost of providing clean water and sanitation for all: $9 billion. Annual amount spent on perfumes in Europe and the United States: $12 billion.
- A person born in a high-income country can expect to live more than 50 percent longer than a person born in a least-developed country (78 years to 51 years).
- The richest 1 percent of the world's people receives as much income as the poorest 57 percent.
- A person in a least-developed country is almost 25 times more likely to die from tuberculosis than a person in a high-income country.

By now, some may be asking what all these conditions abroad have to do with the United States? Start with health. AIDS was imported, bringing devastating levels of death and illness. Tuberculosis takes two million lives yearly in the world. It was virtually stopped in the United States in the 1950s, but is returning with drug-resistant strains. And other tropical diseases, mutating or jolted by environmental disruptions, head stateside.

National Security?

After the 9/11 massacre, even Donald Rumsfeld and George W. Bush acknowledged that despotism, poverty, disease, and illiteracy help breed stateless terrorism. The suicide attackers did not come from Scandinavia. Justice is the ultimate breeding ground for peace.

Bush, however, is bleeding our public budgets, over-militarizing our foreign policy, distorting our priorities for domestic programs, and shredding our civil liberties in a climate of politically promoted fear and anxiety. Overseas convulsions distract us from the best within us. We can offer so much to the world's neediest from our reformist past, our present science, and our deepest humanitarian traditions. Instead, we are adopting foreign policies that rely heavily on waging war rather than waging peace, and ultimately produce the opposite of what our leaders claim to want—the effect is "blowback," to borrow a phrase from the CIA.

Our political and economic leaders are not paying enough attention to America. It is too easy, as retired General Wesley Clark declared, "to play politics with national security," especially when the public feels intimidated. In 1957, retired General Douglas MacArthur warned the American people about government exaggerating foreign threats to expand military budgets. Budgets driven ever larger and more wastefully by what another retired general, Dwight D. Eisenhower, warned about in his farewell presidential address three years later— the "military-industrial complex." This vast complex includes the large military weapons corporations and their former executives in high Pentagon civilian positions.

Exaggerating external threats to frighten the populace has long been a technique of control by unscrupulous politicians and the businesses that derive profits from them. "Terrorism" has replaced "communism" as the dreaded enemy. And when the threat is blown out of proportion compared to larger and preventable casualties, it serves to entrench incumbent politicians. George W. Bush repeatedly raises the specter of terrorism to chill dissent, to stifle or co-opt the Democratic Party, to distract from domestic necessities (where he is at his weakest), and to favor his corporate buddies with profitable contracts.

He does all this and hopes to remain steady in the polls. Not bad for a selected president.

This is very bad for our country. An imperial power whose military budget is roughly as large as the combined military budgets of all other nations, and which has bases in more than a hundred countries thirteen years after the fall of the Soviet Union, cannot help but experience weakened democracy at home. Half of the federal government's discretionary budget (excluding social insurance programs like Social Security and Medicare) goes to military programs. Millions of underpaid American workers make this country run every day and do not receive their just rewards. Our ever-expanding gross national product is skewed heavily toward the rich and super-rich.

Suppose during their congested daily drive to work, Americans turned off their radios and cell phones and started questioning what they and their families and neighbors must put up with for no good reason. Call it *daydreaming into reality*. There are quite a few questions they might think to ask:

- Why must we spend so much of our lives just getting back and forth to work, bumper to bumper, with all the noise, fumes, road rage, and overall fatigue? Why aren't there modern public transit systems flexible enough to allow us to snooze, read the newspaper, or chat, instead of fighting the traffic?
- Why can't we make enough to pay our bills, even with our spouses working? It seems we're getting deeper into debt and hearing about more and more layoffs and outsourcing, or cutbacks in wages and benefits.
- Why are our bosses paid so much more than we are, and so much, much more than our parents' bosses ever were? Don't they know that it affects our morale and our attitude toward them? Is it right that while these bosses are getting richer, they are demanding that we become poorer?

- Why do we have to go without health insurance or pay more for the insurance we have from our employer? Why are there so many exclusions, deductions, co-payments, and other fine print loopholes that take away our access to medical care when we need it most—during an illness?
- Why can our bosses get away with forcing us to train our own imported substitutes before they ship our jobs to India and elsewhere?

Stop daydreaming. Turn on the radio and listen to the heaving voice of giant corporatism, Rush Limbaugh. Hear him say that "Americans have this sense that they are entitled to their job. Ridiculous." So says Rush, the cowardly purveyor of unrebutted soliloquy and war hawk who escaped the Vietnam draft. Rush exudes nonstop plutocratic bile to please his corporate paymasters who make him $20 million a year. Keep listening to those corporatist radio talk show jocks who pit us against one another while the bosses laugh all the way to the bank. They tell us about the quarterly increases in productivity while never wondering who is receiving the gains from this productivity.

Our economy is at least 25 times more productive per person today than in 1900, adjusted for inflation. In 1900, there were many poor people. Today there are many poor people. People are poor in the same ways and in different ways. They are deprived of basic necessities, burdened with debt, often sick, hurting, and lonely, very lonely in America. Why? There should be no involuntary poverty in the wealthiest society in the world. Even Nixon believed this. Where is the benefit from this productivity going?

It is going to the upper classes. It is going to expanding entertainment and minor conveniences, to a bloated military, and to paying heavily for deficiencies resulting from shortsightedness. Who knows where else it goes? Economic theory is so empirically undernourished that economists ought to hit the road and see the other America—in the devastated inner cities, the sprawling waste of the suburbs, the impoverished rural countryside with its closed or decrepit Wal-Marted main streets and shuttered family farms. Maybe you think impoverished Americans are just lazy? Think again. The poor, who have fought our wars since 1776, work harder than the rest of us, and if you had their daily agonies and anxieties, you might be driving into pillville and shrinkland twice a month.

What is poor, by the way? According to the pathetically outdated U.S. Department of Labor's definition, in America you are no longer officially poor if you are a family with Mom and Dad and two children making $19,000 gross a year (before deductions and before the expenses of daycare and just getting to work, expenses such as another used car, repairs, and insurance policy). The Economic Policy Institute (EPI) is more realistic. EPI states that, to receive the basic necessities that lift you from poverty, a family needs, depending on the region, anywhere from $20,000 to $40,000 gross a year. By that definition, roughly 40 percent of American family households live in or near poverty!

Robert Fellmeth, a professor at the University of San Diego Law School and the leading children's advocate in California, took the two official categories of "poverty" and "near poverty" and applied them to that state where the rich and famous roam. Forty-six percent of all children in California fall within those two categories—poor or near poor.

In our advanced economy, relatively few families achieve a modest middle-class standard of living with just one breadwinner. Many cannot reach that objective with two breadwinners—imagine one working at Wal-Mart and the other in one of the few remaining textile factories. Now the bad news. Official unemployment is over 8 million. Add another 4.7 million Americans who work part-time jobs while looking for a full-time job. (The Department of Labor considers them employed.) Another 5 million want jobs but have given up looking—they don't count as officially unemployed either. A total of 18 million people, almost 12 percent of the labor force, cannot find full-time work.

Various veneers obscure the reality of our economy. The few winners are very visible in the local or mass media. The struggles of the vastly greater number of invisible families are concealed by macro data on aggregate economic growth. And such data can be misleading as well. It is not well known that, adjusted for inflation, wages for a majority of Americans peaked in 1973. Real gross national product (GNP) has nearly doubled since then, but wages are lower—adjusted for inflation, but not adjusted for increased daycare costs, commuting, and other larger-than-ever work-related expenses. The $5.15 an hour federal minimum wage is almost three dollars less in purchasing power than it was in 1968. No wonder so many homeless people are from the ranks of the working poor. A one-room occupancy in many large cities costs in rent alone the entire sum produced by the minimum wage.

The economic plight of the American people really registered with me during a conversation I had in the spring of 2000 with Edward Wolff—an economics professor at New York University, managing editor of the *Review of Income and Wealth,* and probably the leading expert on the distribution of wealth in America. Ed related that Bill Gates' financial wealth equaled at the time the combined wealth of the bottom one hundred and twenty million Americans. One hundred and twenty million! More than 40 percent of the population. Of course, those hundred and twenty million Americans are essentially broke, with assets barely (if at all) above liabilities. Bill Gates and a select few others are doing fine, but what about the people who clean for them; serve their food; harvest their crops; make, store, and sell their products; take care of their older relatives; and drive their vehicles? Fight their wars?

And when the struggling workers are seriously injured by workplace hazards, defective cars, toxic chemicals, and medical malpractice, and use our civil justice system, the oligarchy rises up repeatedly to limit their just compensation and restrict their day in court in the twisted name of "tort reform." The same oligarchy of naysayers who still deny all Americans health insurance includes the insurance carriers and health industries. We are the only western nation to say no to our ill and infirm.

This comparison to other democracies irritates apologists for the stagnant status quo. When mention is made of all workers in other countries having four weeks or more paid vacation, health insurance, daycare, paid family sick leave, regardless of whether they belong to a union, the apologists (most of whom can afford all these services or do not need them) grumble inanely, "If you don't like this country, you know where you can go." But why not use our liberties to improve this country and, as my mother once said to me, make it more lovable? Which is the more patriotic attitude?

Are you dismayed by what you see around you—our workers falling behind, our democracy weakening by dirty money-dominated elections, a deteriorating environment, corporate takeovers, unraveling neighborhoods, cultural decay, lack of time for civic duties, fast food, fast talk, fast pace, fast, faster, and fastest, precluding human conversation and community renewal, children spending much of the day staring at screens in a nonhuman world of virtual reality? You should be dismayed, but not demoralized. We need to rebuild democracy, which remains the best system ever devised to pursue happiness. Think of all those great Americans of yesteryear who sweated and battled for the blessings and goodness that they handed down to us. Think of what they must be saying to us now, "Press forward, descendants, on the road to a more just society, help finish the job we started."

When confronted with a blizzard of evidence about the injustices around us and the perils that await future generations, we need to get our dander up, not our despair. The civic personality declares its independence, raises levels of expectations, marshals kindred spirits, assembles the many known solutions and models of success and proceeds steadfastly, courageously to take back the United States. As community organizer Saul Alinsky always said, "The only thing that can overcome organized money is organized people." Who else is there? Not the government, until it is liberated from the moneyed interests. Not the global corporations that have no allegiance to this country and seek only to control or abandon communities as they see fit. If our democracy is to be rebuilt, it must be by the people, organized civically and politically. As the old movement song put it, "The People, Yes."

SPINEWATCH

Cowards in the Parties

arties, parties, parties—there were dozens in the nineteenth century, many paving the way for outlandish reforms that later became accepted as commonplace. There was the party to abolish slavery, so outrageous to the cotton plantation owners, and the party to enfranchise women, so outrageous to the early industrialists (who knew that many women opposed cruel child labor practices and therefore wanted women kept out of the polling booth). There were the post-Civil War parties demanding the forty-hour work week, the right to form trade unions, the right to strike. Other parties pioneered for the great populist-progressive movement launched by East Texas farmers in 1887. Many of these parties had short durations, four or fewer election cycles. They found their issues co-opted in significant measure, as when Franklin Delano Roosevelt adopted key social insurance and regulatory positions of Norman Thomas' Socialist Party. Other parties withered away for lack of resources and leadership. Still others declined from internal conflicts. But they all contributed to the public debate, brought out more voters, raised expectations, and pushed their agendas into the political debate.

Our Constitution made no mention of political parties. Many of the framers despised them, calling them "factions"—narrow-minded, self-interested groups tempted by insidious power. George Washington,

John Adams, and especially James Madison in the Federalist Papers—
how prescient they were regarding today's Democratic-Republican
duopoly. But the founding fathers also established the predicate for
such a duopoly with the Electoral College and winner-take-all elections. That approach, adopted largely to mollify the smaller states, had
unintended effects.

One latter day effect was to desensitize many civil libertarians to
the rights and virtues of small parties or independent candidates who
may siphon votes from their cherished Republican or Democratic
Party. Dissent tends to produce discomfort, which in turn gives rise to
intolerance, an unseemly willingness to look the other way as the two
major parties pass law after law in state after state to exclude multi-
party competition. If ballot-access barriers don't suffice, the major
parties resort to a sequence of arbitrary moves by various bi-partisan
agencies, including: disqualifying signatures, adopting instant new impediments, marginalizing ballot placement, ignoring write-in votes,
excluding candidates from debates, and assorted shenanigans on election day (such as discouraging or intimidating voters) and at ballot-
counting time.

And so, sources of regeneration and reform, the provision of
more choices and voices, the opportunity to vote for a candidate of
one's choice, not the duopoly's choice, are effectively denied. Inside
the electoral system, impediments frustrate free speech, the right to
petition and the right of assembly. Still, civil libertarians are not per-
turbed, unless their party's ox is gored. Most civil libertarians won't
push their party to support Instant Runoff Voting (IRV), which
could promote expression of these rights.

Thwarting or stifling competition has consequences, just as if nature were to keep seeds from sprouting or laws kept entrepreneurs
from starting businesses. In politics, duopoly has become politics as
usual. When just two parties control the electoral scene, they tend to
converge. They are dialing for the same commercial interest dollars

and recruiting mostly candidates willing to grovel and make quid pro quo deals. The parties naturally become more cautious toward the powers-that-be and develop a strategy of protective imitation toward one another. Bill Clinton's welfare "reform" was one example. George W. Bush had his phony but politically effective "leave no child behind" and prescription drug benefit. More and more the major parties become Coke and Pepsi, frantically highlighting their dwindling differences and masking their growing similarities.

The two-party duopoly is redistricting the nation's congressional and state legislative districts into one-party districts. Ninety-five percent of congressional districts are now seen by both parties as safe, not competitive. About 40 percent of state legislative seats are so "safe" that no opponent from the other major party even challenges the incumbent. Entire states are effectively becoming one-party states. In many states, one or the other major presidential candidate makes no effort and thereby further depresses the vote for his party from governor down to city council. In the face of this political monoculture and massive voter turnoff, the liberal intelligentsia plays the least-worst game with the presidential election.

There was a time when the Republican and Democratic Parties more distinctly represented different constituencies. The former bent toward the wealthy, propertied, and protectionist interests, much of rural America and the early ethnic groups. The latter responded to the populist-progressive agendas of the industrial workforce and recent immigrants to the cities. Senator Boies Penrose of Pennsylvania was a flamboyant type of Republican a hundred years ago. A dedicated glutton, he weighed in at 350 pounds. His feasts (which included a dozen oysters, pots of chicken gumbo, a terrapin stew, two ducks, six kinds of vegetables, a quart of coffee, and several cognacs as windups) were often paid for by business buddies. Once he explained his political philosophy to a gathering of supporters: "I believe in a division of labor. You send us to Congress; we pass laws under . . . which you make money . . . and out of your profits you further contribute to our campaign funds to send us back again to pass more laws to enable you to make more money."

By contrast, consider the two wealthy President Roosevelts—considered traitors to their class—who rode the crest of the progressive movement, challenged "the malefactors of great wealth," championed the rights of workers, and developed a regulatory framework that saved business from its own avaricious excesses. The Great Depression of the 1930s imprinted more deeply the line between the two parties—one was for the haves, the other for the have-nots.

After World War II, the parties presented themselves differently. Other image-driven perceptions came to dominate: the Republicans as tough on communism and street crime, the Democrats as more solicitous of minority and elderly rights. Although Republicans talked a better game on the hot button international and military issues, actual differences tended to be exaggerated. The bigger differences were in the civil rights, civil liberties, consumer, worker, and environmental areas—with most Democrats on Capitol Hill and in the White House representing the more progressive party.

Meanwhile corporations, stung in the 1960s and early 1970s by regulatory legislation covering cars, other consumer products, credit, toxic pollution, workplace safety, and the like, resolved to regroup. If there was a marker, it was a Lewis Powell memorandum to the U.S. Chamber of Commerce (CEOs only) in 1971. Powell was a corporate attorney in Richmond, Virginia, before Richard Nixon nominated him to the U.S. Supreme Court. His detailed memorandum warned the business community of a radical turn of forces that was gaining momentum both in Washington and around the nation. Public opinion, especially among the young, was turning against corporations, Powell observed, and he offered a list of what had to be done. The list included more money in campaigns, more lobbying muscle in Washington, and a dedicated expansion of pro–Big Business think tanks and public relations activities.

In the following decade, the business lobby turned Powell's recommendations into reality and benefited from serendipity: they found Congressman Tony Coehlo, the Democratic Party's lead fund-raiser in the House, quite accommodating. Coehlo convinced his fellow Democrats that they could receive an ample share of business campaign contributions if they aped the Republicans. In 1980, prodded by Coelho, the Democrats jump-started their own business cash register politics. Corporate political action committees (PACs) began multiplying like rabbits and buying into both parties. Ronald Reagan's presidency made it easy for Democrats to ignore their better instincts. They failed to push progressive measures in Congress, claiming that Reagan would only veto them. Many veteran progressive stalwarts had left Congress, accelerating the Democrats' slide. A concessionary political culture took hold of the party. And it routinely kowtowed to business lobbyists.

This period was also marked by shifts of power inside the Democratic Party. Trade unions kept losing influence and settling for less and less, becoming mostly defensive in nature. An emergence of corporate and conservative Democrats out-hustled the liberal/progressive wing of the party when it came to setting the policy agenda and mapping electoral strategy. They planned what they claimed was a necessary move to the center. But the Center was more like the Right when it came to populist, regulatory, and union issues. The liberal/progressives inside the party ran out of gas. Many left and weren't replaced. Who wanted to play the rancid money-raising game? More and more, good people decided not to run. Conforming to Gresham's law, bad politics drove out better politics.

Washington, D.C., is not exclusively a federal city with government and business cutting deals. A large number of progressive civic organizations address many areas of injustice; ways to help the poor, the aggrieved, workers, and consumers; ways to protect the environment, civil rights, and civil liberties; and to influence domestic and foreign policy across the board. Twenty-five years ago, many sensed the doors starting to close on their efforts. It wasn't just that they were losing battles; they were getting less and less of a hearing from all three branches of government. They did not like to acknowledge this shift publicly. They had to keep their spirits up to keep fighting against the mounting odds. These citizen groups had to fight the Republican resurgence that threatened the legitimate needs of those Americans for whom they fought.

These Americans numbered in the tens of millions. Why then wasn't the Democratic Party speaking forcefully for these people? Why was the party losing its historic anchors, its soul? Was it just that Republicans had become more clever, more opportunistic, more obsessed with victory? As one who was in Washington, D.C., trying to understand and stem the shift in favor of the Republicans, I found the behavior of the Democrats more frustrating. They fantasized that Republicans were winning for one reason: They had more money. It wasn't the Democrats' absence of message, organizing energy, or reach to the grassroots where the people live. It wasn't the way Democrats increasingly resorted to expensive electronic combat with dull thirty-second television ads instead of relentlessly working the precincts between, not just before, elections. Over and over again, I asked Democratic lawmakers: Don't Republicans oppose the legitimate interests of workers, consumers, low-income people, and people of color? Aren't their policies harmful to the environment and political reform? Of course, they reply. Then why aren't the Democrats winning landslides?

When I put the question to a major Democratic presidential candidate recently, he replied: "The Republicans have so much money to cloud the issues." Such hand-wringing is not good enough. The

Democratic Party has failed to defend our country from the corporate Republicans whose extreme servility to big business actually betrays even conservative principles. Republicans (with Democrats' acquiescence or active complicity) have given us gigantic deficits, uncontrolled business subsidies, and sovereignty-diminishing global trade agreements. For ten years, the Democrats have been losing races to control state legislatures, big city mayoral posts, governorships, and Congress. They even blew a presidential election they had won in 2000. They have become very good at electing very bad Republicans. In the face of all this, their biggest electoral asset is that they are not as bad as the Republicans. Long forgotten is Jimmy Carter's campaign motto—"Why not the best?"

When a party's sole claim to legitimacy is that its major opponent is even worse, idealists in the party have a choice. They can hold their noses and join the interminable slide or they can deny their party their vote until the party shapes up and resumes working for the people. It is clear that the majority of progressives have no intention of either leaving their party or fighting to rescue it from the likes of the powerful Democratic Leadership Council, which bizarrely blames the party's defeats on its being too liberal.

What of the public? What will it take to replace cynicism and powerlessness with a resurgent and robust reform movement? Remember old Senator Penrose, the glutton who openly coddled corporations in exchange for their largesse. Here is his current version: George W. Bush, who pushes through Congress over two trillion dollars worth of tax cuts, mostly for the wealthy, over ten years. The wealthy, saving tens or hundreds of thousands of dollars a year, are predictably grateful. They attend Mr. Bush's huge fund-raisers and return a bit to his re-election coffers. He'll raise over $200 million in hard money, an all-time record, to splash coast-to-coast television ads misleadingly touting his claim to return money back to "the people." But Bush knows who got the lion's share of his tax cuts. His knowledge is personal. In one year, he saved $30,858 on his taxes, Cheney saved more than $88,000 on his, and Rumsfeld saw a benefit of $184,000. In return, Bush continues to run the government to favor the super-rich and the business powers.

Washington has become a much larger bazaar of accounts receivables than ever before. The avarice and abuses have become increasingly complex and institutionalized. What outraged the public thirty or forty years ago is now seen as business as usual. In the 1970s, a five cent increase in the price of natural gas prompted congressional indignation and investigation. Now natural gas sells at ten times what it sold for then and a lone Senator Joseph Lieberman writes an objection. The rest yawn at a 50 percent increase over six months, despite the fact that supply and demand remained about the same during that period. Gasoline prices quickly rise thirty to fifty cents per gallon for no perceptible reason except tight refinery capacity in an industry that for twenty years has been voluntarily closing—and not replacing—domestic refineries. Stretched over a year, thirty cents a gallon takes $45 billion out of motorists' pockets in the U.S.

The people used to cry out for action. Not today. They feel it is useless. Murmurs from Washington about a possible investigation quickly fade away. And why not? Bush has forty-one executives from the oil and gas industry in high government positions. They want an even more lucrative job to return to on the Houston-to-Washington-to-Houston merry-go-round. Beyond that, their mind-set and that of their boss in the White House is marinated in oil. Let the millions of drivers pay, because they have no say.

In 1996, the Federal Communications Commission (FCC) gave away what then presidential candidate Robert Dole estimated to be a $75 billion asset of the American people—the digital spectrum—to the broadcast industry. Dole attacked this heist in a rare expression of anticorporate outrage and demanded congressional action. So did Senator John McCain. But Dole's successor as Senate Majority

Leader, Trent Lott, refused to do anything. His college chum, Eddie Fritts, the executive director of the National Association of Broadcasters, stands watch over the media companies' free use of the public airwaves from his modernist headquarters near DuPont Circle in Washington. This enormous giveaway wasn't an issue in the presidential campaign; Clinton couldn't be bothered since after all it was his FCC that made the decision. Dole did not press the matter.

Each year the shredding of our federal government's public assets and obligations becomes more brazen. Even in the face of ever more outrageous subsidies and handouts to corporations, bloated military contracts, consumer gouging, and environmental destruction, both parties favor less regulatory law enforcement. In the face of a crime wave against small investors, pension holders, consumers, and workers, the Justice Department's corporate crime prosecution budget is starved by Congress and the White House. You'd think trillions of swindled dollars would create a front and center political issue. But not if both parties are hustling business interests for campaign cash and selling out the nation for a "mess of pottage."

The myth persists that the politicians comprise our government. Our government is ruled by corporate executives, thousands of lobbyists, and corporate lawyers who plunder, pillage, and reduce our revered national capital to corporate-occupied territory. The powers-that-be escape their fair share of taxes, attack sacred constitutional rights, and exclude the people from the commonwealth of resource-rich public lands, and the public airwaves. It can be numbing to people who struggle to get by and believe they have no time for anything other than a bit of relaxation after work before the daily grind starts again.

What is occurring here could be an addendum to Machiavelli's classic rules for rulers, *The Prince*. As corruption, robberies, and usurpations become bigger, more complex, and obscured by semantic baloney, opposition diminishes. It is replaced by passivity, resignation, hopelessness, surrender. Yet sometimes something happens that gets our attention. Year after year, Congressional and media investigations and private whistle-blowers document the stupendous waste, incompetence, redundancy, and graft in the military contracting budgets—tens of billions of undeserved dollars steered to prime Pentagon munitions corporations. The people scarcely stir. But when a few intrepid souls disclosed that the Pentagon paid $435 for a $10 claw hammer, which the contractor billed the government for under the description of "multi-directional, impact generator," the public and editorialists took acid notice. When a $1,700 toilet seat cover followed, the reaction was vociferous. When spending is broken down and placed within the framework of ordinary experience, civic sparks start to fly and a rumble from the people can be heard in Washington.

Why did Richard Nixon sign all those historic bills in the late 1960s and early 1970s? Because he wanted to? Probably not. It was because he took notice of marches, rallies, teach-ins, confrontations with power, and agitation. Justice-seekers were on the offensive. That is a key lesson of history: Once those strivings for justice are thrown on the defensive, reacting to the agendas of the corporatists and reactionaries, expectation levels fall, self-confidence declines, and the whole balance of power shifts. That is what started to happen in the mid-1970s. When the organized oligarchs counterattacked, the rumble faded away. This was facilitated by Nixon ending the draft, the end of the Vietnam War, and the end of sheriffs hosing down and handcuffing nonviolent civil rights demonstrators. Those successes reflect the dilemma of liberalism. The more it succeeds, the more it takes the steam out of itself. This necessitates the emergence of new leaders and agendas to revive the rumble of democracy.

Many injustices lack the visceral immediacy of young people conscripted to fight and die in Vietnam, or innocent citizens pummeled on the streets of Birmingham. Today, massive risks are often more abstract, remote, and complex. Farts disturb more people than odor-less pollution or global warming. Thoughtless ethnic slights rile more people than widespread lead poisoning of children and skyrocketing levels of childhood asthma. We must awaken to the many menaces around us and dedicate some civic attention to widespread perils.

Personal irritations shrink as the magnitude of civic challenges is absorbed into one's purposeful self. When people move into the civic arena and take on a cause, they experience stress and uncertainty, but the gratification is deeper, a more truthful part of the summit of their being, to paraphrase Ralph Waldo Emerson. When Anne Witte completed a series of interviews with women who became super-active leaders, for her book *Women Activists: Challenging the Abuse of Power,* I asked her to identify the one over-riding impression she took away from them. Without hesitation she said, "I've never met happier people." Hmmmm.

From whom should the Republican and Democratic parties take instructions? From artificial commercial entities that subjugate the public interest, or from human beings who possess inalienable rights? The question answers itself. But the question is not repeatedly and in-sistently asked in party platforms, on the campaign trail, in media, in the legislative halls, and judicial forums. What are the answers, some-one asked Gertrude Stein? "What are the questions?" she replied. Sci-entists know that the properly formulated question is well on the way to finding an answer. When it comes to politics, we don't ask ourselves enough questions. Here are some:

- Why can't millions of citizens remove Congress from the grip of 1,500 large corporations and their trade associations?
- How much of our time would it take to reassert the people's agenda over the plutocrats', since we clearly have more votes?
- How can we achieve our own mass and local media so we can alert and engage one another and solve problems together, without the

filters and censors of advertising revenues, media stock prices, and conglomeratization?

- How can we become as excited about the prospect of freeing our political parties from corporate domination, so they can return to representing us, as we are watching sports or movies on television?
- Why aren't we willing to spend the same organized time to obtain universal health care as we do watching the festivities of one Super Bowl?
- Why aren't we motivated to correct wrongs when we hear that people like us have said "enough is enough," rolled up their sleeves, and changed things for the better?
- Is life spinning out of our control, leaving us little time to catch our breath or focus on what is important to our children's futures?
- What are we scared of when we balk at performing our civic duties on problems we worry about, in this "land of the free and home of the brave"? Since we revel in these words, why don't we march under their banner?
- How fragile has our democracy become when one party wages war on our Bill of Rights with the other party's complicity and hardly a protest from the people? Whatever happened to the exclusive congressional authority to declare war, to due process of law, freedom of consumer contracts, and equal protection of the laws?
- If the Bill of Rights were abolished, how much of the way you live daily would be disturbed?
- How much disrespect will you tolerate before you end your passivity and join the movement to take control of politics through public financing of public campaigns, a series of commonsense electoral reforms, and establishment of the people's own radio, television, cable, and network stations?
- Would you become more political if you had the opportunity to learn how to become more politically effective?

- Haven't you taken on far more difficult tasks than joining with others to take back our political institutions? Raising children, overcoming illness, acquiring a work skill, building a business, taking care of an elderly parent. . . . Aren't these achievements far more demanding than a modest, consistent engagement in putting the "people" back in politics? Isn't raising your country, overcoming political corruption, building democracy, taking care of injustices, and meeting the necessities of a great nation worth some of your regular time, patience, and talent? What's domestic patriotism all about, anyway?

As these questions imply, we need to summon will power and self-confidence to envision the wonderful benefits of political participation for the quality of life and justice in America and in the world. Asking these questions of oneself in earnest starts one on the road to replacing what irreverent author Sam Smith calls the "don't care, don't know, and don't do" rationalizations of futility with "I care, I know, I do." It brings one closer to what Emerson called "the integrity of your own mind." Some one hundred and fifty years ago he advised, "Absolve you to yourself, and you shall have the suffrage of the world."

CIVIL AND CRIMINAL WRONGS AND RIGHTS

"If we are to keep our democracy, there must be one com-mandment: Thou shalt not ration justice," said Learned Hand. A consistently fair justice system is an essential build-ing block of a thriving democracy—and yet the scales seem to tip too often in favor of the corporate powers-that-be in our country.

Steven Olsen, a two-year-old boy, became permanently blind and brain-damaged because a hospital refused to give him a CAT scan that would have detected a growing brain abscess. A jury awarded Steven $7.1 million in non-economic compensation for a lifetime of dark-ness, pain, and around-the-clock supervision. But the judge was forced by a California law to reduce the amount to $250,000. Similar laws have been enacted in other states, and George W. Bush and his congressional cohorts would like to enact them nationwide.

Bush and company seem to regard the civil justice system as a nuisance that threatens to destroy our economy and way of life. In reality, America's civil justice system plays an indispensable role. When the rights of injured consumers are vindicated in court, our society benefits in countless ways: compensating victims and their families for shattering losses (with the cost borne by the wrongdoers rather than taxpayers); preventing future injuries by deterring dan-gerous products and practices and spurring safety innovation; stim-ulating enforceable safety standards; educating the public to risks associated with certain products and services; and providing society with its moral and ethical fiber by defining appropriate norms of conduct. As Peter Lewis, chairman of Progressive Insurance Company told me, tort law functions as his industry's "quality control."

The justice system also embodies democracy in action. The words EQUAL JUSTICE UNDER LAW, emblazoned on the Supreme Court building, speak volumes. An average citizen will never influence an election or a vote in Congress as much as those corporations and well-heeled individuals who make juicy contributions to a politician's coffers. But when the high and mighty act improperly and cause harm to an ordinary citizen, and she files a lawsuit, she stands before the judge and jury as the equal of her more powerful opponent.

That, at least, is the theory. Sometimes it works that way. But the reality is often different, and the playing field uneven. Rich and powerful defendants hire big law firms that use their unlimited resources to delay and defeat justice.

One of their favorite tools is "discovery"—the process whereby each side in a case gains access to the relevant information in the hands of the other side. Discovery rests on a sound idea: If it's truth and justice we're after, we want both sides and therefore the fact finder—the jury—to have access to all relevant information. But, in practice, law firms use discovery to defeat rather than promote truth and justice.

Under the federal discovery rule, and its similar state counterparts, when one side requests information or documents, the other side must "fairly meet the substance of the" request. In practice, lawyers do anything but. In the words of Judge William Schwarzer, lawyers generally ask themselves: "How can I interpret this interrogatory, or document request, to avoid giving up what I know my opponent is after?"

Corporate law firms use discovery as a sword as well as a shield—to harass, irritate, and delay. They file countless requests for documents, and conduct numerous depositions, just to keep the other side off balance and prevent a case from getting to trial. If justice delayed is justice denied, millions of ordinary citizens are denied justice by their opponents' abuse of the discovery process. Moreover, except where the law provides for awards of prejudgment interest, delays enable corporations to benefit from returns on investment. The longer it takes to get to trial, the more witnesses become unavailable or their memories dimmed, leading to inaccurate and unjust outcomes.

A solution to discovery abuse begins with recognition that the very idea of discovery actually makes little sense. If the goal of a trial is truth and justice, it should be unnecessary to dig out the other side's evidence. The idea that each side may conceal information that could be critical to the fact finder, provided the other side doesn't ask for it, makes sense only if we view the trial as a kind of game. We don't expect a competitor to help his opponent. A football coach doesn't share with the other team his own team's tactics or scouting reports. But in a viable system of justice, there is no justification for playing hide and seek with relevant information.

Our civil justice system should require both sides to share all relevant information without prompting. In other words, we should move away from "discovery" and toward "disclosure." Rather than put the burden on a party to discover information it doesn't know exists and rely on opposing counsel to cooperate, we should require each side to disclose all relevant information in the early stages of every action. (Reformers have proposed such a rule, but no action has been taken.)

Lawyers would still have to decide what information is relevant, so the rule should be bolstered by a declaration that any uncertainty must be resolved in favor of disclosure. Lawyers would unambiguously know that they must produce all relevant information without regard to how a discovery request happens to be drafted, and without the benefit of self-serving interpretations. If violations were punished severely, such a rule would make the legal system more of a forum for justice rather than an arena for game playing and attrition.

Discovery abuse is one of many advantages enjoyed by the wealthy (often corporate) litigant at the expense of the ordinary citizen. Does this trouble our lawmakers? Are they clamoring for reforms that level the playing field? No, our elected representatives have looked around and reached a startling conclusion: Ordinary citizens have an *unfair advantage* in our tort system, and the system needs to be changed to help corporations and insurance companies and physicians!

That's the amazing thinking underlying the so-called "tort reform" that has become a major issue in American politics, including presidential elections. The corporate community clamors that runaway juries, overcome by emotion and sympathy, routinely dispense outlandish awards that drive companies and physicians out of business, notwithstanding the hundreds of thousands of fatalities and serious injuries that occur yearly. Actual payments and settlements amount to less than what we spend on dog and cat care. (Ninety percent of injured persons do not even file a claim.) No impartial studies document these claims; in fact, studies suggest the opposite. The Center for Justice and Democracy reports that median jury awards dropped 30 percent in 2002 to $30,000 from $43, 000 in 2001. Nevertheless, the Republican Party has taken up the cause.

The GOP solution? A series of legislated measures that prevent injured citizens from receiving fair or full compensation in courts of law. The most significant measures cap the amount of compensation victims can receive for pain and suffering and limit or eliminate a jury's ability to award "punitive damages" designed to punish particularly egregious actions and deter the wrongdoer and others from repeating such misconduct. Other measures, such as elimination of strict liability in product liability actions and the elimination of joint and several liability, make it impossible for some victims to receive *any* compensation.

The full anti-victim package, more accurately called tort deform than tort reform, damages Americans' cherished constitutional right to trial by jury. It ties the hands of jurors, preventing them from doing justice as the case before them requires. Only the judges and juries see, hear, and evaluate the evidence in these cases. But it is the politicians, absent from the courtrooms, who push bills greased by campaign cash that send a perverse message to judge and jury: Too much justice is a bad thing when it comes at the expense of the rich and powerful.

Consider the case of George W. Bush, a leading proponent of tort deform. In their book *Bush's Brain,* Wayne Slater and Jim Moore recount their interview with Karl Rove, Bush's top White House political adviser. Rove said that he "sort of talked [Bush] into" tort reform. Why? "Rove wanted that issue elevated because he knew that its most ardent advocates in Texas could provide millions of dollars in campaign contributions needed to unseat [former Texas governor Ann] Richards."

Such political pandering has a vicious cost to innocent people. Take legislation adopted in some states and pending at the federal level, supported by Bush, the insurance industry, and many physician associations, which would place a cap of $250,000 on a lifetime of pain and suffering. Some insurance company bosses make $250,000 or more every week! No matter how serious the injury (such as brain damage) or how inexcusable or outrageous the misconduct (for example, a doctor removing the wrong organ) causing the injury, this legislation would forbid juries from awarding more than the predetermined amount. It's already the case that injured persons receive zero compensation unless they can prove that they were wronged to the satisfaction of jurors and judges with no personal stake in the outcome. The tort deformers are determined to limit the amount of recovery for those who successfully meet that strict burden. Backwards thinking.

Other legislation, already passed in some states, limits punitive damage awards. Punitive damages, which may be meted out only in extreme cases of misconduct, such as the Exxon Valdez disaster, are often the best means of deterring future wrongdoing. Such awards are infrequent and, if they are excessive, may be reduced by trial judges and courts of appeal. But pandering politicians have decided to take the matter into their own hands. Ignoring the crucial deterrent purpose of punitive damages, they seek to eviscerate or eliminate this valuable benefit—the ability of a body of ordinary citizens representing the community to send a message that certain bad behavior is beyond the pale.

If we are to restrict the legal rights of victims of wrongdoing, those damaged by hazardous goods, toxic chemicals, and the like, we ought to have some sound public policy basis. What is the basis for tort deform? In a nutshell, a mishmash of self-serving propaganda—lurid, often false anecdotes involving unnamed physicians allegedly forced to abandon medical practice because of high insurance premiums and corporations driven to the brink of bankruptcy by excessive verdicts. These anecdotes, and the self-serving lesson drawn from them, are spread through a massive disinformation campaign.

Then there is the McDonald's coffee spill case. When a jury awarded a woman $2.9 million against McDonald's because of burns she sustained from a coffee spill, editorial writers, pundits, and talk shows went to town. The Chamber of Commerce even ran a radio ad mocking the verdict. The case became the poster child for tort deform.

The propagandists emphasized that millions drink coffee every day without spilling it, and those who do spill it accept minor burns as the price of their carelessness. Here are some things they forgot to tell us: (1) McDonald's coffee was far hotter than normal coffee, causing a greatly accelerated burn rate; (2) McDonald's had received 700 complaints of burns, but stubbornly refused to lower the temperature or place a clearer warning on coffee cups; (3) the seventy-nine-year-old victim, Stella Liebeck, suffered third-degree burns on her thighs, buttocks, and genitals, requiring a week of hospitalization and subsequent skin grafts; (4) Shortly after the incident she wrote McDonald's a letter explaining that she had no intention of suing and requesting only that McDonald's cover her medical and recuperation costs and look into its coffee-making process to avoid future injuries; (5) McDonald's declined to change its policies and offered Liebeck an insulting $800; (6) Only $160,000 out of the $2.9 million verdict went to compensate Liebeck. (The jury arrived at $200,000 for compensatory damages, including pain and suffering, then knocked off 20 percent because Liebeck's negligence contributed to her injury.) The rest was for punitive damages; (7) A major goal of punitive damages is to deter future misconduct, and in this case it worked—McDonald's in Albuquerque, New Mexico, cooled its coffee after the verdict; (8) The trial judge reduced the punitive damages by 82 percent to $480,000, bringing the overall liability down to $640,000. To avoid the expense and uncertainty of an appeal, the parties reached a settlement for less still.

In sum, an arrogant, megabillion dollar corporation, indifferent to numerous injuries caused by its scalding product, was brought to heel by a jury of ordinary citizens. The verdict compensated an elderly woman for severe suffering and forced the company (and perhaps other companies) to take action that spared future victims. To the extent the verdict was excessive, a built-in corrective mechanism in the courts reduced it.

In other words, the system worked. But why let the facts (pointed out by *Newsweek* and the *Wall Street Journal*) interfere with a perfect propaganda opportunity? Similar distortions and dishonesty are seen across the board. Company spokesmen and CEOs insist that lawsuits and insurance premiums are financially devastating. Yet, the very companies most loudly proclaiming hardship and demanding tort reform (such as Dow Chemical, Corning, Monsanto, Textron, Upjohn,

Coleman Company, Cooper Industries) report megaprofits on an annual basis! Moreover, according to Ernst & Young and the Insurance Risk Management Society, in 1999 the total of *all* business liability costs combined were $5.20 for every $1,000 in revenue.

Supporters of tort reform invoke one myth after another: a litigation explosion, juries automatically ruling in favor of plaintiffs and routinely awarding punitive damages, an economy shattered by these awards. Each of these notions is demonstrably false. Rather than bombard you with data, I refer the interested reader to the web site of the Center for Justice and Democracy: www.centerjd.org. As the Center's data demonstrate, only a tiny percentage of persons injured bring lawsuits, and an even tinier percentage of those who do so receive large verdicts. Tort deform is a justice-destroying solution to a trumped-up scare tactic to escape accountability.

A driving force behind this dishonest campaign is the insurance industry. Whenever insurers face low interest rates and declining stock investments, they start the drumbeat against justice for victims. They've made a particular cause célèbre of medical malpractice. Instead of demanding disciplinary action against incompetent physicians and urging medical associations to police their own ranks, the insurance industry gouges the specialized physicians and then lobbies state and federal legislatures to curtail victims' rights and remedies. Physician policyholders have joined the insurance industry's call and paraded to the legislature.

Why do physicians allow themselves to be tools of insurance companies which gouge them regardless of whether they are among the incompetent few who account for most malpractice claims (5 percent of doctors are involved in roughly 50 percent of malpractice payouts)? One answer is that insurance companies frighten physicians with false data suggesting that malpractice suits run amok. A persuasive case can be made that there are far *too few* malpractice suits. A Harvard School of Public Health study estimated that gross malpractice in hospitals alone takes eighty thousand American lives a year and causes hundreds of thousands of serious injuries. Yet studies show that roughly 90 percent of people harmed by medical malpractice do not file suit.

If you total the entire amount of premiums all physicians pay in a year and divide it evenly by all the physicians practicing in the United States, the average annual premium is $10,000 per doctor. Very manageable. So why are some doctors paying $50,000 or $100,000 a year or more to their malpractice insurers? Because the insurance companies have learned to over-classify and reduce their risk pools, thereby charging exorbitant amounts to specific specialists like obstetricians and orthopedic surgeons. In addition, because insurers fail to surcharge the few incompetent physicians in these specialties, the competent specialists pay far more than they should.

There is another benefit to the insurance industry from this kind of over-classification. When obstetricians are gouged, they protest loudly, threaten not to deliver babies, and sometimes actually go on strike. This makes great television—crying babies and physicians in their garb blaming lawyers—and deflects blame from the insurers, who laugh their way to greater profits. (During almost the entire period in which they pushed tort deform, claiming hardship, the insurance industry made money. For much of the period, their profits soared.) Last year, the property-casualty insurance industry reported a 1,000 percent increase in profits over the previous year.

There are no television visuals of the human victims who receive neither compassion nor compensation, and little air time for people like Donald J. Zuk, chief executive of SCPIE Holdings Inc., a leading malpractice insurer in the West. Mr. Zuk assails fellow insurance company executives who blame the legal system for the malpractice crisis. As Zuk candidly acknowledged to the *Wall Street Journal,* the problem is "self-inflicted."

Neither organized medicine nor the insurance companies go after bad doctors. The AMA's website does not report any data about incompetent or crooked physicians, and the insurance companies have shown little interest in loss prevention. Instead, both physicians' and insurers' lobbies fund and press legislators to enact laws that politicize the courts, tie the hands of judges and juries, and make it harder for innocent people to receive just compensation for terrible suffering.

Are malpractice awards the national crisis physicians and insurers suggest? In fact, the entire malpractice insurance premium business represents one half of one percent of the nation's health care costs (amounting to roughly what the country spends on dog food). Isn't it time to focus on malpractice prevention instead of trying to restrict the rights of hundreds of thousands of Americans harmed by their doctors' negligence? We mustn't ignore the severe plight of these suffering human beings. People like Colin Gourley, a Nebraska boy who suffered devastating injuries at birth because of medical malpractice by his mother's obstetrician. A jury found that $5.625 million was needed to compensate Colin for a lifetime of medical care and suffering, but a cruel Nebraska law required that the verdict be slashed to one-quarter that amount. Tragically, there are similar stories from around the country.

Whether it's malpractice, products liability, or any other aspect of the civil justice system, we need to ask whether proposed reforms level the playing field or tilt an already unlevel field even further by making it more difficult for ordinary citizens to receive justice.

The tort deform movement amounts to a perverse rewriting of history. Tort law produced decades of slow but steady progress in state after state respecting the physical integrity of human beings against harm and recognition that even the weak and defenseless deserve justice. Instead of seeing this evolution as a source of national and global pride, a coalition of insurance companies, corporate defendants' lobbies, and craven politicians, led by George W. Bush, depict it as a source of shame and instability that must be stopped.

If this campaign succeeds, the results are sadly predictable. Tort deform means less deterrence, which means more injuries, more uncompensated victims, and tremendous overall costs to society. As the countless victims still experiencing horrors as a result of exposure to asbestos, lead poisoning, and use of dangerous products like the Dalkon Shield know all too well, America needs a stronger, not weaker, civil justice system.

Problems with Our Prison System

The criminal justice system is also broken—so badly that one hardly knows where to begin describing the breakdown. We can start with the war on drugs, since commentators across the political spectrum recognize its lunacy. We pour almost endless resources (roughly $50 billion each year) into catching, trying, and incarcerating people who primarily harm themselves, thereby damaging and endangering communities and draining crucial resources from the police, courts, and prisons that could be used to combat serious street crime (and suite crime—see the chapter "Corporate Crime and Violence") that directly violate the public's liberty, health, safety, trust, and financial well-being. As with alcoholics and nicotine addicts, the approach to drug addicts should be rehabilitation, not incarceration.

The war on drugs also contributes to other negative features of the criminal justice system, including discriminatory treatment of African Americans. Racial profiling results in harassment and invasion of privacy of people who have done nothing to justify suspicion—people whose only crime is the color of their skin. Proponents of racial profiling claim it is justified on the ground that African Americans commit a disproportionate amount of crime. It's certainly the case that African Americans constitute a disproportionate and growing portion of the prison population, but that is in large part because of the war on drugs.

Between 1980 and 1999, the incarceration rate for African Americans more than tripled. According to the Urban Institute, black men today have a 28 percent lifetime chance of incarceration, compared to 7 percent for white men. This was largely the result of tougher sentencing laws enacted in the 1980s that made the punishment for distributing crack cocaine 100 times greater than the punishment for powder cocaine. Persons convicted of crack cocaine offenses, who tend to be African Americans, received substantially harsher sentences than white citizens who are more likely users of the powder form of the drug. (A person convicted in federal court of distributing five grams of crack cocaine receives a mandatory five-year minimum sentence while it takes 500 grams of powdered cocaine to trigger a five-year mandatory sentence.) A 2002 study titled "Reducing Racial Disparities in Juvenile Detention: Eight Pathways to Juvenile Detention Reform" by the Annie E. Casey Foundation found that African-American youth with no prior record were six times more likely to be incarcerated than white youth with no prior record when charged with the same offense. The Urban Institute and others document how the incarceration of Blacks for nonviolent drug offenses has a devastating effect on inner-city neighborhoods.

The discriminatory treatment of African Americans occurs with respect to the most serious crimes as well. Among the many problems with the death penalty is its discriminatory impact resulting from racial prejudice—a black man convicted of killing a white is far more likely to be sentenced to death than a white man convicted of killing a black. More generally, the death penalty is disproportionately sought and administered against racial minorities. Studies ordered by then-Attorney General Janet Reno revealed that from 1995 to 2000 roughly 75 percent of those against whom federal prosecutors sought the death penalty were blacks or ethnic minorities, even though far less than 75 percent of the people who commit federal capital crimes are members of such groups.

Of all the arguments in favor of capital punishment, supporters have neglected one—given the state of our prisons, inmates must often feel they are better off dead. As our penal system has abandoned all pretense of rehabilitation, prisons and their internal culture of violence turn even minor drug offenders into hardened criminals. Those who are eventually released have little chance of leading productive lives. In November 2000, the *New York Times* reported that many states even prohibit ex-felons, who have served their time, from voting. (Jim Morris, the famous impersonator, used to do a clever routine that captured the absurdity of the war on drugs. He impersonated the first George Bush giving a macho spiel about the war on drugs: "If you do drugs, you will get caught, and if you get caught you will do time, and if you do time, you will do . . . drugs.")

To some extent, government's response to failed prisons has been an overt abandonment of responsibility. Over the past few decades, many state and local governments, seduced by the siren call for privatization of public services, turned to private corporate prisons that made grandiose promises of cost saving. There is no evidence that they have delivered on those promises.

A series of academic and government studies and General Accounting Office reports offer little evidence of cost savings from prison privatization. Worse still, a study by Good Jobs First, a national research center that tracks state and local development practices, suggests that "prisons for profit" projects are often cesspools of corporate welfare that rip off taxpayers. Good Jobs First studied sixty privately built and operated prisons and found that three-fourths of them received valuable subsidies—tax-advantaged financing, property tax reductions, and tax credits.

Has the corporate prison served other penal objectives? Hardly. In 2001, the *American Prospect* reported that the search for profits through cost cutting has resulted in significantly higher employee turnover, with dramatic ill effects on quality and safety. The magazine cites a survey conducted by George Washington University that found 49 percent more inmate-on-staff assaults and 65 percent more inmate-on-inmate assaults in medium and minimum security private facilities than in similar prisons run by government.

American Prospect, Good Jobs First, and other watchdogs have documented numerous abuses and security lapses in prisons run by some of the nation's leading private-prison companies. On the one hand, there have been easy prison escapes while guards looked away; on the other hand, extreme physical abuse of prisoners, widespread denial of medical care, and failure to segregate inmates from more dangerous inmates. In some states, conditions were so poor that the government (at times under pressure from the federal government) has been forced to take control from the private operator.

Privatization of prisons was a dubious idea that has often proven to be a costly mistake, yet another drain on taxpayers to feed the profits of private corporations that fail to deliver on their claims to benefit the public. Governing bodies at all levels should abandon this failed experiment.

As is often the case with criminal justice policy, one foolish initiative begets another. The ill-conceived war on drugs helped create the need for the ill-conceived privatization of prisons by greatly expanding the prison population beyond the capacity of public prisons. We can begin to undo this knot by replacing the failed war on drugs with regulation, rehabilitation, and education. But such an idea will face resistance because this phony war is a symptom of a larger problem: a mindless "get tough" crime policy that substitutes slogans for common sense.

"Three strikes and you're out" sounds good, until it leads to a life sentence for marijuana possession or shoplifting. We need to get tough on rapists, muggers, murderers who make our streets unsafe, and corporate criminals who swindle shareholders and the taxpaying public of millions of dollars. All too often law enforcement ignores such offenders and reserve its toughness for relatively minor violators.

As if lengthy periods of incarceration for minor offenders weren't bad enough, our criminal justice system also punishes altogether innocent persons. In the past decade, DNA testing, pushed by Barry Scheck's Innocence Project, has exonerated well over one hundred persons wrongly convicted of serious crimes. All states should create an innocence commission to monitor and investigate such errors, and Congress should pass pending legislation (the Advancing Justice Through DNA Technology Act) which makes post-conviction DNA testing available to inmates.

Roughly one-fourth of those exonerated by DNA had confessed to the crime in question (before recanting the confession and protesting their innocence). False confessions have turned out to be a surprisingly widespread problem, encouraged by certain pervasive police practices, such as threats and promises that overwhelm frightened or mentally retarded suspects. To make matters worse, juries are not in position to evaluate false confessions because the police often choose not to videotape interrogations. A few states now require videotaping, a positive step that all states and the federal government should adopt.

Another positive step would be better representation for death row inmates, both at trial and on appeal. Among those exonerated by DNA testing and other means are an alarming number of people who were on death row. Experts say that a major cause of their wrongful convictions was inexperienced and under-resourced defense attorneys. Judges need to appoint more able and experienced counsel in capital cases, and legislatures need to establish a system that facilitates this process.

Better still, the death penalty should be abolished. Given the inevitable execution of innocent persons, the racial bias in implementation, the costly appeals process (without which there would surely be more innocent people executed), the cost exceeds the cost of life in prison, and the absence of any reliable evidence showing a deterrent effect, the case for abolition is compelling. Indeed, most civilized nations long ago abandoned capital punishment. During this decade, the murder rates in countries and states without the death penalty have remained consistently lower than the rates in states and countries with the death penalty.

Assorted other desirable reforms in the criminal justice area should be considered, including greater reliance on community policing, greater emphasis on rehabilitation and community development, and, as discussed earlier, reform of drug and mandatory sentencing laws and replacement of for-profit corporate prisons with more accountable superior public institutions.

Our justice system is designed primarily to vindicate rights established by our elected officials. What happens when our "leaders" fail to establish or recognize an appropriate body of rights to begin with? For example, residents of the inner city don't find that the law and law enforcement is on their side against the business predators and loan sharks who take their earnings. Instead, the crooks are the ones who summon the law to enforce their rip-offs. So too, African Americans and Hispanics can testify that the existence of a well-designed justice system amounts to very little for those groups excluded, in whole or in part, from the very concept of justice.

Persistent Inequalities

Many groups today still face high levels of discrimination. Women continue to receive unfair treatment in a number of areas. A study by the General Accounting Office, released in April 2004, shows that women's wages still lag substantially behind men's. Amazingly, the hourly pay gap has narrowed by just half a penny a year since the move for wage equality began in earnest four decades ago. At this rate, it will take another four decades for women to reach pay parity with men.

Congress should strengthen the Equal Pay Act by closing loopholes that permit discrimination, and should enact legislation prohibiting employers from firing employees who share their salary data. Enforced secrecy sustains inequality: Many women are unaware of discriminatory pay scales because they are prohibited from discussing their salary with coworkers.

Wage inequality is part cause and part effect of a larger phenomenon: gross inequality in economic and political power. Although women are well represented as students in colleges and professional schools, as they move up the ladder they eventually face the glass ceiling. The upper echelons of the business world remain virtually a males-only club, as indicated by some telling statistics: only 16 percent of partners in law firms are women, 16 percent of corporate officers, and 12 percent of Fortune 500 boards. Only eight Fortune 500 companies have female CEOs. Women represent 50 percent of the population, but just 15 percent of the U.S. Congress.

Such discriminatory patterns tend to reinforce themselves, depriving companies, consumers, and citizens of diverse viewpoints—which result in less enlightened policies. We are also sending a depressing message to young girls that contradicts the official pieties about equal opportunity: The good old boy network remains a powerful force in America's economy and social and political life.

Women's professional advance is inextricably linked with their personal freedom. Progress in the workplace would be reversed if we turn back the clock on reproductive rights. But while celebrating women's autonomy, we should not celebrate abortion. To the contrary, we should take reasonable measures to reduce the number of unwanted pregnancies. The debate over how to accomplish this objective has come to resemble a beer commercial ("less filling"; "tastes great"), with both sides shouting competing slogans ("abstinence"; "birth control") that rest on a false dichotomy. We need *both* to preach the virtues of abstinence and to educate young people about contraception, since it is unrealistic to expect everyone to heed lessons about abstinence. Equally important, we need to provide better support services for pregnant women and children born into poverty. One recalls Congressman Barney Frank's observation that some right-wingers believe that life begins at conception and ends in birth. Those who insist that every pregnancy should result in birth should not oppose the programs (such as infant nutrition and pre-K education) that give children a decent chance in life.

Progress for women in other areas is often less impressive than we're led to believe. For example, despite real gains under Title IX, resources for women's sports have never caught up to resources for men's sports at most colleges and universities. Women's athletic programs continue to lag behind men's by all measurable criteria. While 55 percent of our college populations are female, female athletes receive only 42 percent of participation opportunities, and 36 percent of operating expenditures.

Why are women still second-class citizens in athletics despite Title IX's promise of equality? Because laws on the books mean little unless adequately enforced. The federal agency responsible for enforcing Title IX, the U.S. Department of Education's Office for Civil Rights (OCR), has not initiated a single proceeding to remove federal funds at any school or college failing to comply. Instead, OCR has negotiated settlements that are usually far less than the law requires.

Gay men and lesbians constantly confront unequal treatment. The denial of same-sex marriage, much in the news lately, is only one example of discrimination based on sexual orientation. By denying gays marriage status (or at least a fully equivalent legal status), a state also denies gay couples access to scores of state and federal benefits—pertaining to health insurance, hospital visitation, probate rights, tax benefits, and much more. The comprehensive package of benefits accompanying marriage makes it far easier to raise a family. Those who promote the fear that gays will do harm to children should instead recognize the harm to children of gay couples that comes from discriminatory laws making it difficult for such couples to provide for them.

Politicians who oppose equal rights for same-sex couples (which is most politicians, reflecting timidity as well as prejudice) go to great pains to deny any animosity against gays. For example, in his state of the union address, President Bush noted that "the same moral tradition that defines marriage also teaches that each individual has dignity and value in God's sight." But such rhetoric is unmatched by deeds. If the Republican Party truly cares about gays as individuals warranting proper treatment, why not protect them from discrimination in the workplace?

For ten years now, Republicans have blocked the Employment Non-Discrimination Act (ENDA), which would prohibit employment discrimination against gays (while exempting from its terms businesses with fewer than fifteen employees, religious organizations, and the armed forces). In many states, there is no legal remedy for workplace discrimination based on sexual orientation, even though firing or refusing to hire people because they are gay clearly fails to treat them with the value and dignity the president claims they deserve.

Although ENDA exempts the armed forces, gays in the military deserve more protection. The "don't ask, don't tell" policy, a well-meaning initiative, has failed to reverse the policy of harassing and expelling gays. Those willing to take up arms to serve their country are the last people who should run up against government bigotry or acquiescence in private bigotry. (Many countries recognize as much, treating gays as equals in the armed forces.) The tombstone of

Leonard Matlovich carries this inscription: "When I was in the military, they gave me a medal for killing two men, and a discharge for loving one."

Attacks on Civil Liberties

Inseparable from civil rights are "civil liberties." Today, civil liberties are under siege from a president and attorney general (abetted by a panicked Congress that overwhelmingly passed the Patriot Act in the wake of the terrorist attack on September 11) who view violations of the Constitution by the executive branch as mere technicalities rather than a growing threat to the constitutional fabric of liberty, privacy, due process, and fair trials.

Of course, they are verbally reassuring about the "war on terrorism." President Bush says, "We will not allow this enemy to win the war by restricting our freedoms." Last September, Attorney General Ashcroft said, "We're not sacrificing civil liberties. We're securing civil liberties." Then they swing into action, making arrests without charges followed by indefinite imprisonment without lawyers. They jail indefinitely "material witnesses," not accused of any crimes. To shove the courts aside, they need only call someone—even an American citizen—an "enemy combatant." That permits them to throw him into the brig without charges and without a lawyer, so no one can question the all-powerful White House prosecutors. Over two centuries ago, James Madison warned that "the accumulation of all powers, legislative, executive, and judicial, in the same hands, whether of one, a few, or many, may justly be pronounced the very definition of tyranny." Imagine what Madison and Thomas Jefferson would think of the Bush administration!

What would they think of the dragnet law enforcement approach where everyone is a suspect until proven otherwise? With perfunctory judicial approvals facilitated by recent statutes, federal snoopers can secretly search our homes and businesses simply by asking a secret court for a warrant—a court that rarely says no. The government can go to libraries and bookstores to find out what we've been reading and prohibit the librarian or storeowner from telling us or anyone about their demands. It can listen in on conversations between lawyers and their clients in federal prisons. It can access our computer records, e-mails, medical files, and financial information based on what is essentially an enforcement whim.

The Constitution's great phrase of restraint, "probable cause," has been swept away. Without "probable cause," government agents can covertly attend and monitor public meetings, including places of worship. Wantonly brandishing the word "terror," the Bush White House is becoming a law unto itself—chilling Congress, intimidating Democrats, diminishing legal review, distracting the nation from domestic necessities, and draining the federal budget into a swamp of deficits to pay for a garrison state and its foreign adventures. And most important for Bush, attempting to frighten the public into his re-election.

To their credit, conservative Republicans have opposed some executive overreaching, such as a TIPS program ("Total Information Awareness Program") that would have enlisted millions of postal workers, delivery people, truckers, and service workers who have access to homes and offices to report on any "suspicious" talk or activities. Congressional conservatives and liberals joined together to stop this crazy move toward a nation of snoopers, part of a Rumsfeldian fantasy of a gigantic computer dragnet of detailed information about all Americans.

Give George W. Bush credit for keeping one campaign promise— to be "a uniter, not a divider." Bush has united liberals and conservatives in rising opposition to his government of men, not laws.

In this chapter, I've touched on some of the problems with our laws and legal system and proposed solutions that would provide greater protection to ordinary citizens and the most vulnerable among us. Yet rather than considering implementation of such measures, state and federal legislatures are busy working to restrict the rights of ordinary citizens and to protect wealthy corporations and professions, even though such immunities harm the public interest and result in more innocent victims. Meanwhile, in the name of protecting our liberties, the federal executive branch assumes junta-like powers. Does all this reflect a proper set of priorities? A well-functioning political process?

CONSUMER WONDERLAND

One spring morning in 1972, I went to National Airport in Washington, D.C., to catch an Allegheny Airlines plane to Hartford, Connecticut. A large audience in downtown Hartford was gathering at noon to hear me and other speakers. Hurrying to the ticket counter by the jetway, I arrived in time with my confirmed reservation in hand. But the passenger clerk told me and the legislative aide to Connecticut Senator Abraham Ribicoff that we could not board because the plane was full.

"What?" I protested, "You can't be serious. I have a reserved seat."

"Sorry," he said, "you can take a small plane to Philadelphia and change planes to Hartford arriving in several hours."

Too late for my speaking engagement. Thanks a lot.

Attorney Reuben Robertson took my case all the way to the Supreme Court, which unanimously ruled that bumped consumers could sue an airline for illegal and deceptive practices. As a result, all the airlines changed their deliberate overbooking practices. Since then, when an airline overbooks, it offers seated passengers money to get off the plane and take the next flight, which allows overbooked passengers to get on board. This solution has worked well.

In this instance, I was able to make a difference. Unfortunately, we consumers are amateurs increasingly controlled by large vendors who are staggeringly skilled at relieving us of our dollars and our ability to fight back. They are remorseless and organized; consumers are voiceless, isolated, and unsupported by the supposed forces of law and order. Neither regulation nor litigation offers adequate protection. As I have pointed out, our state and federal legislators are making it more and more difficult for us to take corporate crooks to court no matter how serious our injuries, widespread the frauds, or unconscionable the conduct. The big business lobby (small business, having to face customers and larger competitors, is a different story) is so powerful that it writes and unwrites the legal rules. Large corporations have become the law unto themselves.

But, say the theoretical free enterprisers, it is the market that rules, not the big sellers. The market is king. Well, the market is only king when quality competition rules, and vendors get around it by destroying, attenuating, or avoiding competition and maintaining control of consumers. The nullification of authentic competition goes well beyond monopolistic practices; it is an immensely intricate artifice of the ingenious commercial mind. Ever see a television ad for a new car in congested traffic? Ever see an ad for a modern public transit system with comfortable commuting passengers reading, chatting, or snoozing while their super-rail zooms by a highway clogged with trucks, vans, and cars? Sixty years of automobile company propaganda, and of course we believe that mass transit is inefficient compared to the gas guzzling, polluting motor vehicles that fill up one seat out of five on expensive congested roadways. When we think of mass transit, we envision old-style buses, conventional trains, and their incomplete routes in suburbs designed for highways and motor vehicles.

Smarter Consumers, Better Markets

Ever wonder what we mean when we say certain food is delicious? Is it the sugar added for our taste buds by the processors? What's in the food may not delight our arteries, kidneys, liver, heart, or cells, but as unenlightened consumers, we figure that what doesn't immediately pinch can't possibly hurt. Meanwhile, our children pollute their bodies with the ominous fat and sugar from the McDonalds pumping machine.

See all those advertisement for double cheeseburgers, and those fat-immersed hot dogs that are the dietary equivalent of deadly pink missiles. Millions of ads everywhere, despite studies connecting fatty food to diet-related diseases costing over three hundred thousand lives a year. You never see an anti-ad that gives dietary cat-scans for the sake of real knowledge—that elusive thing that makes a market work. You've never seen one of these anti-ads on television, although it's a sight I bet millions of physicians, dieticians, nutritionists, and vegetarians would welcome. You are surely not getting the other side of the story.

The market respects the consumer only to the extent that the consumer brings knowledge to the market. In the 1950s, the jukebox era of automotive design, GM would say "we're giving the consumers what they want and that's why we're making our profit." How can they say that's what motorists wanted when they were selling them style, speed, and power but keeping them in the dark about seat belts and other safety devices, lower auto insurance rates, fuel efficiency, pollution control, protective bumpers, and ease of maintenance and repair? All those issues were off the boards because the other car companies copied the GM giant. Economists call this habit "protective imitation." When many functional features became publicized by consumer and Congressional advocacy and became subject to regulation and European-Japanese competition, surveys showed an upward curve of consumer receptiveness. Things started to change. Before long, car companies were bragging about features they had opposed for years. Regulation and higher quality competition brought motorists more life-saving, money-saving, and lung-saving products.

One sees the same sequence of progress in the food market. When I was a teenager, my father's restaurant had a Polish-American baker who made good, solid, fresh loaves of bread daily. Some people liked them, but they were never as popular as the Wonder and Tiptop breads in the grocery stores. You know it's Wonder Bread without looking, because you can pick up a loaf, squeeze, and find your fingers colliding with your palm. There might have been a whole wheat loaf on the shelves, but, by and large, the choice back then was limited to bleached white flour bread. Then came knowledge—Senate hearings, articles in newspapers about nutrition, diet, weight, and disease citing independent experts, followed by national television shows like Phil Donahue's showcasing nutritious whole foods. That knowledge was carried into the supermarkets as forty million Americans embraced diets more conducive to good health. The stores diversified their offering with more bread varieties and more fresh vegetables and fruits. Later, grocery shelves offered organic foods, low-fat foods, less sugared foods, and fewer empty calories. Not everyone, to be sure, but millions of eaters have gotten on the right track. Larger consumer frames of reference make markets tick, and smaller competitors can move into the markets ignored by obtuse vendors.

But not always. It depends whether the markets are truly open to competitors. Until the 1970s, cartel regulation froze out new airlines. The big airlines specifically demanded and received this regulation, called the Civil Aeronautics Board, in the late 1930s. When that barrier was finally removed, some new airlines (such as People's) were created that offered cheap fares. The big airlines, with their greater reserves and credit lines, had several ways to fight back. They could merge with the smaller airlines, or drive out their limited-route competitors by predatory pricing. They also controlled the finite number of jetway slots at airports.

In a twenty-year span, more than twenty-five airline mergers were approved by the Department of Transportation. Many fares were outrageously high, especially on essentially monopoly or duopoly routes such as Washington to Pittsburgh, Hartford, and New York. Travelers adjusted, pacified in part by frequent flyer miles and senior packs. The business traveler, naturally not wanting a Saturday stay-over, paid dearly. Then came Herbert Kelleher's Southwest Airlines and its methodical expansion out of Texas. Gradually, travelers came to see that they did not have to spend long minutes pressing recorded announcements one, two, three, four, and then waiting while music or advertisements assaulted their ears. Why, sometimes when I wanted to hear classical music while working late hours, I dialed United Airlines.

By contrast, most of the time after three or four rings one found a real person with real answers at the other end of the Southwest Airlines phone. We did not have to pay extra to change a ticket. Southwest's employees went to work wanting to say *yes* to customers, not a variety of defiant *no*'s. In 2000, 2001, and 2002, this cheapest airline with the best service on the newest planes made more profits than its three biggest competitors combined—United, Delta, and American. At least while Southwest's superiority lasts, the awful quality of big airline management, so addicted to self-pampering and rewarding itself with unmerited bonuses, is exposed. Kelleher has been receiving much lower pay than the heads of those diminishing companies.

Often, it takes a long time for a company like Southwest to break through and raise expectation levels of consumers and market to those levels. Typically, mimicry feeds the craving for control by businesses that like to avoid the uncertainties of competition. In addition to overt price-rigging, as has often occurred in the highway construction in-dustry, there are endless ways to suppress competition. Signaling for parallel pricing (which avoids smoke-filled rooms that invite antitrust prosecutors) occurs throughout the economy right down to the local banking, repair, and medical-dental service markets.

Then there are all those unfair, fine-print contracts we dutifully sign on the dotted line with nary a glance at the oceans of words in their pages. Lawyers call these "contracts of adhesion" and, indeed, they stick it to you when you sign a lease, buy a car, purchase a home with a mortgage, obtain an insurance policy, purchase software, open a bank account, or end up in the hospital. Recall that one of the pillars of our presumed free economy is freedom of contract. Suppose you want to exercise this freedom. You are appalled by the fine-print sales contract at the GM dealer and stomp down the street to the Ford or Toyota dealership. Same fine print. You see the State Farm auto insurance policy and hop over to the Allstate office. Same fine print. You recoil from the Visa credit card application form with its stream of conditions and trundle over to Mastercard. Priceless, but find the same fine print!

These private corporate legislatures lock up consumers in a tighter and tighter vise. These fine print contracts, representing corporate regulation of consumers, are so unbalanced as to be comical—were they not so tragic. A spreading contract provision keeps you from going to court in a dispute, and restricts you to compulsory arbitration. Some of these so-called contracts contain a provision stating that the vendor reserves the right to change unilaterally the terms of the agreement. That is why the airlines, for instance, can decide arbitrarily to require more frequent-flyer miles and pile on more onerous restrictions than you initially were accepting with good faith.

A contract is a meeting of the minds with reciprocal obligations. When was the last time you met the mind of Microsoft Windows, Wal-Mart, Sears, or your HMO? The whole system is an outrageous farce with a noncompetitive corporate government taking away our constitutional rights (especially to a trial by jury) in ever more brazen fashion. Some courts uphold one-sided fine print by resorting to absurd legal fictions, such as the presumed consent of the buyer. When there are no choices, consent is effectively coerced. Some excellent judicial decisions in the 1960s invalidated certain "unconscionable" landlord leases. Such judicial wisdom is rare today.

Year after year, the pseudo-contract squeeze intensifies and tips the balance of negotiating power even further in favor of sellers. The more these vendors get away with, the more they seek to get away with, until the consumer becomes a contractual serf. This serfdom is illustrated in the inability of medical malpractice victims to sue their HMOs for the most serious injuries. In such cases, the fine print was not just in the contracts but also in an arcane provision in a federal law called Employment Retirement Income Security Act (ERISA), enacted in 1974.

The most egregious injustices are inflicted on the poor. They have always paid more because their powerlessness attracts predators. Thanks to fine-print contracts, pay-day loans, rent-to-own rackets, predatory lending, landlord abuses, and check-cashing gouges are legal and crushingly enforceable. The results? Four hundred percent cumulating interest rates on pay-day loans, forfeiture of one's small home for missing payments on a television set, and countless other horror stories. Economic abuses in the inner city define the indifference or corruption of elected officials and their uninterested or underbudgeted prosecutors. Much financing of these rip-offs comes from Wall Street financial companies whose executives, not wanting to dirty their hands, act through intermediaries. The lawmakers are often their agents. In the 1970s, usury was illegal. What to do? Presto, repeal the state usury laws and watch interest rates on consumer loans skyrocket.

Another ticket to consumer serfdom is the blizzard of fees and penalties imposed on unconsenting customers by banks, credit card companies, airlines, and numerous other firms. These charges become profit centers, not just a way to unbundle general prices. You inadvertently bounce a check, which costs your bank under two dollars, and you're charged thirty dollars. These and other bank charges—there are over three hundred different varieties—total over $29 billion a year. Plunder!

The smelly avarice takes many forms. Your series of checks that are presented for clearance are chosen so that the big one comes first—so you can bounce three smaller ones for three penalties instead of one. ATMs were introduced as a free service to help banks become more efficient and cut the cost of banking services. Now ATM fees are profit centers. All these charges breed less revolt or resistance because you do not have to write a check.

Your monies are in their hands so they can just debit them, thereby inducing passive nonresistance. (The government, by the way, does not include fees and penalties as part of its inflation index because they are not considered prices.)

Similar rip-offs abound. The computerized consumer credit and debit systems of charges and payments make possible unilateral impositions that would have been laughed out of the country not too many years ago. The coercive, often unannounced, packing of fees and charges during real estate settlements amount to $10 billion a year, according to Bush's Secretary of Housing and Urban Development Mel Martinez. In the late 1990s, Advanta credit card company announced that as of July that year if any of its customers quit doing business with it, they would be charged twenty-five dollars. Now, imagine the year is 1950, and the only payment is by cash or check. A company says to its customers that anyone quitting it would be charged twenty-five dollars. How many customers would have rushed to make out the check?

A Chicago bank declared that any customers using a live teller would be assessed a fee. Another bank stated that calling the bank more than twice a month would incur a fee of two dollars a call. The same bank charged fifty cents for a deposit slip—the kind that used to be piled up for the asking under the glass tables. Similarly, General Electric (GE) Credit stated it would charge customers more if they paid their credit balance on time! How's that for punishing prudence and punctuality? GE Credit makes its money from late payments. Perverse.

So much data on consumer purchases are in computer banks that one-stop banking can mean a one-stop octopus. Just try and leave for another bank once you have all your various financial transactions locked in a matrix of charges, credit ratings, credit scores whirling around the nation or the world to whomever without your consent. And this is just the beginning. Control over your financial transactions is a prime objective of financial institutions these days. That is why they oppose opt-in rights for consumers and why they are increasingly surcharging you if you pay or order the old fashioned ways. The power to debit is the power to control. It's convenient to a shopper, and you just won't feel a thing.

Under-Investment in Fraud Control

Some of the largest crimes and frauds are the ones you do not know about or feel, such as third-party payments. But all of us pay for them. Take the rapacious computerized billing fraud in the $1.6 trillion health care and pharmaceutical industry. In 1992, the General Accounting Office (GAO) estimated that 10 percent of health care spending is defrauded. Today, that would be $160 billion down the drain. The nation's leading expert on this rake-off, Malcolm Sparrow, who teaches at the Kennedy School of Government at Harvard University, estimates that health care fraud costs could actually be three times that amount. With a doctorate in applied mathematics and experience in police law enforcement against fraud, Sparrow, author of *License to Steal,* asserts that the federal government is seriously under-investing in fraud control and doesn't even want to know its scope. Under Bush, the Inspector General of the Department of Health and Human Services has stopped reporting the amount it is overpaying doctors, hospitals, and other health care sellers for Medicare. The audits themselves are not comprehensive. They exclude, for example, services not provided, and the auditors do not contact the patients to verify that the billed services were actually provided. Sparrow told the weekly *Corporate Crime Reporter* that "most kinds of fraud would go unnoticed by such an audit protocol."

The savvy know the codes and know how to provide bogus documentation when they submit claims. Sparrow sees new legislation leading to bigger crimes, such as pharmacy-related frauds in the Medicaid programs. He believes that enforcement budgets are pitifully small—"one tenth of one percent of what is being spent on the program, or less. Multiply that budget ten or twenty fold and it will pay off handsomely. Typically, return rates are five to one, ten to one, in some cases 200 to one." As for effective penalties that deter "corporate crime," Sparrow sees two. "One is the threat of exclusion from major public programs like Medicare and Medicaid," The other? "Personal criminal liability for executives. That does get their attention."

Ever hear of Malcolm Sparrow? Ever see him on the television news or the network magazine shows? All he has is meticulous knowledge of how intricate gigantic frauds are perpetuated, and how to document and do something about them so that health care consumers get what they pay for. Think about it: $150 billion to $450 billion a year and growing. This is real money, enough to cover the tens of millions of Americans who lack health insurance. Sparrow toils in his office in Cambridge, rarely called by the media, very rarely consulted by members of Congress about enacting effective, funded fraud control systems. Law and order goes out the window when such corporations are involved, when scams are so rampant that they become the accepted way of doing business. A form of looting.

As taxpayers and consumers, we pay for this seamy kind of business. Stealth forms of fraud that escape the attention of regular people going about their lives is the mark of a complex, multitiered economy able to shift heavy costs onto innocent citizens. Consumers ultimately pay all the bills, because they are the path of least resistance.

The worst penalties consumers pay are death, injury, and sickness due to marketplace failures. The ultimate abuse consumers endure stems from hazardous products, toxic chemicals, and the compulsory consumption called "pollution." The toll is terrible, though historically it is occasionally reduced by protests of those afflicted and their families and friends.

It is a reflection of our current powerlessness that politicians running for office rarely place these human casualties on their campaign agenda. According to OSHA, 58 thousand Americans die yearly from workplace-related disease and trauma. The Natural Resources Defense Council estimates 64 thousand people die every year from air pollution. The Harvard School of Public Health physicians put the number of deaths due to medical malpractice in hospitals, excluding emergency rooms, at 80 thousand a year. The Institute of Medicine reports an annual loss of about 18 thousand lives due to lack of health insurance coverage. Medical journal articles estimate 100 thousand Americans lose their lives each year due to adverse effects of medical drugs. The National Highway Traffic Safety Administration reports annual deaths of roughly 42 thousand (to either motorists or pedestrians) from motor vehicle crashes.

Most of these casualties are preventable, but this kind of violence doesn't much interest legislators, governors, or presidents—except when the people rise up and protest. Imagine if all these preventable human losses together, occurring month after month with dismal predictability, produced the hue and cry that the September 11, 2001, terrorist attacks provoked. One, of course, is deliberate premeditated violence, the other usually results from incompetence, carelessness, crime or rationalized willfulness such as dirty electric generating plants and drug industry greed. But it hardly consoles a mother who loses her child to malpractice, to respiratory disease, or a reckless construction workplace cave-in to be told that the cause of death was not terrorism. The crux is the preventability of all styles of violence. Stopping preventable violence should be our cause.

Look at how the tobacco industry's manipulation of youthful emotions and fantasies was challenged after millions of tobacco-related deaths in the United States. It started with the release by

Dr. Luther Terry of the Surgeon General's first report on tobacco and health in 1964. Our society was puffing away when this bombshell dropped on a population divided almost evenly between smokers and nonsmokers. Smokers were aggressive, blowing smoke in your face and superseding the rights of nonsmokers to breathe tobacco-free air. I recall in college, lecture hall after lecture hall filled with cigarette smoke. Most nonsmokers didn't dare to demand that smokers refrain.

This first report was followed by annual reports, regularly adding to the evidence and findings. By the late 1960s, the nonsmoking movement was underway. My associates and I were in the vanguard of pressing for smoke-free airplanes, interstate buses, and railroads. Smokers were not pleased, but the tide was unstoppable, notwithstanding the tobacco industry's hiring of scientists to deny repeatedly the connection between cigarettes and lung cancer and other ailments. Official reports led to breakthroughs in the hitherto self-censored media. Physicians began counseling more of their patients. The early, unsuccessful lawsuits that were filed against Big Tobacco were followed by more successful ones that uncovered incriminating internal company documents about the deliberate hooking of youngsters. Inside, whistleblowers came forward. *Sixty Minutes* and *20/20* commenced a series of exposés. The fight over tobacco became a more regular beat for newspapers and magazines. Accumulating medical research about the varieties of tobacco-related harms was reported on the evening news.

Word of mouth spread. Local antismoking groups were formed all over the country, their members trained in tobacco-control and tobacco-free areas strategies. Community health leaders began to meet and plan. The decisive blow came when trial lawyers and state attorneys general got together to file the now celebrated lawsuits against Big Tobacco. The resulting settlement of $206 billion over twenty-five years and disgorgement of millions of pages of internal company documents lifted the profile of a scourge that was taking well over

420 thousand American lives a year. (That's more than the total number of American lives lost in World War II.)

Smoking adults now comprise less than 25 percent of the adult population, from 45 percent in 1965. This great, ongoing consumer health victory reflects the efforts of millions of people. Each time a person objected to smoking in public areas, it helped the cause. Each time the managers of a public institution declared a public space off-limits to smoking, it advanced the cause. The once all-powerful tobacco companies were thrown on the defensive, forced to acknowledge the harm of tobacco addiction that their century of clever ads helped foster. Now, Philip Morris asks Congress to give the Food and Drug Administration regulatory authority over tobacco, Maryland proposes a buyout of tobacco farms, and other states consider this approach.

In the midst of this activity, the trial lawyers were unfairly reviled. To be sure, they had an economic interest, but it was contingent on a verdict or settlement. Their investment in these costly cases reaps no fees when they lose. Without any regulation of the industry, the courts were the only fairly level playing field left. This instrument of justice must be preserved in the face of recurrent assaults by immunity-minded corporations.

Needless to say, tobacco is not the only addictive product dutifully proffered to young and adult alike. The liquor industry entices the young with its ads and sponsored events. Street drug dealers seduce the youth with their substances. The addicted bear some responsibility for sure, but so do the far more driven, calculating, and organized addictors. Legal or illegal, it is all about making money by preying on the vulnerable, the young, the impoverished.

Consumers, however, bear little responsibility when they are harmed by what they cannot see, smell, taste, or touch, such as radiation, carbon monoxide, pesticides, herbicides, toxic additives, leachings like lead, and contaminated foodstuffs. The recent hikes in gasoline, heating oil, and natural gas prices represent forces beyond the reach of individual consumers. With no change in supply and demand, the industry's hikes will take billions of dollars from consumer pocket-books while promoting fuel-guzzling vehicles. When it comes to tax cuts, George W. Bush tells us incessantly that the "people" should be able to keep more of their own money. Of course, those tax cuts go mostly to the wealthy. Why doesn't he ever defend the consumer from his avaricious oil and gas buddies? Why doesn't George W. say that consumers should be able to keep more of their own money?

Moving Forward

What can the individual consumer do when corporate lobbies push for reduced regulations so that they can take the federal cop off the corporate beat? They succeeded in weakening banking and securities regulations. Hundreds of billions of lost dollars resulted from the savings and loan scandals of the early 1980s to the ongoing Wall Street scandals. Paid for by the people.

Regulation does matter! Government subsidizes costly synthetic fuel projects for companies to produce energy that is then given government price supports, illustrating Bush's and the industry's utter contempt for consumers and the marketplace. Without regulation or de facto deregulation, electric, gas, and telephone utilities are like private governments wherever they have monopoly. But even in deregulated industries, such as the price-competitive long-distance telephone area, the companies get on new rip-off tracks to trick consumers. "Competing by cheating, scams, and schemes," was Connecticut Attorney General Richard Blumenthal's explanation for his lawsuits against AT&T, MCI WorldCom, Sprint, and Quest. Complexity and latency are the nefarious modes of rolling shoppers. If food buyers want to know whether the supermarket food is irradiated, the industry arranges with the FDA for the least visible emblem. For genetically engineered foodstuffs, the industry has fought any labeling favored by over 90 percent of the people. Deregulation of the cable industry has sent cable rates higher as giant mergers leave viewers with less and less competition and choice of quality programming.

Powerlessness leads to paying ever-higher drug prices to an immensely profitable industry that consumers subsidize heavily through tax credits and free research and development from the National Institutes of Health. Five years ago, I received a letter from a woman with ovarian cancer who lost her $19-thousand-a-year job and her health insurance. Her doctor recommended Taxol sold by Bristol-Meyers-Squibb and a series of treatments that would cost $14 thousand. What she may not have known is that the National Institutes of Health programs discovered Taxol and tested it in human clinical trials. Then, under federal policy, the agency gave it to Bristol Meyers to sell under a monopoly marketing agreement with no royalty clause or reasonable pricing provision. What can an individual consumer do about this and many other medical discoveries that are developed by the taxpayer and handed off to the drug firms, who put out ads taking the credit?

What can consumers do when, even with a second breadwinner, a family can't make ends meet and the debt trap creeps up on it? Consumer debt, including home mortgages, is nearing $8 trillion. There are record numbers of bankruptcy filings. The two major causes of personal bankruptcy are medical expenses and job loss. Still, the credit and financial industries press Congress to make it much harder to declare bankruptcy. These and other lobbying drives are part of a big business strategy to increase the corporate regulation of government to achieve corporate goals and not the goals of the American people our agencies are sworn to represent. A persistent testament to the short-sightedness of industry is that it never recognizes the future benefits of regulation even as it advertises the past benefits (like federal meat inspection) or boasts about the safety features of products (such as seat belts and air bags) brought about by previous regulatory standards.

The corporate propaganda machines, and those of the think tanks they fund, strive to get people to hate their system of protection—often exaggerating costs, ignoring benefits, and peddling cock and bull stories about the destruction of innovation and productivity. These corporate behemoths peddle the canard that health and safety regulations inhibit freedom, when, in fact, the opposite is true. Such regulations produce freedom from harm and fraud. Maybe they have been listening too much to President Ronald Reagan who, when campaigning in 1980 in Michigan, called air bags an impediment to freedom. Maybe in a narrow technical way, he was correct—air bags block the freedom to travel through the windshield.

Credit scores, debit charges, contracts of adhesion, collusion, refusals to sell (as in red-lining), latent defects, overwhelming complexity of goods and services, no outlets for grievances, little time for comparison shopping—it all amounts to a steady loss of consumer control in the marketplace, and it mandates development of a more rigorous consumer consciousness. Lying, cheating, and stealing from consumers is equivalent to a pay cut at the office or the plant. In the 1970s, Senator Philip Hart (D.-Mich.) estimated that 25 percent of consumer income is gobbled up by frauds and abuses. Customarily, a pay cut hurts a lot more than an equivalent depletion of the consumer dollars that a worker's pay makes possible. An attitudinal upgrade is needed here. Workers will labor hundreds of hours to buy a new motor vehicle or pay for food, but spending three or four hours learning how to buy those products will save them far more dollars per hour than their pay per hour at work.

One radio talk show host read my book *Winning the Insurance Game* (coauthored with Wesley J. Smith), took the advice, called his brokers and saved $500 on his yearly insurance buys. Shoppers flock to Wal-Mart for a good deal. But these deals hurt shoppers in hidden ways. Wal-Mart's low-wage policies, which also demand that suppliers cut costs by driving down wages and benefits, or exporting jobs to China, reduce purchasing power and increase dependency on governmental social service programs. Wal-Mart has crushed Main Street and replaced the community of family-owned small businesses that constitute community and pay local taxes. All this reduces the scope of the consumer's supposed bargain. Polls have shown that American consumers are willing to pay more for improved conditions in foreign sweat-shops, which produce goods for export to the United States.

Consciousness grows when skills are acquired. During my final days as a senior at Princeton, we were visited by an insurance salesman trying to sell us life insurance. We never thought to ask the obvious question: "We have no dependents, so why life insurance?" When I mentioned this episode to my father, he replied: "Don't confuse schooling with intelligence."

The marketing madness and deceptive promotions and advertising have filled books (one of the best is by Michael F. Jacobson and Laurie Ann Mazur, *Marketing Madness*). Commercialism runs rampant, plastering logos and ads in schools, on public buses, on floors and ceilings, zoos, museums, operas, athletes' uniforms, and lately, on some college student's bodies. When commercialism reigns, everything is for sale, even civic sanctuaries and childhood itself. Its insidious energy and creativity undermine an independent consumer consciousness and the desire for consumer skills. Young students can learn more about our economy by acquiring consumer skills than by rote reading. How should they best fend for themselves? How should they shop for credit, for a car, for competent health care or clothing? Absent the assertive consumer, a dependency takes hold and the student grows up corporate, making what Pavlov called conditioned responses.

Sixty years ago, we could have graduated from our schools skilled consumers who would have placed a greater value on renewable, self-reliant, safe solar energy; more modern public transit; universal health insurance; and other positive transformations of our economy and environment. Skilled consumers are far less likely to be hoodwinked, to be denied information, to have their grievances ignored, and their horizons restricted from broader possibilities for consumer sovereignty. Smart consumers make the economy more efficient, more productive, and more competitive. They should be the quality control for sellers. They would be more likely to band together to negotiate terms of exchange with vendors—banks, insurance companies, real estate brokers, manufacturers, and other lines of industry and commerce. Companies are organized. Consumers need to be as well. The approaches to organization vary, including buying clubs, cooperatives, specialized consumer groups for complaint-handling, lobbying, their own media, negotiating the basic terms of trade from contracts to product specifications to pricing levels. The Internet can make this less expensive and quicker with ease of entry.

It is necessary for enough consumers to think of their role in broad terms, beyond their pocketbooks and immediate purchases. If motorists had thought big and organized to instruct their elected officials and the leaders of auto companies early on, motorists today would reach their destinations more safely, healthfully, economically, and inexpensively. Every day, motorists on congested highways pay the price of neglect. Since the true measure of a sustainable economic system is the health, safety, and economic well-being of consumers, buyers can properly see themselves organized as the shapers of such an economy. Otherwise, the rat race continues in a downward spiral of debt, depletion, and dependency. Not a nice prospect, given invasive new technologies, to hand down to defenseless children and grandchildren.

Ten Simple Ways to Shaft
Yourself as a Consumer

1. Buy before you think.
2. Buy before you read.
3. Buy before you ask questions.
4. Buy before you can afford to buy.
5. Buy before you see through the seller's smile and smooth tongue.
6. Buy before you comparison shop.
7. Buy when you are tired or hungry.
8. Buy when you are rushed.
9. Buy to dote on your child or because you child demands the product.
10. Buy just to keep up with your friends or neighbors.

From: *The Frugal Shopper Checklist Book: What You Need to Know to Win in the Marketplace* (Washington, D.C.: Center for the Study of Responsive Law, 1995).

WHEN LITTLE
TAXPAYERS SHRUGGED

I n the late 1970s, I had lunch with the commissioner of the Internal Revenue Service and several others. During the wide-ranging conversation, I offered my check-off proposal for the 1040 tax return. Over one hundred million of these forms are sent out every January. Since the tax system exists for the benefit of the people, why not allow prominent space where taxpayers can voluntarily check off minimum dues to join an independent, nationwide, membership-controlled taxpayers association? Its full-time, independent, non-government staff would be vigilant on the fairness of the tax system, its enforcement, and how the money is spent or misspent. The commissioner seemed to like my proposal, but after reflecting a moment or two he said he could not support it. Why, I asked? Then came one of the most memorable replies in all my experience with governmental officials. "Because," he explained, "it would cause undue clutter on the tax return."

Clutter? I murmured something about the existing clutter throughout the individual tax returns. I'm sure he had other objections, for he was a serious man.

Engraved in stone at the top of the IRS headquarters are the words of Oliver Wendell Holmes Jr., a Justice of the Supreme Court of the United States: "Taxes are what we pay for civilized society." Holmes practiced what he preached and then some, leaving his entire estate of one million dollars to the U.S. government.

By his example, Justice Holmes was directing our attention to the public or common good, and away from the individual discomfort over contributing tax revenues. Today, many prominent corporatists would scoff at such a view. For them, taxes are something to be diminished, avoided, or evaded whether by exemptions, deductions, depreciations or other write-offs, shelters and tax havens, forgiveness or waivers, safe harbors, outright statutory tax cuts, and acquiescent regulatory opinions. Holmes would have greeted such schemes with patrician contempt. Taxes helped the people become a community with decent public services, prevented clear and present dangers, filled gaps in the private economy, built and maintained public works (now called infrastructure), delivered the mail, and provided law and order (through the courts, through the regulatory and law enforcement agencies).

For millions of individuals, acceptance of their tax obligations would increase if they thought everyone was paying their fair share and the monies were being used efficiently and wisely. Since that is not the case, cynicism reigns and much manual or clerical work is done off the books. The attitude of cynicism is buttressed by selfishness—looking out for number one. There are plenty of tax preparation services and unscrupulous outfits touting "pay no tax" schemes, which cater to this desire to exit.

It is difficult to square fiscal abandonment of country and community with patriotism. But when Congress and the president allow massive escapes from tax responsibilities for large corporations and the wealthy, the sense of patriotism attached to paying taxes goes out the window for many people. To check out, instead of forcefully voicing one's grievances, only worsens the situation. Because the indentured government demands that smaller taxpayers pay a larger share than is fair, these taxpayers should be more demanding of their government.

When some taxpayers complained bitterly to their representatives about mistreatment by the IRS, the resulting public hearings excoriated the IRS in the full glare of mass media. Many television viewers enjoyed seeing the tax collectors get their comeuppance. However, other consequences of IRS-bashing were not so widely publicized. Despite more taxpayers and a growing complex economy, the IRS budget has been slashed or blocked from expanding, which only benefits tax avoidance and evasion schemes of the multinational corporations and the super-rich. Moreover, Congress pressured the IRS to go after low-income workers for alleged fraud in the earned income tax credit. Less money for the IRS to corral the big fish and more pressure on go after the poor—grotesque priorities. Television viewers witnessed a congressional hearing extravaganza in exchange for more burdens on their 1040 returns.

In 1998, Charles O. Rossotti, head of the IRS, testified that tax avoidance and tax evasion cost each taxpayer an average of more than $1,600 per year. That's based on what he knows. What Rossotti doesn't know, nor does anyone, is the aggregate amount of avoidances and evasions offshore (parking trillions of dollars outside U.S. jurisdiction) and the size of the business conducted off the books. In addition, Rossotti's estimates are limited to the confines of drastic reductions on taxes from capital gains and dividends. His $1,600 figure, therefore, is very much an understatement. In any case, hotel magnate Leona Helmsley's immortal utterance that "only the little people pay taxes" correctly implied that wealthy people and large companies who rig the system burden the rest of America. Instead of thanking Ms. Helmsley for her candor, the editorial writers expressed outrage over her arrogance.

If the "little people" pay a higher total percentage of their income in various taxes than the very rich, why not think of a way to dramatize this situation? Frequent media exposés of tax dodges by companies and the wealthy have failed to produce the necessary agitation for change. Even the proposed moves to Bermuda tax havens by companies such as Stanley Works, based in New Britain, Connecticut, failed to move Congress to pass legislation to limit these offshore tax havens, a bill introduced by the late Senator Paul Wellstone and Senator Charles Grassley. These offshore tax *escapees* still operate in the United States and receive all the public services and contracts as if they were paying their taxes to the U.S. Treasury.

The Stanley Works caper created an uproar. Before announcing his intention, the new CEO, John M. Trani, laid off thousands of workers making $14 an hour and shifted the work to China where their counterparts were making 25 to 30 cents an hour. The workers in New Britain spent their last hours packing machinery for shipment to Shanghai. The proposed Bermuda move was the last straw for the workers, many of whom were shareholders who had to vote on Trani's decision. Mass demonstrations ensued, while Connecticut Attorney General Richard Blumenthal charged Trani with rigging the forthcoming vote—a charge with serious ramifications for Trani's future with the company he was strip-mining.

At a subsequent Congressional hearing, conservative Republicans and Democrats joined to condemn Trani and other companies contemplating the abandonment of their community and country for a Bermuda mail drop. The House Republican leadership faced a revolt of its rank and file. One hundred and ten Republicans joined the Democrats and passed legislation in 2002 to bar the corporate tax haven companies from obtaining contracts with the new Department of Homeland Security. Since then nothing has happened either in the Senate or the House. The gesture, although a factor in ending Trani's trip to Bermuda, was primarily for the benefit of incumbent candidates in the 2002 elections.

All this gives you the idea that no matter how clear it is to people, liberals and conservatives alike, that tax havens and other tax avoidance schemes are wrong and unfair, and no matter how much media is devoted to exposing them, nothing has changed by way of legislative corrections.

Taxpayer Appreciation Day

Over the years, you may have watched *ABC Nightly News* and its series "It's Your Money," which has documented how special privileges and wasteful federal projects benefited the cloying companies featured. There's scarce evidence that these reports on abuses of taxpayer dollars, seen by millions of people, led to reforms. So why not a new approach? First taxpayers should develop a proprietary interest in where their tax dollars are going instead of simply listening to pandering politicians talking tax cuts for them when they really mean for the wealthy. "It's Your Money," so why not launch a Taxpayer Appreciation Day on April 15 of each year? Millions of individual taxpayers would demand that all those corporations that receive taxpayer subsidies, giveaways, bailouts, and other forms of corporate welfare take a day off from feeding at our trough and express their thanks at various public events.

Although most taxpayers may not realize it, much of our economy—including flashy, "urban renewal" sports complexes and gallerias, scientific advances, and many emerging industries—result from taxpayer-financed programs whose fruits go mostly to big businesses. The commercial real estate industry is permeated with tax subsidies called "incentives." Taxpayer dollars have funded the discoveries at NASA, the Department of Defense, the National Institutes of Health, and other federal agencies—and yet these innovations are given away to companies that brag about them as if they'd played a role in the progress.

Taxpayer dollars have been a major factor in the growth or emergence of the aviation and aerospace industry, the biotechnology industry, the pharmaceutical firms, the semiconductor and computer businesses, the telecommunications, containerization, and medical device industries, among others. These industries are not needy, but greedy. Uncle Sam, without us looking over his shoulder, is a soft touch. A few years ago, in testimony before Congress, Andrew Grove, CEO of the hugely profitable Intel Corporation, urged legislators to appropriate more taxpayer money for basic research in his industry, which he said concentrated its capital on product development and production. Talk about entitlements!

Some may say that corporations send income taxes to Washington, too. Less and less, even in the face of record-setting profits. Corporate tax payments in 2003 constituted a mere 7.4 percent of federal revenues, down from 28 percent during Eisenhower's term in office. Some large corporations are heading for tax-exempt land. The General Accounting Office reported that during the booming late nineties, over half of U.S. corporations paid no federal income taxes at all, and others sheltered most of their income. Individuals pay more than four to five times as much in federal income tax revenues, apart from payroll taxes.

So back to the Taxpayer Appreciation Day and some exciting events of gratitude:

- General Electric bought RCA, which owned NBC in the mid-1980s, with the billions from an outrageous tax loophole that Reagan demanded and Congress passed in 1981. This bonanza allowed GE to pay no federal income taxes on three years of large profits, a savings totaling over $6 billion. The company received a refund of $125 million to boot. All these tax cuts gave GE the money to buy RCA. GE should arrange one of its media extravaganzas on NBC television to say "Thank You, Taxpayers." One of these featured taxpayers could be any one of the hundreds of thousands of GE employees who *single-handedly* paid more in federal income taxes than the major multinational company at which she worked during those three years.

- The drug companies, already benefiting from generous tax credits, constantly use their ads to ballyhoo their discoveries. What they don't say is that many of the important nonredundant therapeutic drugs, including most of the anticancer drugs, were developed in whole or in part with taxpayer money. The medicines developed under the auspices of both the National Institutes of Health and the Department of Defense have been given away free, under monopoly marketing rights, to individual drug companies. Since the drug companies spend deductible billions on advertisements each year, they can spare a day on April 15 to advertise a "Thank You, Taxpayers" message. For our part, we might start questioning why drug prices are so high when we taxpayers are paying so much of the research bill in the first place.

- The timber and mining companies receive vast sweetheart deals from taxpayers. We build the roads in our national forests for Big Timber companies to use. Under the 1872 Mining Act, hard rock mining companies get our minerals (on our public land) free on discovery. No matter how rich the minerals beneath the ground, these companies pay us no more than the maximum $5 per acre designated in that 132-year-old law. Only in America can they get such a deal. As an example of the giveaway, a Canadian company received ownership of $9 billion worth of gold (our gold) on federal land in Nevada from the Department of the Interior for about $30,000. Private timber companies can cut down ancient, giant trees for a pittance in the Tongass National Forest. Timber and mining companies support many timber museums around the country. How about a graphic display of appreciation to taxpayers at these museums, as well as on their websites: "Thanks from Weyerhauser, the taxpayer draining company."

- Television broadcasters were given $70 billion worth of digital spectrum by a supine Congress in 1997. Starting in 1927, radio and later television stations have received a free license for the use of our public airwaves. Wouldn't take much for these broad-casters to say thank you. They control our public airwaves for free and can easily communicate their gratitude. Please do it in prime-time, guys.

- What about all those professional sports corporations that play and profit in taxpayer funded stadiums, ballparks, and arenas? A parade of the owners and players would serve as a Thank You to the tax-paying fans, who, despite such subsidized largess, still pay through the nose for tickets and parking.

- McDonald's for years received taxpayer subsidies to promote the company overseas as part of a foreign marketing access program. Marriott, Intel, and other companies receive local tax abatements and other facilities. They've got the restaurants and the ballrooms to accommodate smashing appreciation parties in hometown America. Ronald McDonald can be the Master of Ceremonies.

- Corporate welfare is everywhere. How about the HMOs and the for-profit hospital chains? Or the military weapons contractors with their reimbursed over-runs and other runaway expenses. These companies have great public relations firms that can develop flamboyant displays of gratitude to taxpayers. We just have to make sure that these outlays are not tax-deductible because they are certainly "not ordinary and necessary business expenses."

Taxpayer Appreciation Day will launch a longer, much more en-gaging public debate about our tax system and its vast behavioral impact. Which do you think most people would prefer to have de-ductible: tobacco and liquor consumption at business occasions or their children's college tuition? The tax laws say *yes* to the former and *no* to the latter. Hiring a belly-dancer to entertain clients is de-ductible; going for an uncovered physical checkup is not.

Tax incentives don't reflect our societal needs. Instead they direct savings toward our crassest activities, such as gambling casinos. These incentives can undermine the common good and enhance the lifestyles of the rich and famous. Jimmy Carter used to call our tax system a "disgrace to the human race" and he was not just referring to its complexity and unfairness. It sways us, individually and collectively, toward behavior that drains the best intentions of our society and the greatest promise of its future. It compels individual taxpayers, trying to pay their own bills, to subsidize big companies to make more of a profit. Why, for example, in the early 1980s, should General Motors and the city of Detroit demand and receive over $300 million in local, state, and federal subsidies to build a luxury car factory in Detroit, with the city further agreeing to demolish, through eminent domain, a peaceful neighborhood of hundreds of homes, small businesses, and churches to make room? GM, which could have built the plant nearby on an abandoned auto plant site, had assured these city officials that the factory would employ 6,000 workers when, in fact, the highly automated facility hired only 3,000 laborers. But the company's subsidy was not cut proportionately.

The courts allow such condemnation proceedings, a form of corporate socialism, that transfers private property to corporations. The disparities between the corporate plutocrats and plain citizens who sweat it out every day transcend dollars. Companies can fly their lobbyists to Washington for their goodies and deduct the expenses. When individual citizens do the same, it's on them. The binding of a book is not large enough to chronicle the crude power plays and money deals embedded in thousands of pages of tax statutes, tax regulations, and special tax advisories. But I'll highlight just a few of the favors bestowed upon the demanding rich to get your dander up:

- Why should the Treasury write out virtual checks, called tax credits, in the millions of dollars to Microsoft, a company which had $62 billion cash in the bank in Spring 2004—probably a world record. The fact that Microsoft was judged in federal court to be a monopolist should have disqualified it from receiving welfare.

- For a long time, Washington has been giving a cornucopia of tax benefits to U.S. companies for shipping jobs and factories abroad. Similarly, the government gives big-time aircraft, tank, and other weapons exporters (who often export to the most repressive regimes) tax subsidies and export credits exceeding over a billion dollars a year. In years past, these tax subsidies were even extended to U.S. tobacco companies setting up production facilities for their cancer sticks in foreign countries.

- The estate tax is slated to be eliminated altogether by 2010, even though fewer than 2 percent (a declining percentage, as the phase-out continues) of persons who leave the richest estates pay *any* federal estate tax at all. With exemptions for estates rising each year, apart from free spousal transfers and a welter of other ways to arrange estate planning to minimize taxes, by 2009 only 3,000 of the wealthiest estates would be subject to the estate tax. So brazen was this estate tax abolition drive, which was geared to Bush's affluent circles of friends, that then candidate George W. Bush went around rural America justifying repeal on the basis of saving family farms: "To keep farms in the family, we are going to get rid of the death tax." He gave not one example where a farm loss had actually been due to the estate tax. After being selected president, he was still unable to give one example of any farms lost because of the estate tax. No one in his government or at the American Farm Bureau Federation could give him one instance.

This ploy was just one of the false premises that made it easy for a majority in Congress both to go along with Bush and receive grateful campaign cash from contributors. Another was the claim that administering the estate tax, and paying lawyers to avoid it, cost as much as the tax raised. The more accurate figure is

6 cents for every $1 raised, according to Rutgers University business professors Charles Davenport and Jay Soled.

In a remarkable transcendence of their own interests, over 1,000 rich people, led by Bill Gates Sr., Warren Buffett, and George Soros, declared their opposition to estate tax repeal. What is more, Mr. Gates has started a series of personal testimonials by his group called "We did not do it by ourselves." Gates Sr. began his own testimonial by saying he went to college on the GI Bill. After he married, he and his wife bought their first home with a Veterans' Administration loan. He later became successful as a Seattle attorney and gave his son, Bill Gates Jr., seed money to start a company called Microsoft which benefited almost immediately from additional federal tax credits.

• There is a Wisconsin law requiring the state's Department of Revenue to provide Wisconsin residents meeting certain conditions with the amount of state income tax reported by corporations. These companies are not human beings deserving the sanctity of privacy, nor are they entitled to a privileged relationship with the Treasury Department. These companies are artificial legal entities, endowed with privileges, powers, and advantages that no individual can possess. Corporate tax returns should also be made public for a reason outlined by Charles Lewis and Bill Allison in their book *The Cheating of America:* If corporate tax returns were public, investors would have another tool to determine whether the glowing earnings statements companies like to release have any basis in reality. The truth of the matter is that many profitable companies tell the public one thing and the IRS something else entirely. Corporations might be less willing to engage in elaborate tax shelters if they had to reconcile the bottom lines they report to the public with the ones they report confidentially to the government.

Tax Avoidance + the Lack of Enforcement

Tax avoidance, which is legal, and tax evasion, which is not, are more related than distinct. The large companies employ skilled attorneys to draft the provisions, popularly known as loopholes, and then send lobbyists to Capitol Hill to muscle key staffers of key members of the tax-writing House and Senate Committees (many of whom probably have received contributions from these same attorneys or their clients). Regularly, well-honed amendments are buried in bills that run hundreds of pages long. These amendments are often so obscure, and so part of the swapping customs between legislators, few people in Congress know who they are benefiting or how much shifting the burden or reducing services will cost the little taxpayer. Occasionally, reporters are tipped off, but often months after the legislation has passed. GM and Ford benefited handsomely from one short paragraph that got through in a lengthy bill over a decade ago. The *Washington Post* was the first to expose its presence—about five months after the bill became law. The champions among the tax bar are those adroit attorneys who can transform what was an evasion into an avoidance. But even if they cross the line back into evasion for their clients, as their tax shelter production factory often does, the risk of persecution is minimal. These matters are routinely settled, if the IRS brings any action at all.

During my aforementioned lunch with the IRS commissioner, I teasingly asked whether he agreed with those who said the insurance section of the tax code is so complex and obscure that Einstein's theory of relativity is comprehensible to more people. He replied that he would not be at all surprised if that were true. "Then how can the IRS enforce such provisions?" I asked. He said that it's difficult to enforce these rules, in part because it is very hard to find an available expert to consult and to testify for the IRS.

Try to put yourself in the place of the IRS. Tax compliance by the rich and powerful is vanishing, but the agency can't publicize their awareness of this trend for obvious reasons. Conventional "tax avoidance schemes and crimes," says the Center for Public Integrity, "are frankly beyond the current competence and budget of the Internal Revenue Service." But this worrisome pattern is nothing compared to what is emerging: As corporations evolve due to new technology and globalization, they simultaneously evolve new loopholes and ways of manipulating the tax system. The Center puts it this way: "Because of exploding technologies and their inability to regulate cyberspace, governments today find themselves impotent to tax trillions of dollars in potential new revenue from electronic commerce." A book titled *The Sovereign Individual* by James Dale Davidson calls cyberspace "the ultimate offshore jurisdiction. An economy with no taxes. Bermuda in the sky with diamonds." Global corporations are reaching a stage where they can decide how, where, and even *if* they want to be taxed.

During the past twenty-five years, the trend has been unmistakable. Both relatively and absolutely, corporations pay less income tax. Relative to the middle class and the poor, the super wealthy are paying on the whole a smaller percentage of their income in overall taxes. Nominal corporate tax rates, the effective rate actually paid, and the taxes on capital gains and dividends all have been dropping. The tax burden continues to shift from the wealthy to the working class. These trends exacerbate already sharp disparities in wealth and income in the United States—the worst disparities in the Western World.

The slide into deeper plutocracy has continued under Republican and Democratic administrations, at both the federal and state levels. Apart from blocking the repeal of the estate tax under Clinton, the Democrats appear helpless. A clutch of them have essentially joined the Republicans, and the party as a whole cannot muster the unity or energy to stop the Republicrats from further plundering the American middle class. In the words of David Cay Johnston, the *New York Times* Pulitzer Prize winner and author of the excellent bestseller *Perfectly Legal: The Covert Campaign to Rig Our Tax System to Benefit the Super Rich and Cheat Everybody Else:* "There is an underground economy among the super rich that lets them understate their true income and overstate their tax deductions. . . . The major change taking place is a shifting of burdens off the super-rich and onto everyone below them. It is a shift that began with the Democrats in 1983 and that has been increased dramatically since the Republicans won control of the House in 1995," five years before Bill Clinton left office.

Where have the Democrats been? If they couldn't play offense, what about defense? Well, for starters, they were dialing for the same corporate dollars. Second, many seemed to have lost their moorings regarding the public philosophy and rationale of progressive taxation, including that of unearned income. Third, some bought into the theory that cutting taxes on the wealthy and corporations automatically increased investment and economic growth. They forgot that taxes were much higher in the prosperous 1960s, and that tax-cuts can cause ballooning deficits (hugely generated by Ronald Reagan) that inflict their own pain on the economy. Last, they've lost the semantic advantage in the debate over taxes. Johnston writes of the Republicans' chief semanticist, Frank Luntz, promoting the use of the phrase "death tax" instead of estate tax or inheritance tax. For a drive to eliminate the capital gains tax, he recommended use of the phrase "savings and investment tax." For the effort to privatize social security, he said "Social Security" should never be mentioned, and instead should be replaced by "retirement security." Personalize, personalize, personalize, said Luntz, and you win the debate over tax policy. Luntz was so contemptuous of the Democrats that he even openly advised them on how to develop their own effective language, such as describing the estate tax as "billionaire's tax." The Democrats' response—grumble, mumble, and jumble their message. Writing in *Harper's* magazine last December, even a mellowed George McGovern could say that "most of today's liberals are too intimidated for my taste." He mentioned the poet Robert Frost's observation that a liberal is someone who "won't take his own side in a quarrel."

In the midst of the tax fairness crisis, there is an easy initiative for the Democrats: press Congress to give the IRS an adequate budget, skilled staff, and the authority to go after the tax evasions and tax avoidance schemes of the global corporations and the super-affluent classes. They need go no further than the rationale given and documented by Johnston:

> Our tax system is being used to create a nation with fewer stable jobs and less secure retirement income. The tax system is being used by the rich, through their allies in Congress, to shift risks off themselves and onto everyone else. And perhaps worst of all, our tax system now forces most Americans to subsidize the lifestyles of the very rich, who enjoy the benefits of our democracy without paying their fair share of its price.

The triumph of the oligarchs extends further still. Not only is the IRS inadequately funded to cope with the increasing assaults on its enforcement duties in areas offering the greatest revenue recovery, but its resources are getting squeezed even tighter. Under Clinton and a Republican Congress, the number of revenue agents decreased, as did the number of audits of the corporate wealthy. During the fiscal year 1989 to 1999, with 14 percent more returns being filed, Lewis and Allison report that "the number of permanent IRS employees dropped 26 percent (from 111,980 to 82,563). The President and Congress also cut the staff of the IRS Office of Examination staff, including revenue agents and tax auditors, by 34 percent, from 31,315 to 20,736. . . . Under political pressure, the IRS is auditing poor people more often then well-heeled taxpayers. And tax-related prosecutions are half what they were nearly twenty years ago." The two authors couldn't get answers from officials as to why this was happening. So, they posed a series of questions "that no one in Washington is particularly able or anxious to answer . . . without considerable squirming, hemming, and hawing":

> How serious are our federal officials in both parties, at both ends of Pennsylvania Avenue, about upholding the current tax laws today for all Americans? Politicians should be asked bluntly whether they favor or not increased enforcement of the existing tax laws. Do they think the poor should be audited more often than the rich? Should billionaires be able to renounce their U.S. citizenship in order to avoid taxes, and still be able to return home for months on end because the law barring their reentry is rarely, if ever, enforced.

Increasing enforcement resources, now being requested by the IRS, would certainly produce more revenue. But what happens instead? Audits of the biggest corporations, which pay 85 percent of the corporate income tax, declined: two out of three were investigated in the late 1980s, but that number has slipped to one out of three.

In terms of the IRS itself not allocating small resources for big gains, Johnston found the work of IRS partnership specialist Jerry Curnutt most astonishing. Out of his small Dallas office, Curnutt's pair of CD-ROMs contained financial details reported by all two million partnerships in the United States. He found that a huge amount of tax cheating had escaped the Service's attention because a key question was not asked on the partnership tax return form: whether the partner had a domestic tax-exempt partner. After constant requests, Curnutt, staying on long after he was eligible for retirement, could not persuade the IRS to find room in its "budget to pay for the keystrokes to capture this data," wrote Johnston, "even though it was costing the government billions and billions of dollars." Commissioner Charles O. Rossotti, in his final report, confirmed Curnutt's claims—"that a few dollars to capture one more line of data from partnership tax returns could bring in billions of dollars in taxes"—with figures ranging from Rossotti's $7 billion to other much higher estimates annually. To date, neither the IRS nor congressional tax committees have moved to correct this data gap.

By the time he was ready to leave his five-year term of office as commissioner of the IRS, Charles Rossotti was prepared to speak out more forcefully. When Republican Congressman Amory Houghton, chairman of the IRS Oversight Subcommittee, could not answer questions from the press about widespread tax dodges and the implosion of tax law enforcement at the IRS, he was embarrassed enough to schedule a tax cheat hearing in October 2002. Commissioner Rossotti was scheduled to be the lead-off witness. But the hearing was cancelled without explanation. Somehow Johnston got a hold of Rossotti's testimony that included the following message to Houghton:

> The tax system continues to grow in complexity, while the resource base of the IRS is not growing and in real terms is shrinking. Basically, demands and resources are going in the opposite direction. This is systematically undermining one of the most important foundations of the American economy.

The last point raises a fundamental question: whether the federal income tax is salvageable or even deserves to be saved in its present form. The powers that be and the campaign contributors are one and the same, and unlikely to adopt the patriotic wisdom of Oliver Wendell Holmes. There will become ever-more evasive tax escapees, continuing to shift the tax burden to work and away from wealth. It is time for a raging public debate about reversing this trend. As *Business-Week*'s chief economist William Wolman pointed out in his book *The Judas Economy,* there is a relentless increase in the returns on capital as compared with the returns on labor. Beyond shifting the tax burden back to wealth and away from work, a rational society would tax those things we like the least—pollution, gambling, the addictive industries, lurid luxuries, and high turnover currency trading and stock, bond, and derivatives transactions. The latter alone, given its vast volumes and velocity, can become the subject of an international treaty to provide enormous revenues from tiny taxes for the signatory nations.

It is time for integrated thought about taxes to clarify goals, collect revenues, and expend them efficiently. The taxpayers who have the greatest stake in progressive tax fairness, tax simplicity, and the spending of tax revenues are the far larger number of small taxpayers who have the votes, who collectively have the vision and who are not expatriating. They remain in the United States. They should be given the same standing to sue the federal government. They should also seek a well-promoted check-off on that 1040 tax return so that they can voluntarily contribute up to $300 to a public campaign election fund as the first step toward reforming the monetized political climate that is corrupting both federal and state tax systems. We are a long way from a goal of taxation espoused by Adam Smith: "to remedy inequality of riches as much as possible by relieving the poor and burdening the rich." Corporatism is also a long way from conservatism.

SELLING OUR CHILDREN

T he word corporate Republicans like most is "conservative." They constantly use it as a fig leaf to hide their true ideology—the supremacy of commercialism over values more spiritual, nurturing, moral, and truly conservative. In no area does marketing madness run roughshod more than in its insidious grip on childhood and children's traditional sanctuaries. In no area is the distinction between avaricious corporatism and authentic conservatism clearer. For no other age group is it more important for true conservatives to declare their independence and take a stand against these modern day Mammons. No other trend is more subversive of parental authority, more penetrating at an early age of the mind and body of the child, and more deliberative in strategic planning for expanding the violent, addictive and pornographic world of the child.

A New Byrd School

Let's look at an inner city fifth-grade class to provide a contrast to these forces of greed and profit, and to illuminate the hypocrisy of Bush's "leave no child behind" policies also embedded within the testing industry. Recently, after speaking to an assembly of students at Columbia University in Chicago, a young fifth-grade teacher, Brian

Schultz, gave me a folder describing "Project Citizen: A New Byrd School." In early December 2003, Schultz asked the 16 African American students in his class to select a project. They chose to study their Robert E. Byrd Academy School, documenting its decrepit condition and launching an initiative for a new school. Since Schultz has these pupils the entire day, the project became the epicenter for teaching the various core subjects like math, data analysis, politics, economics, reading, and writing. Attendance is at a high for the school—98 percent. Motivation is intense. Discipline problems have almost disappeared. They developed the Action Plan that included, in their words, "researching, petitioning, surveying, writing, photographing, and interviewing people we think can help us fix the policy." Ranging in age from ten to twelve, and living in the low-income Cabrini Green housing projects, the students focused on five major conditions, starting with filthy restrooms (often without soap, paper towels, or garbage cans). "We do not have doors on the stalls and have no privacy. The sinks have bugs in them and water is everywhere. As an example of how bad they are, sinks move and water leaks on the floor. The hot water faucets have cold water."

Next was temperature in the classrooms. "The heat is not turned on. It is really cold in the classrooms," the students report, adding that they have to put their coats on "during class because it is so cold. They cannot fix it because the pipes are broken. It is uncomfortable and hard to learn. Our hands are cold and we cannot write. This needs to be changed!"

Next came the windows cracked with bullet holes, held together by tape. "We cannot see through the windows and it is dark in the classrooms," wrote the children, "We can hardly see what we are doing because it is so dark. This is not a good place to learn."

There is no lunchroom; children eat in a hallway, which is distracting to ongoing classrooms. The school has no gym, no auditorium or stage. The school borrows a gym across a busy street. In their letter to dozens of people, the students plead: "We would like to invite you to see our school for yourself. We do not think that you would let your kids come to a school that is falling apart." Vice-President Richard Cheney responded to the children in a letter supporting a new elementary school. Mr. Cheney, vigorous supporter of the wasteful defense budget, did not mention any federal financial support. But the students are not stopping at letters to politicians; they are organizing everyone they can envision helping, including fifth graders from other more fortunate schools and a wide array of persons with various occupations and positions. They circulated a petition and obtained more than 900 signatures. Children are learning citizen skills, maturity, self-reliance, seriousness, dedication, and ingenuity in this classroom and from their most immediate surroundings—their school.

For five months, this project has become the entire day's curriculum, Schultz told me. He has the full approval of his principal, and the other teachers are supportive. He can do this because his students meet the conventional standards for their grade without having to go through the rote memorization process that youngsters find so tedious. All this decay and the resurgence of demand for decent facilities takes place in Chicago, whose motto is "The City that Works"; Chicago, a metropolis gleaming with tax-subsidized office buildings, undertaxed business executives and companies, galleries and cultural institutions. Its schools and clinics for low-income people are not given comparable attention. This neglected school and its children should shame and inspire us at the same time. Each school day the minds of these children expand and they learn to *think,* not vacuously believe. Tax dollars are short for teaching needs and facilities, but available for bureaucratic layers that don't educate our young. Our country has creative teachers like Schultz and more will come forward if learning impulses and the innate curiosity of youngsters are accorded priority. (The reflections of Barbara A. Lewis, a fifth-grade teacher in a Salt Lake City school, in her book *Kids and Social Action* also shows what can be done effectively and inexpensively.)

There is underinvestment in many public school systems. However, regular tax rebellions by residents against school bond issues or tax increases occur because they hear horror stories about what is going wrong and they resent bearing the financial burden. Public schools are part of civil society. They will rise or fall in correlation with the participation of parents, together with boards of education, principals, and teachers who define their success not by fraudulent multiple-choice standardized test results, but by the multiple intelligences that are aroused, informed, and sharpened within the developing minds of their students.

The Corporate Barrage

There are no shortages of corporate investment dollars in direct marketing to those same youngsters. There is little spared in separating impressionable children from their parents so that they can be sold on deliberately seductive advertising and programs. "For the first time in human history, most children are born into homes where most of the stories do not come from the parents, schools, churches, communities, and in many places even from their native countries, but from a handful of conglomerates who have something to sell," wrote George Gerbner in the *Prospectus for the Cultural Environment Movement.*

The inability of young children to distinguish television programming from its advertising led, years ago, to Western European nations prohibiting the use of children in television ads. Now, in our country, ads and their characters often are so interspersed within the programs themselves that even adults can miss the distinction.

It is in the nature of commercialism to push the envelope, to know no boundaries or self-restraint. Nearly ten years ago, our researchers asked some marketers where they would set the limit in weekly hours for children's television programs—twenty, thirty, forty, fifty, or sixty. They declined to answer. Instead, they said, whatever the market can attract is the guide. It is not up to them; it is up to the children and their parents. It is not the seducer but the seduced little ones who guilt-trip their often absent-at-work parents. When a creative ad person from Madison Avenue develops a children's ad, a "high nag factor" is considered a plus. Each year some $20 billion is directly spent by children twelve and younger, while around $200 billion is spent by the parents goaded by their "nagging" children.

The premeditation and planning that transformed these companies into proficient electronic child molesters shock parents. The old days of occasional bubble gum, ice cream cones, and a Saturday afternoon movie at the BiJou theatre have been replaced by 24/7 entertainment and product placements and logos that pepper the brains of children two-years-old on up. Assisted by applied and developmental psychologists, companies target every psyche, every child vulnerability, every sensual sensitivity, every peer group development these hucksters can contrive to foment or grasp and turn into dollars. To get a sense of their laser-like zealotry, a marketing report in 1994 was titled "Kids are not just kids! 0–2, 3–7, 8–12, 13–15, 16–19: Accurate Targeting Through Age Segmentation." In the same year, Bob Garfield in *Advertising Age* wrote a column headlined "Nintendo Aims to 'Be Heard' by Exploiting Kids' Distress." In the past ten years, the pace of commercializing childhood and schools has quickened, pushing youth into growing up even more commercialized in their bodies and minds. Advocates of holistic medicine weighing the mind-body connection would not imagine the advanced Pavlovian states of conditioned responses coming out of these marketed to children.

There's a great deal of hypocrisy at work. To take just one example, Steven Spielberg admitted he would not let his eight-year-old watch *Jurassic Park,* but he did not complain that many children that age and younger were seeing his hit movie. In a similar vein, the same corporations whose executives pontificate about the need to upgrade standards in the schools are part of the marketing madness that undermines education.

A new coalition of parents and friends called the Center for a New American Dream is organizing public opinion and resistance. According to a poll commissioned by the Center, 70 percent of parents with children ages two to seventeen believe that marketing negatively affects kids' values and worldview, making them too materialistic and putting pressure on them to purchase things that are harmful to them. More telling, over half of the parents polled admitted to buying things for their children that they disapproved of, because the youngsters felt they needed the product in order to fit in with the crowd.

Why are parents losing the war over their children? It's partly a matter of resources, and the destructive use of those resources dictated by the perverse logic of the marketplace. Driven by billions of dollars in sales, profits, bonuses, and stock options, the men atop giant companies are in a race to the bottom with their competitors, ever expanding the range of filth and junk they peddle through ever more manipulative delivery systems. Parents cannot match the vast sums of capital, technology, and influential connections of these highly focused men and their battalions, and parents have other obligations to tend to—working to make ends meet and dealing with the various stresses of workplace, household, and community. Unless they throw out their televisions, radios, VCRs and DVDs, and home-school their children, parents cannot insulate kids from the marketers' multilevel commercial assault.

In single-parent homes, the over-worked, over-stressed parent finds it impossible to shield her children. The situation is not much better in two-parent homes where both parents work full-time and can't adequately monitor their children's activities or exposure to commercial culture. Frequently, parents learn about such exposure only after the fact, when they see their children imitating behavior and language picked up from television, radio, and movies. With parents absent or too busy to inculcate values, children adopt values from the entertainment industry.

Granted, there are some fine commercial videos for children, along with some wholesome children's programming, mostly by the Public Broadcasting System and a handful of educational channels. However, the Big Business, the Big Profits, the Big Promotions are those programs and products that target children at the lowest rungs of the sensuality ladder—taste, texture, supersonic scenes, sound, color, and an assortment of visceral stimuli requiring very little reflection or digestion from the mind, but instead instant reflexive response. It is almost impossible to count the change of pictures from an MTV video or advertisement per minute. The eyes of the viewer are pulled so quickly that the brain doesn't have a chance to digest and react. The brain surrenders.

The latest of several studies conclude that children age two to four who watch more television than the average child register higher rates of attention-deficit disorder by the time they are seven and in school. Overdosing on television or videos at a very young age shrinks attention spans, impedes socialization, and hinders development of vocabulary. All these effects, of course, produce in their wake further deleterious consequences for slower development and personality afflictions.

Nevertheless, direct and indirect sales to the kids' markets are booming, as are related conventions, seminars, consulting firms, and endless marketing studies and publications. Just what are these companies pushing? The fast-food companies persuade children to eat large portions of fatty and sugary food and desserts that will increase their weight and predispose them to diabetes, high blood pressure, and other diet-related ailments. Child obesity has doubled since 1980 and diabetes is surging also. The situation is so out of control that it has even alarmed Bush's Department of Health and Human Services. The U.S. Surgeon General has estimated that about 350,000 deaths a year can be attributed to obesity in adults. Trial attorneys are moving to file lawsuits charging fast-food chains with deceptive advertisements and labeling beamed directly at vulnerable children. They want the nutritional truth to be conveyed, not images and words connoting health and strength, whether by omission or commission.

The soft drink companies induce children to drink their sugary concoctions even for breakfast. Nutritionists warn that the decline in full fruit juice and milk consumption diminishes bone strength. Over the years, the tobacco and alcoholic industries have slyly and not so slyly been reaching youngsters. They know that the earlier kids can be hooked on these powerful drugs, the more likely addiction to or over-consumption of their brands will ensue. The illness and fatalities from such addictions are enormous. Yes, the addicted have a central responsibility, but the addictors going after young persons are malicious. Their thirst for profits seemingly blinds them to the tragedy of over 400,000 American deaths each year from tobacco-related disease—and 100,000 fatalities from alcoholism.

Children's commercial television programming conveys the message that violence is a solution to life's problems, and pushes low-grade sensuality, from junk food and drink to pornography and addiction, as a way of life. Children stare at screens while munching on damaging, fatty foods. Violent video games are sadistic and ghoulish and the T-rated games for children thirteen and over find their way to younger children. Harvard University researchers reported in 2004 that the number of "deaths" per hour in eighty-one "T-rated" video games they analyzed averaged a hundred and twenty-two. Ninety-eight percent of the games contained intentional violence, with 42 percent showing blood, according to their tally. Sixty-nine percent rewarded the youngsters for killing characters or required them to do so. The technology of interactive mayhem is replacing the spectator role in ever more vicious and mutilating ways. Billions of dollars flow into company coffers every year.

Retired Lt. Colonel and West Point Professor Dave Grossman's book *Stop Teaching Our Kids to Kill* relied on hundreds of scientifically designed studies linking video game violence and aggressive behavior. Before these videos, studies abounded linking television violence to violent behavior by some young viewers mimicking in real life what they saw in virtual reality.

Drug Pushers

Meanwhile, the drug companies are busy expanding their pediatric divisions and turning personality problems into newly characterized diseases that, violá, their products will treat. Some physicians call this barrage the "medicalization of childhood." Overmedication of children is not restricted to Ritalin and the greatly expanded sales definition of attention-deficit disorder.

This field is literally exploding on youngsters, their frightened parents, and drug company promotion-saturated physicians. Consider the late arrival of real science confronting the deceptive corporate medical claims relating to the treatment of depressed children. Moving away from applying love and attention to these afflicted children, our society is driven to the drug (or drug abuse) solution. In early 2004, Australian researchers concluded, according to the *New York Times,* that "pediatricians and family physicians should not prescribe antidepressants for depressed children and adolescents because the drugs barely work and their side effects are often significant." The study, published in the *British Medical Journal* (BMJ), zeroed in on three antidepressants, Prozac, Zoloft and Paxil, used on patients under age eighteen. While there is still more to be known, medical researchers point to increased incidences of suicidal thoughts and behavior associated with these drugs. The Food and Drug Administration, always cautiously averse to challenging the powerful drug industry, did issue a warning on March 22, 2004, that ten antidepressant drugs can lead to worse depression, mania, and violent activity, including suicide. The agency is reviewing more data.

There's no lack of certainty when it comes to overuse of antibiotics in our medical treatments and meat products. One result is more resistance by mutating organisms that cause life-threatening infections. Some of these bacteria are now resistant to all or all but one antibiotic on the market. The World Health Organization and outspoken pediatricians are increasingly fearful of returning to what they call a "pre-antibiotic era" in which fatalities would no longer be preventable. In 1998, the British House of Lords held extensive hearings on this accelerating problem of bacterial resistance. According to author John Humphreys, in his book *The Great Food Gamble,* the Lords' final report recognized a "vicious circle repeatedly witnessed during the last half of the century, in which the value of each new antibiotic has been progressively eroded by resistance, leading to the introduction of a new and usually more expensive agent, only for this in its turn to suffer the same fate." Tuberculosis, which takes over two million lives a year around the world, is now occurring in drug resistant strains, especially in the countries of the former Soviet Union.

Children, of course, are far more vulnerable to these drugs (and pesticides, herbicides, and many toxins for that matter). Yet, the over-prescribing continues by uninformed, demanding parents, uncritical physicians, and a meat and poultry industry bent on routine therapeutic insertion of drugs into the daily meals of the animals that get into our stomachs. The incessant advertising and promotion of these drugs pours out of the frenzied marketing divisions of the large drug companies. The sheer profits render them oblivious to the medical literature on their desks.

The overmedication, the legal drugging of our children, only gets worse by the year as many children march to the school nurse to pick up their pills. Shouldn't the schools be the sane, educational sanctuary for children and teenagers to learn good eating and good health habits? Not to the corporatists. Schools, public and private, are to them just another marketing opportunity. Their "free" materials have generated some parental opposition—but not enough.

Consider the big business, Channel One, which has contracted with thousands of high schools to hijack twelve minutes at the beginning of the school day for MTV-paced news and two minutes of ads promoting junk food, soft drinks, underarm deodorants, sneakers, music CDs, and other such products. This amounts to awarding six full school days a year to the hucksters, paid for by taxpayers. The schools allow this because Channel One lets them use the television equipment that the company installs for its early morning access to public high school students for the rest of the day. As UNPLUG and Commercial Alert have repeatedly pointed out, this is a costly tradeoff. Would these schools allow the nonprofit Urban League and the League of Women Voters to program twelve minutes of civic skills education, including stories about students improving their community by taking on injustice?

Now the rush is on, in Seattle and elsewhere, to conclude secret contracts between soft drink companies and entire public school districts and universities. Their aim is to obtain exclusive rights to sell the sugar, water, and formula to a captive student body. These contracts usually provide that the company will make the decision about what other drinks will be allowed in the vending machines on school property. Company logos appear on school buses and the walls of the schools in Colorado Springs. Schools are even considering selling naming rights. Commercialization of big-time high school sports is also on the rise.

Just when you think you've heard it all, another outrage is reported. A few years ago, the lead industry tried to discredit and have fired Professor Herbert Needleman of the University of Pittsburgh, who did the groundbreaking scientific work on the deadly effects of lead-based paint and gasoline on little children. Over the past half century, millions of inner-city children have ingested this peeling paint. The lead has damaged their brains and other body organs. Whatever is being done to test and protect these children is due in no small part to Dr. Needleman's pioneering studies. Fortunately, his scientific colleagues came to his rescue, and he remains on the faculty.

Commercializing childhood seems to have no limits. Urging children directly to consume bad products and entertainment harmful to their physical and mental health and safety is bad enough, especially since it often leads to angry exchanges between parents and children. The companies are always on the prowl for ways to hook children; they just won't let childhood be. Who could have anticipated that when the gambling casinos in Las Vegas began marketing their hotels as "family entertainment," they would teach children how to gamble (though without money) in these comfortable surroundings? The companies prefer the term "gaming" to "gambling," for obvious reasons.

When a grade school teacher in Maryland held up a picture of George Washington and asked the children to identify him, a cluster of them said "he sells cars." Corporate hucksters have used former presidents, such as Washington, Thomas Jefferson, Abraham Lincoln, along with Benjamin Franklin, as television commercial pitchmen for car dealers, furniture stores, carpet sellers, banks, and insurance companies. Teenagers have told reporters that "you are what you buy." The sense of the heroic for preteens is almost entirely drawn from celluloid celebrities such as the Ninja Turtles or the Power Rangers. Real history does not exist in their frame of reference, their aspirations, or their dialogue. Culture becomes commercial culture with children as spectators, not participants in community culture that nourishes family upbringing and togetherness.

In a 1996 survey on the Nickelodeon area of America Online, a majority of children said they trusted their computers more than their parents. Corporations are taking children away from their parents and into a commercial world that knows no time restraints, shows no concern for the child's development, and is under little or no regulation. Accordingly, companies figured out how to overcome or circumvent parental control over spending. First, they entice children to nag their parents. Second, they take advantage of the absence of parents who travel or work long hours outside the home. Third, they undermine the authority, dignity, and judgment of parents in the eyes of their children, thereby inducing kids to purchase or demand items regardless of their parents' opinions.

Pushing Back

The parents and clergy members who sound the alarm about the surrender of self-sustaining human values to commercialism must wonder how our society can fight back. There are plenty of ways outlined in books, pamphlets, catalogues, and advisories to recover our cultural traditions and build on them for our children. First, however, we must become more aware of what these conscious corporate predations are doing to our children and will do in an ever-more intrusive way if they are not rolled back. Parents must then become deeply receptive to ways they can recover control of their children from the grips of commercialism. *Marketing Madness,* a survival guide for a consumer society (as mentioned earlier) by Michael. F. Jacobson and Laurie Ann Mazur is a book that all parents would benefit from reading.

A larger picture can provide the activating civic jolt. All this money—the marketing energy, overwhelming advertising and promotion to sell, sell, sell so much violent, addictive, useless, harmful, tasteless, deceptive junk that happens to connect with the provoked sensualities of children or the consent of harried parents— produces a quarter of a trillion dollars a year in sales and much more in unintended consequences. Children's attention spans and vocabularies shrink, and the necessities, needs, and legitimate nurturing of children go begging. Schools crumble, books and other educational materials are short on budgets, cutbacks in arts and physical education are announced, conditions in juvenile detention facilities deteriorate, foster care abuses are rampant, millions of children are without health insurance or proper nutrition, housing, or clothing. Well-to-do youngsters feel purposeless—their parents grow afraid of what they might do to themselves.

What's going on here? Why have we lost so much control over our descendents, our future, our neglected, lonely, little loved ones? Where is our civic enterprise? Slogans by politicians will get us nowhere. Only deeds. Only determination by parents and other citizens. Cuts in taxes for the wealthy come at the same time as cuts in budgets for children's programs, as law professor Robert C. Fellmeth, head of the Children's Advocacy Center in San Diego, points out regularly. Fellmeth has brought together rich documentation of the brutish plight of children in the Golden State (it bears repeating)—over 45 percent of them live in poverty or near poverty. The absence of mass indignation tells us something about public resignation in today's America.

I am reminded of what one of Canada's wisest social essayists, John Raulston Saul, wrote in his best-selling book *The Unconscious Civilization:*

> The place to begin is with the more basic questions of need, advantage and viability. . . . Each way we look, the need is not for reforms but for a change in dynamics. . . . One way of examining our dynamics and how they might be changed is to ask ourselves

what it is that we reward and punish in our society. I think you would be surprised if you drew up your own lists to discover that most of what we reward works against the public good and most of what we discourage or even punish would work in its favour.

I have spoken from the beginning about our slippage into the unconscious and our susceptibility to imbalance. We could call this the unconsciousness of imbalance or unbalanced unconsciousness. They feed each other. But if a society insists upon rewarding primarily that which weakens it and punishing that which can strengthen it, surely it is a clinically identifiable victim of both imbalance and the unconscious.

Yes, we need consciousness, balance, attention to the common good, the recovery of common sense, prudence, and reassertion of parental authority. We need to replace the false deity of corporatism that is bringing up our children. But first our voices must be heard. For corporatism dominates the very public airwaves and cable channels that we the people own or license and are excluded from twenty-four hours a day. Shut out. People have the power to put their children first. Do we have the time, dedication, and horizons to defend and rescue our children? It is assuredly a matter of perceived values and priorities.

We can stretch our familial imaginations away from the coarseness of corporatism. We can delve into the literature of small, human-scale, community and neighborhood self-reliance. As Andrew Kimbrell says, that means being more a creator than a consumer. He explains: "With the food I buy I'll create a different kind of earth, a different kind of farming system. . . . Instead of consuming music, I'll make music. Instead of consuming poetry, I'll write poetry." There are alternative economies evolving in local areas of our country, using both old and new knowledge to commune with the local natural resource base to meet material needs in sustainable and renewable ways. The E. F.

Schumacher Society (www.smallisbeautiful.org) provides a wealth of practical approaches. Children need to be given vistas other than television and computer screens. They need to be introduced to nature—their forgotten natural habitat. Gardening, hiking, swimming, field studies in the woods open their senses to the sounds of nature as respites from the technological and entertainment noises that saturate them day after day. Father Thomas Berry has written about raising a child in harmony with the grandeur of nature—our commonwealth: "The star-filled sky, meadows in bloom, tumbling rivers, soaring raven songs—all of these are needed to shape the spirit of the child who is capable of growing up to an emerging creativity with the commons."

We must strive to become good ancestors.

Commercial Alert (www.commercialalert.org), a fine citizen's organization, backs various measures to restore balance to our ultra-commercialized society. The organization, which I launched, recently announced a campaign for a worldwide ban on marketing of junk food to children 12 years of age and under. This sensible proposal, championed by director Gary Ruskin, would combat the rising global epidemic of childhood obesity—and thus help save or enhance millions of young lives. Numerous health professionals and organizations have called on the World Health Organization to incorporate such a ban into its global anti-obesity initiative, or to enact the ban through international health regulations. (Such regulations are legally binding on countries unless they affirmatively opt out.)

Commercial Alert is also pushing a package of measures it calls a *Parents' Bill of Rights* to help combat the destructive commercial influences on children, promote wholesome values and products, and resist the epidemic of marketing-related diseases (including obesity, alcoholism, addictive gambling, and deadly smoking-related illnesses).

This Parents' Bill of Rights includes nine proposed pieces of legislation (a few of which have already been introduced in the Congress) for federal and/or state legislatures:

- **Leave Children Alone Act,** banning television advertising aimed at children under twelve years of age.
- **Child Privacy Act,** giving parents the right to control any commercial use of personal information concerning their children, and the right to know precisely how such information is used.
- **Advertising to Children Accountability Act,** requiring corporations to disclose who created each of their advertisements, and who did the market research for each ad directed at children under twelve years of age.
- **Commercial-Free Schools Act,** prohibiting corporations from using the schools and compulsory school laws to bypass parents and pitch their products to impressionable schoolchildren.
- **Fairness Doctrine for Parents Act,** applying the Fairness Doctrine to all advertising to children under twelve years of age, thereby providing parents and community with response time on broadcast television and radio for advertising to children.
- **Product Placement Disclosure Act,** requiring corporations to disclose, on packaging and at the outset, any and all product placements on television and videos, and in movies, video games, and books. This prevents advertisers from sneaking ads into media that parents assume to be ad-free.
- **Child Harm Disclosure Act,** creating a legal duty for corporations to publicly disclose all information suggesting that their product(s) could substantially harm the health of children.
- **Children's Food Labeling Act,** requiring fast food restaurant chains to label contents of food, and provide basic nutritional information about it.

- **Children's Advertising Subsidy Revocation Act,** eliminating federal subsidies, deductions, and preferences for advertising aimed at children under twelve years of age.

Our culture should actively teach children critical thinking and promote wholesome activities and learning experiences with family, neighbors, and teachers. Instead, concerned adults need to focus their energies on warding off the depraved commercial saturation of childhood. Still, the measures listed above would go a long way toward restoring parental control over child-raising, and countering the nefarious effects of rampant commercialization. But the significance of the work by Commercial Alert transcends the potential value of the proposed legislation it supports. The very existence of this and other citizen groups suggests that parents will not simply roll over and allow corporate America to subordinate the notion of a healthy childhood to the goal of mega-profits.

A new amalgam of both selling our children and selling out our children has provoked more and more parents and teachers to do anything but roll over. The Leave No Child Behind (LNCB) law bids to become the biggest "blowback" in the history of public education.

Ballyhooed through Congress by George W. Bush, his Republicans, and overly trusting Democrats, LNCB offered hope of greater accountability and higher educational standards.

Instead, it's spawned a miasma of bureaucracies, testing fanaticism, underfunded mandates, detonated expectations, massive evasions, rebellious state legislators, and a retreating Bush administration that remains resistant to the gathering storm of protest that is unifying more Americans than at any time since World War II.

At the core of the revolt are frequently administered standardized tests, which are a narrow, fraudulent measure of academic performance that distort the curriculum and other learning processes. We studied these tests' failures in our groundbreaking report, *The Reign of ETS,* by Allan Nairn in 1980. This federal regulatory tyranny, collapsing from its own freighted foolishness, comes from a numerically fascinated Republican administration that has ignored legions of sensible studies and innovative successes that show how to educate children so that they desire to learn themselves about the world around them. It is a super-irony that this octopus-like Washington regulation of local education comes in Republican garb, which puts the lie to traditional Republican ideology.

Commercialism is the lurking force that makes a business of replacing ideology with dreams of profits. For over a decade, the business of education has drooled over the prospect of taking over the $300 billion public education budget in America. The testing takeover is just one of several ways to set up the public schools for corporate management, consulting, contracting out, and eventual displacement with Edison-type commercial schools.

One of the fastest growing lines of commerce in the country is the test-making, test-preparing, and tutoring business. Who can afford them? Families with money. As author and educator Deborah Meier writes: "We use as our only measure of academic performance the one tool that most reliably reflects family assets: standardized, paper-and-pencil tests. . . Meanwhile, pressure mounts to replace public schools with the private marketplace."

Down at the local school level, the idiotic complexions of LNCB are working their corrosive wills on teachers and students. Education anthropologist Dr. Penny Owen, whose success with demoralized elementary schoolchildren has excited teachers in Winsted, Connecticut, has this to say: "Testing children as young as third grade produces inaccurate results. I have seen students break down in tears, incapable of functioning when presented with yet another test. More significant than a child's anxiety level however is their own awareness that their brains develop at different times than other children, an awareness that adults do not seem to have no matter how much brain research has been done. Teachers call it the "Ah Hah" moment, the moment the light comes on and abstractions finally make sense to their students. Expecting all children to be at the same place at the same time defeats the children, their schools, and in the long run the country."

Children need our time. There is no quick fix, certainly not one that comes with a number. Or with a "For Sale" sign.

ENVIRONMENT
Self-Devouring

During a stretch of years in the late 1960s and 1970s, the young environmental movement, rippling with exuberant grassroots power and loaded with powerful arguments, pushed through bedrock federal laws: the National Environmental Policy Act, Clean Air and Clean Water Act amendments, the Environmental Protection Act, the Endangered Species Act, the Safe Drinking Water Act, the Toxic Substances Control Act, and the Automobile Fuel Efficiency and Conservation Act. The sensitivities and perceptions of millions of Americans toward their environment shifted to demanding action. Reflecting on these accomplishments inspires pride but also disappointment. Our society is still coasting on those advances and, with some exceptions, now has a twenty-five-year record of failure.

Considering what we knew then about energy production, air and water contamination, and dwindling forests, how is it that so many solutions remain unused? In so many cases, we are failing to advance—turning the Texas-Mexico border into a toxic sewer in the name of trade, wantonly allowing our national forests to be cut, allowing fuel efficiency improvements to stall, destroying precious habitat, letting people drink contaminated water and breathe polluted air. Today, even more than in the 1970s, we know what our environment needs and we know how to meet those needs. We know how to provide cleaner, more efficient energy, how to clean the air and water, how to protect crucial habitat that allows us to survive.

But we can't seem to get from A to B. There are more environmental groups producing first-rate research and plans than one could ever have imagined thirty years ago. Some of these groups are spectacularly well funded. They have reams of data supporting their positions. Yet careful consideration of the environmental state of our nation would indicate only diminishing returns to environmental advocacy. Take a look around.

Razing the Landscape

For many residents of the Powder River Basin in Wyoming and Montana, "Home on the Range" is now a nightmare. Life there through harsh winters and sometimes drought-plagued summers was never for the faint of heart, but it was a quintessentially American frontier life with a pervasive sense of freedom. Now, in more and more areas, the landscape reverberates around the clock with the screaming of gas compressors and the rumbling of water pumps. Dust rises behind heavy truck traffic barreling down the new dirt roads that crisscross the land. Salt contamination, left by evaporating water pumped from deep underground, spreads across the soil. Coal-bed methane companies seeking a fast buck are smothering the freedom right out of the range.

Only in the past two decades has a scattershot technique been adopted for relieving coal seams of the methane gas they hold. Shallow, clustered wells can be cheaply drilled into coal deposits where groundwater traps methane in the porous coal. Pumping the water to the surface releases the gas for surface capture. Most of the land in the Powder River Basin is privately owned only on its surface; subsurface mineral rights belong to the federal government, which leases them to gas companies. According to the *New York Times,* "most of the basin's 4,000 ranch families will have no choice but to put up with strangers on their land for the next ten to fifteen years. Except for nominal access fees, most ranchers will get little financial benefit from the hundreds of millions of dollars in gas revenue generated beneath their land." More than 50,000 gas wells are planned for this one area alone, not to mention the coal-bed methane fields in Colorado, New Mexico, and Alabama.

Despite a federal court ruling that water pumped from coal-bed methane wells is "industrial waste" under the Clean Water Act, and therefore subject to regulation, the *New York Times* reports that "coal-bed methane extraction is continuing to hurtle forward across much of the West, thanks to policies put in place by the Clinton administration and accelerated under President Bush."

This isn't surprising. The Bush Department of the Interior sets a new standard for conflict of interest: Steven Griles, before he joined the Bush team as Deputy Secretary of Interior, worked as a lobbyist for several corporations now drilling through the backyards, pastures, and rangelands of Powder River Basin. A recent investigation by the department's own inspector general into Griles' continued association with his former corporate clients found "evidence of and the perception that the department's leadership did not take ethics seriously." This anemic finding is no consolation for rural people whose water wells are being contaminated and depleted, who watch the wrecking of an ecosystem that is an extension of themselves, and whose lives are increasingly shaped by the big corporate hand that grips Washington, D.C.

According to the federal government, proven coal-bed methane reserves account for around 9 percent of the country's total natural gas reserves. The Gulf of Mexico holds around 14 percent, to be tapped by many fewer, though more expensive, wells. But the mercantile mind, ever externalizing the costs—long-term damage to ecosystems and rural community health—sees only short-term profits achieved by politically sanctioned corporate violence. The claim is that we cannot have the energy we need without this violence. But any number of analyses of alternative energy solutions shows that even a modest implementation of proven conservation and renewable energy technologies would eliminate the need for coal-bed methane drilling.

Consider the 150 million refrigerators and freezers in the United States, as Dr. Arthur Rosenfeld, the renowned energy efficiency innovator, often does to illustrate the kind of spectacular potential there is for saving energy. In the first half of the 1970s, refrigerator size was steadily increasing, while the energy used by each unit increased at an even greater rate. Along came a series of California state standards mandating increased efficiency followed by several federal standards. As a result, despite a continuing increase in size and a steady decrease in price, increased refrigerator and freezer efficiency now save 200 billion kilowatt hours over 1974 efficiency levels every year. This energy savings from refrigerator efficiency alone roughly equals 36,000 coal-bed methane wells. Further examples abound.

Dr. Rosenfeld has another success story to relate: With the latest federal air conditioner efficiency standard in place in 2006, the annual energy use for cooling a new California home will be less than 33 percent of what it was in 1970. In their important book *Natural Capitalism,* Paul Hawken and Amory and Hunter Lovins describe the inefficiencies of electric pumping systems, which use 12 percent of the world's electric power. A simple series of innovations involving smaller motors and the lowered resistance of larger diameter pipes made one such system 92 percent more efficient and less costly. Passive solar design is even less sophisticated. Simply orienting a building to absorb heat from the sun can save 10 percent to 20 percent of heating energy.

Executives in the energy extraction business may swagger about the latest gas play, but it's chicken feed compared to saving energy, which carries nearly three times the dollar benefits of extracted fossil fuels. Energy conservation—better for the environment—is also cheaper than destructive extraction.

Across the country to the East, violent extractive practices literally reshape the landscape. In West Virginia, they don't mince words: mountain-top removal is as plain a description as might be found, though it carries with it an air of undeserved surgical precision. Enormous earth-moving machines give mountain-top removal coal-mining astonishing destructive power. First, the forests are ripped out, then soil and rock are carved away and sent tumbling into streams in adjacent valleys, and then the coal is dug out. Industry officials occasionally claim that an important collateral benefit of their activity is a leveling of the landscape from which future strip malls and other development might sprout.

Adding to the violence and horror, slurry dams above valley communities hold back water that is toxic with heavy metals left behind as coal is processed onsite. These dams have failed in the past. The Buffalo Creek Dam, owned by Pittson Coal, gave way in 1972, killing 125 people, injuring 1,121, and leaving 4,000 homeless, in what a Pittson vice-president later called an "act of God." In 2000, the Massey Energy Company slurry spill released 250 million gallons of coal sludge in Kentucky, creating a toxic wasteland.

Hundreds of miles of streams have been buried by coal companies in what a federal judge in 1999 ruled a clear violation of the Clean Water Act. Section 404 of the Act has allowed the U.S. Army Corps of Engineers to authorize the filling of streams and wetlands, but until recently, the "fill material" allowed under these permits did not include any type of waste. This left an avenue open for citizens to challenge mountain-top removal mining in court because mining "spoils" were considered waste.

In May 2002, the EPA and the Corps finalized a rule change which redefined "fill" to encompass mining spoils resulting from mountain-top removal. The rule change had originated with the

Clinton administration in April 2000 as an attempt to appease West Virginia Democratic Senator Robert Byrd, faithful servant of King Coal. Remarkably, a dozen GOP lawmakers wrote President Bush, as they had Clinton two years earlier, in opposition to the rule change: "Allowing coal mining spoil and other types of waste material to be dumped into lakes, rivers, streams, and wetlands is contrary to the central goal of the Clean Water Act: preserving the physical, chemical, and biological integrity of the nation's waters. This rulemaking, if carried forward, would represent a major weakening of current law."

The original rule was seldom enforced in any case. Despite sharp growth in mountain-top removal in the 1990s, the number of federal inspectors whose job it was to identify the impacts of the practice on waterways was cut in half. Inspections in West Virginia fell from 470 in 1993 to only 92 in 1998, with violations decreasing by eightfold, according to the Citizens Coal Council.

So the coal companies have their way with some of the most extensive intact hardwood forest ecosystems in the United States, and continue to flatten the land and the spirits of local people trying to maintain a centuries-old rural existence in their hollows (small valleys) of West Virginia and neighboring states. Ubiquitous dust, massive explosions, debris, rain, flooding and fouled water supplies mark the lives of the few who reject skimpy buyout offers from coal companies—or have no such option. One holdout, Jim Weekley, told the *New York Times* in 1999 that, as a former miner, he was not against mining, but that at least he knew that digging coal in the old deep shaft mines was not fouling his nest in the hollow above.

Mountain-top removal is much more mechanized than mining was in the past; while coal production rose 32 percent from 1987 to 1997, jobs decreased by 29 percent. The Citizens Coal Council points out that the top 15 coal-producing counties in West Virginia have the worst poverty levels in the nation, even though they produce 15 percent of the nation's coal. The economic rationale for laying waste to the landscape, then, is largely one of shareholder value, executive salaries, perks, and bonuses. Judy Bonds, a sixth generation West Virginia hollow resident, and winner of the 2003 Goldman Environmental Prize for her efforts to stop mountain-top removal, calls it "rape and take." As is the case with coal-bed methane drilling, mountain-top removal coal mining is a crime against nature, especially considering the proven potential of energy conservation and renewable energy sources.

The ravaging of the range and the stunning destruction of whole forested mountains are deep violations of freedom, perhaps the central value of a conservative American tradition in the broadest sense. While the word "freedom" has been cheapened by its extended overuse in political platitudes, especially by politicians indentured to big business, it should be used more often and have greater impact when it retains a meaning grounded in truth. Trashing the environment for short-term profit amounts to a radical assault on freedom perpetrated by corporations who have bought our state and federal politicians. Coal-bed methane drilling and mountain-top removal mining are just two examples of largely unseen, cumulative environmental violence that affects the air we breathe, the water we drink, the food we eat, and the complex web of life to which we are permanently tied.

Freedom . . . to Breathe Dirty Air and Drink Toxic Water

In La Oroya, a town of 30,000 high in the Peruvian Andes, residents breathe environmental violence. In 1998, the Peruvian Health Ministry determined that 99 percent of the children in the area suffered from lead poisoning, which can have a devastating impact on their developing brains and organ systems. When it purchased a lead smelter in La Oroya from the Peruvian government in 1997, the Doe Run Company committed to "fixing the blood lead issue" by 2006 with a projected expenditure of $174 million. Now, citing a lack of resources, the company wants to take an additional five years—and spend 20 million less total dollars—to make a "a serious contribution to reduce blood lead levels," the head of the company in Peru recently told the *Associated Press*.

Lead poisoning might be something we associate with the ancient Romans, crowded cities in the Third World where leaded gas is still widely used, or far away smelters in the Andes. But, it turns out, the United States still has serious problems with lead—in peeling paint on the walls of old tenements, mining spoils in places like Picher, Oklahoma, industrial dust, and discarded cell phones and computers in cities. Recently, high levels of lead were revealed in the drinking water in many Washington, D.C. homes and apartments. Doe Run, the same company damaging children's health in the mountains of Peru, admits releasing 226,513 pounds of lead into the air from its smelter in the small town of Herculaneum, Missouri, in 2001 alone. Of children under age six in the town, 28 percent showed unsafe lead levels in their blood, according to the Missouri Department of Natural Resources, and that figure rises to over 50 percent of children within half a mile of the smelter.

According to documents released by the EPA Region 7 office, Doe Run was to have met the EPA's air standard for lead back in 1995 for a projected cost of $8 million. As in Peru, the company now claims that it doesn't have the resources needed to stop itself from spewing lead into the bodies of children. The *St. Louis Post Dispatch* recently reported an unfortunate underlying truth to these claims, thanks to the financial shenanigans of minor junk bond king Ira Rennert. Mr. Rennert has used hundreds of millions of dollars in junk bonds written against the industrial assets he owns, including the Doe Run Company, to pay dividends to Renco Group, Inc., his holding company. Thus, Mr. Rennert has left Doe Run staggering under debt. And Renco continues to poison children with lead in order to subsidize its greed. If only George W. Bush would do his West Texas Sheriff routine on Mr. Rennert.

Instead, the Bush administration announces broad regulatory rollbacks in the Clean Air Act's new-source review program that will allow 17,000 power plants, chemical plants, steel mills, and other major sources of pollution to expand or modify their facilities and increase emissions without modernizing air pollution controls as they had been required to do.

The *New York Times* reports that toward the end of the Clinton administration, EPA officials realized that utility companies across the country were breaking the law en masse. Here was an opportunity to force these companies to modernize and make tremendous strides toward cleaner air nationwide. While the EPA was able to settle with some utilities, reports the *Times,* such as the deal with Tampa Electric that took 123,000 annual tons of pollution out of the sky, most companies held out hope for (and gave money toward) Bush's election, for which they have been richly rewarded. They are allowed to continue killing Americans—disproportionately the poor and non-White.

The EPA estimates that 30 percent of Americans breathe unhealthy air. In a 1996 analysis of epidemiological data collected by Harvard University and the American Cancer Society, the Natural Resources Defense Council concluded that 64,000 Americans die prematurely from cardiopulmonary causes linked to fine particulate air pollution. NRDC recommended a new standard for particulate matter less than 2.5 microns in size of 10 micrograms per cubic meter, but in 1997 President Clinton's EPA settled on a weaker standard of 15. Now even that standard may be moot as President Bush offers the nation more dirty air to breathe.

In the town of Riviera Beach, Palm Beach County, Florida, environmental violence threatens residents' through their water pipes. Organic solvents, the low-tech horror behind the past forty years of high-tech revolutions in Silicon Valley and elsewhere, contaminate the groundwater in this predominantly African American working class community in a classic case of environmental racism—toxics dumped in poor communities of color. For years, Solitron Devices, Inc, a subsidiary of Honeywell Corporation, dumped highly acidic wastewaters down drains, corroding plumbing, holding tanks, and portions of the city sewer, releasing chlorinated solvents and metals to the soil and groundwater, according to the Florida Department of Health. Contaminants then moved in groundwater to off-site municipal wells.

In 1974, the local water utility received numerous complaints from irate consumers about a "pesticide" odor within an hour of pumping water from one of the wells. Subsequent testing of groundwater identified high levels of chromium, chlorobenzene, tetrachloroethene, trichloroethene, and vinyl chloride, chemical compounds known to cause kidney, liver, and neurological damage and cancer. Contamination from another electronics manufacturer, Trans Circuit, Inc. compounded the problem. Trans Circuit had built an evaporation pond, but it was inadequate to hold the 336,000 gallons of effluent the company produced per month. Waste spilled over the liner when it rained and the company was warned several times. The city of Riviera Beach began using air strippers to remove contaminants from municipal well water in 1988, footing the bill itself.

For years, the mayor of Riviera Beach, Michael Brown, sought help from the EPA in vain. The *Palm Beach Post* reports that when he first met with EPA officials in 1999, they offered a do-nothing solution: natural attenuation, according to Mayor Brown. In 2002, the EPA approved a $500,000 reimbursement toward purification costs—upwards of five million dollars—that the city had carried for fourteen years. Recently the EPA held meetings with the mayor to discuss a plan to clean up the aquifer, presumably with money from Honeywell, although the company made no firm commitment. The *Post* reported Mr. Brown's perhaps ironic reaction: "Nobody really knows with this recommendation today if it will take 20 years, 50 years or 100 years [to complete]. We're delighted."

There may be no town in America as polluted as Anniston, Alabama. "In my judgment, there's no question this is the most contaminated site in the U.S.," Dr. David Carpenter, a professor of environmental health at the State University of New York in Albany, told the country on CBS's *60 Minutes*. Anniston's 24,000 residents live in an environment saturated with PCBs, probable human carcinogens banned by the EPA in 1979. Monsanto Corporation, the manufacturers of PCBs in Anniston for years, ran a plant that leaked 50,000 pounds of PCBs into a local creek every year and buried more than one million pounds of PCB-laced waste in its antiquated landfills, reported the *Washington Post* after examining Monsanto's internal documents.

The *Post* reports that, in 1996, PCB levels in the area "were as high as 940 times the federal level of concern in yard soils, 200 times that level in dust inside people's homes, 2,000 times that level in Monsanto's drainage ditches. The PCB levels in the air were also too high. And in blood tests, nearly one-third of the residents of the working-class Sweet Valley and Cobbtown neighborhoods near the plant were found to have elevated PCB levels." In addition, Anniston is now home to an Army chemical weapons incinerator run by part of the most polluting enterprise in the country (including its contractors): the U.S. Department of Defense. Local residents' concerns that the incinerator is unsafe (substantiated by incomplete burning, toxic releases and safety problems at the Army's similar Tooele incinerator in Utah) have been ignored.

President Bush is asking American taxpayers to foot the bill for cleaning up some of the more than 11,000 toxic Superfund sites across the nation. The 2005 budget will require at least 1.27 billion dollars of tax money to clean up after the worst polluters in corporate America. The law requiring that polluters pay expired in 1995 and has not been renewed. Some of the most polluted sites are the toxic legacy of corporate welfare mining. According to a Green Scissors report, mines have polluted more than 40 percent of the headwaters of Western watersheds. The antiquated General Mining Act of 1872 allows mining companies to buy federal land for five dollars an acre (1872 prices) and pay no royalties for gold, copper, zinc and other minerals extracted from our land. So taxpayers are robbed of billions of dollars in mineral wealth and then are expected to pay the stiff costs associated with cleaning up abandoned mine sites. Needless to say, countless other contaminated sites lie untouched.

Along with clean air, there is no more basic environmental right than clean drinking water. Since the passage of the Safe Drinking Water Act in 1974, too few drinking water standards have been set compared to the many hundreds of contaminants found in drinking water across the United States. According to the Natural Resources Defense Council (NRDC), the pesticide atrazine is present in the water of more than one million Americans, while perchlorate from rocket fuel is present in the water supplies of more than 20 million Americans. Lead contamination continues to be a problem. Antiquated pipes mean more organic matter in drinking water combining with chlorine residues to form toxic trihalomethanes. Twenty years after the passage of legislation to deal with leaking underground fuel storage tanks, 136,265 tanks remained leaking in September 2003, according to the EPA. The gasoline additive MTBE has migrated into drinking water supplies in Santa Monica, California, and many other municipalities.

In 2002, the Congressional Budget Office found that $232 to $402 billion in investments will be needed over the next two decades to upgrade and repair the nation's drinking water systems. The United States remains well behind Europe in water treatment. Organic pollutants, the largest class of contaminants, can be dealt with wholesale using activated carbon filters, while ozonation is effective against viruses, bacteria and certain parasites. A handful of U.S. cities use these technologies; many more could benefit from them.

A visionary approach to cleaning up water supplies comes from a sadly unique corner of the manufacturing sector. In Atlanta, Georgia, one of the world's largest commercial carpet and tile companies, the Interface Corporation, run by Ray Anderson, set the astonishing goal of having its effluent be pure water. The idea is that chemicals used to make tile and carpet will be entirely re-used and recycled in the manufacturing process. This has the happy effect of reducing pollution and also company cost.

Erasing Habitats and Killing Off Species

Clearly, some environmental problems have effective solutions that can prevent or reverse damage. Species extinctions resulting from habitat erasure, however, are permanent. And the loss of old growth forests and regional biodiversity might as well be permanent with respect to human life cycles. It is axiomatic that as we lose wilderness, protecting what remains becomes evermore urgent. Such is the case with our national forests.

After the massive clear-cutting of the Reagan years, timber harvested from federal lands dropped to 12 percent of the total timber harvest in the United States. Old growth was down to less than 5 percent of its original extent and urgently needed protection. By the time Bill Clinton was elected president, the case for ending timber harvests in national forests was already very clear.

Damage to cut-over national forests could be partially reversed, at least to the extent that forest ecosystems are understood. With the U.S. Forest Service pouring over one billion dollars every year into the timber cut, the potential for using that money instead for a major subsidizing effort to restore our national forests would add the benefit of creating many needed jobs in logging communities. Recreation, hunting, and fishing already contribute at least $111 billion to the overall economy each year, according to the National Forest Protection

Alliance, far more than logging does. While ending timber harvests on federal lands seemed extreme to some touting compromise a dozen years ago, it was in fact the only reasonable option given the levels of exploitation that had occurred and the damage that exploitation caused, both within forest ecosystems and outside of them—for example, the devastating impact clear-cutting has had on salmon fisheries.

Far from seeking a moratorium on logging in national forests, in July 1995, President Clinton signed into law a bill that contained the now notorious "salvage rider." Though the rider was deviously attached to a bill providing extra relief to victims of the bombings in Oklahoma City, the president was well aware of the logging provisions therein, having criticized those very provisions when he initially vetoed the bill. The law called for salvage timber sales to be offered and stipulated that they be subject to only a very narrow judicial review. Salvage timber was to include not only damaged trees, but green trees "imminently susceptible to fire or insect attack," an amorphously broad definition that the Forest Service then adopted. The rider also stipulated that green timber sales from an earlier appropriations bill that had been halted over environmental concerns be carried out.

By the time the rider expired on December 31, 1996, the Forest Service had offered 4.6 billion board feet of timber as part of salvage sales. Though Clinton did not support efforts in Congress to repeal the rider, the Forest Service did halt sales of 672 million board feet—enough wood to surface a four-lane highway from coast to coast with inch-thick planks—because these proposed sales clearly had little to do with salvaging dead or diseased trees. The areas in dispute had excessive content of green timber, were not imminently susceptible to insect attack or fire, or were in road-less areas, among other objections. But when in 1997 the Government Accounting Office (GAO) reported that these sales had not been offered before the rider expired, Secretary of Agriculture Dan Glickman hastened to respond that, "In fact, the majority of the volume was simply delayed. It is anticipated that only a small fraction of this volume will be cancelled."

The salvage rider had the effect of increasing timber sales 35 percent over what the Forest Service had planned for the same period. Far worse than this increase was the precedent set for *lawless* timber sales. Environmental groups have only a limited ability to monitor and challenge sales offered on an accelerated schedule. According to the GAO, of 11,435 salvage timber sales governed by the rider, only sixteen faced legal challenges.

Widespread forest fires in 1994 provided the impetus for the original salvage rider; the fires of 2002 are causing history to repeat itself, only now the political situation is considerably worse. Mark Rey, Bush's Under Secretary of Agriculture who now oversees the Forest Service, was a principle author of the salvage rider.

Still, the target volume of timber to be cut from national forests shrinks; the volume of wood materials from national forests now comprises only 2 percent of the U.S. wood supply. The situation is worse simply because that much less old growth forest remains. Removing from the market the 2 percent of the nation's wood supply now derived from national forests would have a negligible effect on the price of lumber, especially with the advent of engineered wood products, wood recycling and alternative fibers. But protecting all federally owned old growth and carefully restoring clear-cut areas in national forests would have immeasurable environmental and recreational value to the nation and future generations as the years pass. Posterity needs our trees.

As staggering as it is that corporations and the government have managed to reduce our virgin forests to a tiny fraction of what they once were, the condition of the world's oceans even more clearly reveals the stranglehold over the planet. The Pew Oceans Commission (POC) reports that "we are depleting the oceans of fish, and have been for decades. The government can only assure us that 22 percent of managed fish stocks are being fished sustainably. The decline of New England fisheries is most notorious. By 1989, New England cod, haddock, and yellowtail flounder had reached historic lows. . . . Populations of . . . Pacific red snapper, have been driven to less than 10 percent of their historic numbers."

The POC documented occurrences of thirty-six "dead zones" on the U.S. coastline between 1970 and 2000. These zones are depleted of oxygen after nutrient-rich run-off causes huge algal blooms and subsequent overgrowth of bacteria. Many locations have had several repeat occurrences. The most well known of these, at the mouth of the Mississippi River, is the size of New Jersey. Oceans expert David Helvarg reports that the world's aquatic species are going extinct at a rate fives times faster than that of land animals. In the Gulf of Mexico, for every pound of shrimp trawlers drag in, they waste seven pounds of other marine animals, called simply "bycatch."

The situation is bleak, but Helvarg has a clear solution to America's fisheries crisis. He would start with buybacks of boats by the government in order to reduce the size of the fishing fleet to make entry into fisheries commensurate with sustainable harvest targets. In the past, the U.S. fishing fleet was hugely overcapitalized, thanks to special tax breaks put in place by President Reagan. Undersea reserves are a key, proven component to fisheries recovery. And Helvarg stresses that conflicts of interest (wherein active commercial fishermen serve on oversight boards) that pervade fisheries management must be eliminated.

Looming Large on a Small Planet

We've known for some time that human beings have the capacity to slowly but surely chew our way toward the creation of significant holes in the planet's biosphere, its forests and oceans, and associated creatures. But there are two potential impacts that we know humans will have on life that involve so many feedback consequences—of which we have a still primitive understanding—that we cannot predict their directions, implications or precise magnitudes with much precision at all. The first is human-caused global warming; the second, the widespread release of genetically modified organisms into the environment.

The U.S. National Academy of Sciences (NAS) concluded in June 2001 that: "Greenhouse gases are accumulating in Earth's atmosphere as a result of human activities, causing surface air temperatures and subsurface ocean temperatures to rise. Temperatures, are, in fact, rising." Furthermore, the NAS wrote that "national policy decisions made now and in the longer-term future will influence the extent of any damage suffered by vulnerable human populations and ecosystems later in this century."

What is much more difficult to predict is how this warming, even if we manage to stabilize levels of greenhouse gases, will interact with the extremely complex forces that cause weather patterns. For some, including President Bush, this uncertainty surrounding the exact effects of global warming is reason to dally, to avoid making even the modest changes that the Kyoto agreement stipulates. But there are many clear arguments for these changes besides global warming mitigation.

Even a modest increase in average fuel efficiency could dramatically reduce our dependence on foreign oil, our ground-level air pollution, and greenhouse gases. The temporary cost of raising CAFE (Corporate Average Fuel Efficiency) standards to forty miles per gallon (mpg) for cars and light trucks would be more than offset by the savings in fuel cost in the first 50,000 miles driven. The forty miles per gallon standard carries a projected savings of more than ninety billion gallons of gasoline by 2010. That standard, however, currently looms as a mirage. General Motors, followed by the rest of the world's automakers, has exploited the loophole exempting light trucks from fuel

efficiency standards to generate an explosion of gas-guzzling Sport
Utility Vehicles over the past dozen years. Thus, true average fuel efficiency dropped back to 1980 levels during the Clinton administration,
costing many times more oil than is held in the Arctic National
Wildlife Reserve and adding significantly to global warming. Many
engineers can demonstrate as well how SUV fuel efficiency can be
raised to 35 miles per gallon with simple and inexpensive modifica-
tions, apart from hybrid technology.

Minimizing carbon emissions can be shown to produce healthy
ripple effects throughout the economy. Thus, arguments for fundamental changes in the way we derive and use energy should be made
on all fronts to build the support needed to confront human-caused
global warming.

The Union of Concerned Scientists calculates that achieving a
20 percent reliance on renewable energy sources (up from 6 percent
now) by 2020 would save a total of 20.6 trillion cubic feet of natural
gas, or nearly 50,000 coal-bed methane wells producing strong for
ten years, a huge carbon emissions savings. A recent study by researchers at Stanford University showed that in 24 percent of locations where wind was measured, wind speed in the United States is
fast enough to provide power at the same current cost of coal and natural gas generators. But, in 2002, Denmark, Germany, and Spain together installed 78 percent of the wind-power added worldwide,
leaving the United States lagging far behind, according to the Worldwatch Institute. Though the U.S. Department of Energy's renewable
energy program cites "real potential of cutting solar prices by half,"
the United States continues to progress very slowly on solar development compared to Europe and Japan. What we've known about the
potentials of wind, solar efficiency, and other non-fossil fuel energy
for thirty years is being applied far too slowly, given the urgency of
global warming and the danger of resource wars.

The other human impact with largely unforeseen, though not unimagined, consequences—the release of genetically modified organisms (GMOs) into the environment—is a potentially grave threat. There are innumerable reasons to worry about the ecological consequences for wild organisms and ecosystems of the widespread release of GMOs. Most of these reasons, however, involve thought experiments. Our scientific understanding of the consequences of genetically modifying organisms and releasing them lag far behind the highly sophisticated ability we have to engineer these organisms.

Quite possibly, we will see genetically engineered salmon escape from an aquaculture operation in the future like the 100,000 nonengineered Atlantic salmon that escaped into Puget Sound in 1999. We have terrifyingly little idea of what the effects on wild salmon populations would be of a Franken-species designed for fast growth. Ignacio Chapela's and David Quist's work showing that genes are somehow moving from bioengineered corn to native corn in Mexico has been confirmed, showing a danger to native varieties. In February 2004, the Union of Concerned Scientists released an analysis of seeds of six traditional varieties of canola. All six had been contaminated with DNA from genetically engineered strains. Once again, big business makes these decisions to change the nature of nature, and the corporate grip on our freedom tightens.

Consider the case of Percy Schmeiser, a farmer from Bruno, Saskatchewan, in Canada. For forty years, this farmer—who also served as mayor of Bruno from 1966 to 1983—has developed his own varieties of canola using traditional plant breeding methods. In 1997, Schmeiser was sued by the Monsanto Corporation for allegedly using their patented herbicide-resistant canola seed without paying for it. He was making a decent living with his own seed and had no need for Monsanto's product. Schmeiser had harvested seed from his crop to be planted the following year, as he had always done. The seed he collected inadvertently included seed that had germinated from Monsanto's engineered plants, which had blown onto Schmeiser's land. Some of the GMO seed germinated after the next round of planting and Monsanto inspectors found those plants through testing. The company flexed its muscle, Schmeiser's crop was confiscated—so he lost his own seed as well—and Monsanto sought to punish him financially. From Percy Schmeiser's point of view, Monsanto had contaminated his crop. He used no herbicide and therefore took no advantage of the attributes of Monsanto's engineered seed. It was impossible for him to remove the invading Monsanto seed from his own seed. Despite this logic, two successive courts in Canada found against Schmeiser. But he was not found guilty of *stealing* Monsanto's genetically engineered seed. Simply the presence of Monsanto's plants on Schmeiser's land—regardless of how they got there, and regardless of whether Monsanto's pollen had contaminated other plant stocks—made Schmeiser liable, according to one imaginative judge. Schmeiser's case was finally heard before the Supreme Court of Canada, which concluded that he owed Monsanto nothing, but upheld Monsanto's right to patent life, regardless of how it might become dispersed. Schmeiser views the result as a draw. Monsanto has dozens of such suits pending against farmers across North America.

What if we had the freedom to choose whether or not we support GMO foods in the marketplace? In public hearings all over the United States, over 90 percent of Americans asked for that freedom at the close of the twentieth century: they wanted labeling of GMO foods. President Clinton's Food and Drug Administration said, No, sorry, we won't allow you that freedom; furthermore, we'll give that freedom to large corporations like Monsanto. Most Americans are eating GMO foods without their knowledge. And if the consequences of releasing such organisms into the environment are dire down the road, we will have been robbed of the opportunity to stop such experiments by making a daily choice. Enough! Do we want freedom to pollute the environment, or freedom from self-devouring policies that contaminate our nests?

Once again, the corporate sphere is dominating our ecosphere and blocking known energy-efficient technologies and other environmentally benign methods. We owe it to our descendents to reverse priorities and force corporations to adjust to the sustainability of the planet and its fragile circle of life.

In the 1970s, we had the luxury of giving the bedrock environmental laws a chance to work, to gradually and progressively reclaim the damage done by polluting and pillaging companies. We no longer have time. We thought we had urgency then, but it has failed to carry us through. It is hard to exaggerate the new heights of urgency needed now to clean up our act on the planet. We are up against global trade agreements which erode environmental progress, and technologies old and new that can change the face of the Earth. But we have the awareness to turn it all around. That is what the last 30 years have given us. From the state of California's breakthrough new law passed in 2002 which mandates that motor vehicles reduce their contribution to global warming, to the burgeoning organic food movement, to zero effluent factories, environmental mobilizations are at last starting to move across the land again. We only have to apply focused urgencies to the ready and unused solutions which are parked idly on the shelves.

INCREASING BURDENS ON THE WORKING CLASS

I t's been a dismal three decades for working people in the United States. With big corporations displaying an ever-heightening degree of ruthlessness, business has seen its profits rise dramatically relative to wages.

In the face of aggressive employer demands for concessions, the downward pull of international competition, an overvalued dollar, weak and barely enforced labor and workplace safety laws, relatively high unemployment rates, and a sclerotic labor movement, most workers have seen wage rates stay practically flat over the past several decades—even as CEO salaries and profitability have skyrocketed.

The executive class has captured almost all of the gains in wealth from the growth in gross domestic product (GDP) in recent decades. And George W. Bush's recession and jobless recovery has only worsened the problem.

Here's what a Wall Street analyst said in March 2004: "We'd thought that the labor share of national income was in the process of bottoming out, but whether we're talking outsourcing or just old-style downsizing, the effort by U.S. business to pare costs (and extract productivity gains in services) continues apace."

Meanwhile, employers have slashed benefits for those workers lucky enough to retain a job. And workplaces remain far more hazardous than necessary.

There are glimmers of hope that the situation can be improved. Some unions and communities have won important victories that have made a difference in workers' lives, but they remain a rarity.

Wages

Here's the basic story of wages in this country over the past thirty years: Most people earn no more an hour than they did three decades ago (adjusting for inflation), but those at the top have enjoyed substantial increases in salary and those at the very top—the CEOs and top company executives—have seen their compensation go through the roof.

Most people struggle to get by with rock bottom net worth. They're working more and more—either working longer hours or picking up a second or third job—to pay the bills and meet rent or mortgage payments. (Americans worked on average two hundred hours a year more from 1973 to 2000—the equivalent of five full-time weeks.) In two-parent families, increasingly both parents are in the workforce. Just to meet everyday expenses, they're borrowing more and more from credit cards, home equity loans, or second mortgages, or from legal loan sharks at check-cashing operations. If someone in the family gets sick and lacks health insurance—forty-five million Americans are in that boat—the family is in a jam. Even if they have insurance, the extravagant price of medicine may not be covered, or covered entirely, and paying for the pills can drive a family into despair.

Meanwhile, the executive class rakes in more money than ever before, and indulges new forms of conspicuous consumption. We have competition among CEOs over who has the bigger yacht. If an executive has to go to the hospital, they can check into platinum class luxury suites offered by leading medical institutions—for $10,000 a night. The *New York Times* recently reported on a new convenience for rich New Yorkers: private indoor pools, with start-up costs of $500,000.

Any way you slice the numbers, you get the same result: a deeply divided America with a struggling majority and a super-rich clique. It's a story of a gap between haves and have-nots more severe than anything this country has witnessed for a century, since the start of the Manufacturing Age:

- For the private production and nonsupervisory workers who make up 80 percent of the workforce, it took until the late 1990s to return to the real earnings levels of 1979.
- CEOs at large corporations now make about three hundred times more than the average worker at their firms. In 1982, they made just forty-two times more; in 1965, twenty-six times more.
- The top fifth of households own more than 83 percent of the nation's wealth, the bottom 80 percent less than 17 percent.
- The top 1 percent owns over 38 percent of the nation's wealth, more than double the amount of wealth controlled by the bottom 80 percent. The top 1 percent's financial wealth is equal to that of the bottom 95 percent.
- In 1979, the top 5 percent had eleven times the average income of the bottom 20 percent. By 2000, the top 5 percent had nineteen times the income of the bottom 20 percent.
- Whatever the data examined, it's worse for women and people of color, who receive lower wages and have much less accumulated wealth than White men. Women and minority males earn 70 percent to 80 percent of what White men make. More than a third of single mothers with children live in poverty.

Thanks to low levels of unemployment in the late 1990s, worker wages started rising, eventually catching up to the levels of twenty years earlier. But the recession and high rates of unemployment that have persisted into the new millennium have almost surely ended that trend.

The effective stagnation in worker wages for three decades occurred even though productivity rose steadily. Productivity is the amount of output per person hour worked. In other words, workers were making and producing more, but not receiving any share of the increased wealth. Virtually all of it was captured by increased corporate profit taking.

CEO pay grew at a much faster rate even than corporate profitability. From 1990 to 2003, inflation rose 41 percent. Average worker pay rose 49 percent. Corporate profits jumped 128 percent. CEO compensation rose 313 percent.

If the federal minimum wage had increased as quickly as CEO pay since 1990, it would today be $15.71 per hour, more than three times the actual minimum wage of $5.15 an hour, as calculated by Boston-based United for a Fair Economy.

Reasons for Stagnant Wages

There are many reasons why wages have remained stagnant, although ultimately it comes down to reduced worker power.

Corporate globalization has created a system where workers in the United States must compete with their desperately poor brothers and sisters in countries like China and Mexico. Many manufacturing companies that would like to maintain factories in the United States find they cannot compete with lower cost plants overseas. That has led to the massive outflow of well-paying manufacturing jobs from the United States, and forced many workers who are able to hold on to factory jobs to accept lower wages and benefits. Even employers who operate profitably in the United States frequently move overseas in search of greater profits, or threaten workers with plant closings to extract more concessions.

The U.S. steel industry has shed thousands of jobs in the face of low-wage competition. Warren Dillon, a fifty-five-year-old with thirty-seven years at Bethlehem Steel, is one of the victims, having lost his white-collar job at a Maryland steel plant in April 2003. "I figured it was a stable position," Dillon told the *Daily Record* of Baltimore, Maryland, about his decision to take a job with the steel company decades earlier. "You go down to Bethlehem Steel and just stay there. They stay there until they want to retire. And then they retire and you have a pension and medical coverage and your days are done."

After he'd lost his job, the *Daily Record* reported, Dillon enrolled in resume-writing and job search classes. He thought he might become a computer technician. His career counselors instead suggested courses in truck driving or nursing assistance, areas he wasn't interested in pursuing. Dillon sent out dozens of resumes, with no success. Thirty-seven years experience at the steel plant didn't seem to mean much. He did receive an invitation to interview for a store manager position, with a salary of $36,000 to $42,000. But he was told he was overqualified.

Eventually, he landed a job as an airport screener with the Transportation Security Administration at the Baltimore-Washington International Airport. Salary: $28,000. After looking so hard, Dillon was happy to get anything.

The competitive pressure from corporate globalization is just one component of an economy that has been bad for workers over most of the past three decades. Especially when unemployment rates are high—as they have been for the past several years—people take jobs at whatever wage they can find. Many aren't in a position to hold out for a better job or bargain for a better salary.

When workers try to act collectively, they confront a host of union-busting tactics, including physical intimidation. These actions are often illegal, but legal protections are so flaccid, and the labor rights police so weak, underfunded, compromised, and embattled, that employers can act with virtual impunity.

Unions

Globalization and union-busting reinforce one another. In a 2000 study sponsored by the U.S. Trade Deficit Review Commission, Cornell University researcher Kate Bronfenbrenner found that more than half of all employers facing union-organizing drives threaten to close all or part of their plant, even though such threats are generally illegal. For mobile industries—companies that can more plausibly threaten to move, like auto plants, as opposed to hotels—the plant-closing threat rate approached two-thirds. This study, the most comprehensive ever undertaken, concluded that the "threats are even more pervasive than they were in 1993–1995, and the threat of capital mobility has discernibly affected union organizing strategies."

Bronfenbrenner proved what every worker knows: the threat to move a plant is among an employer's most potent tactics. "The data suggests that most workers take even the most veiled employer plant-closing threats very seriously," she writes. "When combined with other anti-union tactics of employers, as they are in the overwhelming majority of employer campaigns, plant-closing threats are extremely effective in undermining union organizing efforts, even in a context where the majority of workers in the unit seem predisposed to support the union at the onset of the organizing campaign." Bronfenbrenner found that "union election win rates were significantly lower in units where plant-closing threats occurred (38 percent) than in units without plant-closing threats (51 percent). Win rates were especially low (24 percent) in those campaigns where employers made specific threats to move to another country."

Threatening to close the plant is only one device in the employers' toolbox. In at least one out of four union-organizing campaigns, union supporters are illegally fired. Employers facing a union drive frequently give unscheduled wage increases, and make unilateral changes in benefits and working conditions, according to Bronfenbrenner. Many promote union activists out of the bargaining unit. More than a third give bribes or special favors to those who oppose the union, and more than a third assist an anti-union committee. A significant number put union activists under electronic surveillance.

Three quarters of employers facing a union drive hire management consultants and security firms to run anti-union campaigns and intimidate workers. In more than nine out of ten cases, employers facing a union drive require employees to attend captive meetings, where they are forced to listen to anti-union propaganda. In most cases, workers are forced to attend one-on-one meetings with their supervisors. These and other legal and illegal tactics make a huge difference. According to Bronfenbrenner, the union election win rate drops precipitously when employers use more than ten tactics.

There is little to deter corporations from employing these tactics, even when they are illegal. Employers found to have illegally discharged an employee in connection with union organizing are required only to give the employee backpay minus whatever the employee earned in replacement jobs. There are no criminal charges, no civil penalties, no fines. In short, it pays for employers to violate the labor laws.

At its giant meat-packing facility in North Carolina, Smithfield Foods has pulled out all the stops and defeated organizing efforts by the United Food and Commercial Workers. The National Labor Relations Board has cited the company for egregious violations of the law—including conspiring with the local sheriff's department to physically intimidate and assault union supporters—but violating the law pays off. In June, 2002, one manager at the plant told a U.S. Senate committee how she fired workers for supporting the union. "Smithfield Foods ordered me to fire employees who supported the union, telling me it was either my job or theirs."

The plant manager, Sherri Buffkin, said the company promoted racial tension to undermine the union-organizing effort. "Smithfield keeps Black and Latino employees virtually separated in the plant, with the Black workers on the kill floor and Latinos in the cut and conversion departments. The word was that Black workers were going to be replaced with Latino workers because Blacks were more favorable toward unions."

LaTasha Peterson, a former Smithfield worker, told the Senate committee how the company paid her to be part of a group of workers who spied on coworkers and campaigned against the union. "I earned twice as much money campaigning against the union and I didn't have to do any work," she said.

The International Confederation of Free Trade Unions issues periodic reports on countries' respect for labor rights. It regularly rates the United States as a terrible labor rights violator. "There is insufficient protection against anti-union discrimination" in the United States, the Confederation concludes. "The right to strike and the right to collective bargaining are severely restricted."

Assessing the pathetic enforcement of weak labor laws in the United States, the Confederation states, "Remedies for intimidation and coercion are both limited and ineffective. A backlog of some 25,000 cases of unfair labor practices by employers existed in 2002 and it takes an average of 557 days for the National Labor Relations Board to resolve a case, discouraging many workers from using them."

The Confederation points to Wal-Mart to illustrate the point. In 2002, some 43 charges were brought against Wal-Mart in twenty-five states by the United Food and Commercial Workers (UFCW), alleging, among other things, illegal surveillance, threats, and intimidation against union workers. Wal-Mart, the giant global retailer based in the United States, has repeatedly stated that it will not bargain with any union and has taken drastic steps to prevent workers from organizing in stores across North America. Wal-Mart stores routinely violate the legal rights of their employees who try to unionize. Since 1995, the government has issued at least sixty complaints of anti-union activities. However, the maximum penalty Wal-Mart has incurred has been a requirement to post notices in various stores that it will no longer threaten, discipline, or fire employees who engage in "concerted activity" or require employees to report their contacts with unions.

Whether workers unionize makes a big difference in their compensation and treatment. The Economics Policy Institute reports that unionization provides a 28 percent wage premium to workers—meaning the same person in the same job, on average, will earn 11.5 percent more if the job is unionized—and a much larger edge in the area of benefits (more than 100 percent for insurance, nearly 200 percent for pensions).

Given the major economic benefits, not to mention other advantages of union membership, it is not surprising that, unobstructed and unintimidated, workers overwhelmingly choose to join unions. In the government employee sector, for example, where the employer generally does not contest unionization efforts and workers do not fear punishment, unions win approximately 85 percent of elections.

Unfortunately, the story is entirely different in the private sector. Where organized labor once made up about 35 percent of the working population in the United States, the figure has plummeted to below 15 percent—and below 10 percent of private employment.

When workers do manage to unionize, in the face of overwhelming odds, they confront still more employer stubbornness and resistance. In 40 percent of cases, employers refuse to enter into a first contract with a new union.

Even where unions are firmly rooted, their bargaining power has been severely eroded. The factors that have made it harder to organize—corporate globalization, contract labor, high levels of unemployment—have also made it harder for unions to bargain effectively. Declining rates of unionization make it much more complicated; in industries with low unionization rates, unionized firms can plausibly argue that they cannot afford to pay higher wages or benefits because of market pressure from nonunion competitors. Call this the Wal-Mart factor.

Most unions have also practically lost the use of their most powerful tool, the strike. Since 1939, the United States has been burdened by a bizarre Supreme Court decision. While acknowledging that labor laws prohibited firing workers for exercising their protected right to strike, the Court held that employers could "permanently replace" them. To everyone but the Supreme Court, that appeared to be a distinction without a difference.

For decades, employers declined to exercise their right to permanently replace their workers. But things changed in the 1980s. Ronald Reagan's decision to fire striking air traffic controllers (members of the PATCO union) ushered in a new era of strike-breaking. Strike activity diminished dramatically in the 1980s, with labor suffering a series of bitter defeats (and a very occasional victory, such as the coal miners at Pittston, in West Virginia, who used uncommonly aggressive tactics and successfully conveyed their message to the public).

Today, large-scale labor strikes are exceedingly rare. In every year but two in the 1960s and 1970s, there were more than two hundred work stoppages (inclusive of both strikes and lockouts) involving 1,000 or more workers. In the 1980s, the numbers dropped into the dozens, and the past few years have witnessed very few strikes. In 2003, there were only fourteen work stoppages involving 1,000 or more workers. The overwhelming number of missed work days due to stoppages involved the supermarket strike/lockout in Southern

California, and that was entirely provoked by Safeway and other area supermarkets.

The Southern California supermarket situation was an unfortunate bellwether. Safeway provoked a strike, and in a show of corporate solidarity, the other major supermarkets locked out their employees. Citing the competitive threat from Wal-Mart—which had not yet entered the region—the grocery chains demanded major givebacks from their employees. After a long time off the job, the workers capitulated, accepting a two-tier setup that provides for dramatically inferior wages and health benefits for new workers. Over time, as current employees retire and new ones join the workforce, this contract will help drive wage and benefit rates down toward the Wal-Mart goliath's lowest common denominator.

Health Care and Pensions

The slash in health benefits for the Southern California grocery workers is typical. With health care costs skyrocketing, private employers have demanded that their employees pay more and more of their insurance costs—and in many cases, they just don't provide insurance at all.

Pension benefits have also been slashed, often through sleight-of-hand maneuvers that trick employees into thinking they'll have an opportunity to turn a guaranteed steady income stream into a pile of riches upon retirement. Have any doubts what this involves? Just ask former Enron employees.

The key corporate deception was to switch employees from defined-benefit to defined-contribution pension plans. Defined-benefit plans are the traditional plan that guarantees workers a certain monthly payment upon retirement. It's the kind of deal that lets people who worked at solid companies know they would be secure in retirement. It's the kind of commitment that helped define a good job.

In the 1980s, corporations came up with something new. They started switching to defined-contribution plans, which set aside a certain amount of money for employees' retirement accounts (in 401(k)s or similar accounts) which the employees would be able to manage—with some notable restrictions. This became very popular in the 1990s when it seemed to many that they could get rich in the booming stock market.

But a key feature of the defined contribution plan is it shifts risk to employees. When the stock market bubble burst, millions of employees saw their retirement nest egg go up in flames. Under the old system, the burden would have been borne by the employers. But no more.

Another feature of the defined contribution plan is it enables employers to pay employees in their own stock, which has tremendous tax and accounting advantages for the companies. Often, however, that stock comes with limitations, so that employees are not freely able to sell it. Even when employees retain the right to diversify, many corporations urge them to concentrate their share holdings in their employers' stock. CEOs and top executives, however, labor under no such restrictions. In many cases, they sell their stock while it is peaking.

In his book *Perfectly Legal,* David Cay Johnston relates the representative story of John Patrick Pusloskie Jr. A college graduate, Pusloskie decided to follow in his father's footsteps as a telephone repairman for Rochester Telephone Company. He liked the work, and knew it would deliver a decent salary and retirement package that would enable him to raise a family and retire comfortably. He started working for the company in 1989. Then, under an ambitious CEO, Ronald L. Bittner, Rochester Telephone morphed into Frontier, a company that wanted to be a national player. On the last day of 1996, Frontier froze its pension plan and announced it would switch to a defined-contribution plan. The CEO promised workers the sky. The company's contribution was made in Frontier stock, with the condition that it could not be sold for five years. In 1999, Frontier was sold to a high-flying telecom company on the make, Global Crossing. Although Global Crossing never earned a profit, Wall Street mavens sent its stock value soaring. But it was a short-lived flight. In 2002, the company declared bankruptcy. The Global Crossing share of Pusloskie's retirement account, which had peaked at $100,000, was worth nothing. But Global Crossing's executive insiders hadn't been so unlucky. They managed to unload $5.2 billion in stock between August 1998 and the company's bankruptcy in January 2002. So much for secure retirement.

Safe Workplaces

Of course, working is about more than wages and benefits. Work should be organized to give employees some control and influence, so they derive a sense of meaning and fulfillment from their jobs. And no workplace issue is more important than ensuring job sites are safe and devoid of preventable hazards.

The mission of safe and healthful workplaces should be highly visible and backed by an adequately funded and enforced program. Far more Americans have lost their lives due to trauma and toxins in places of employment—especially factories, farms, construction sites, and mines—than in all the nation's wars. Nonetheless, for generations it has been a reluctant push and a strained pull to eke out minimal governmental safety initiatives in these arenas. Until 1970, the states had this jurisdiction to themselves and their expenditures and resolve were minuscule. Only high-profile fatal tragedies nudged their feeble efforts along until customary lethargy reasserted itself.

My associates and I worked to draft and secure passage of the 1970 Occupational Safety and Health Act, that established the Occupational Safety and Health Agency (OSHA), along with the National Institute for Occupational Safety and Health. Along the way, we encountered various syndromes of disinterest among the relevant professions and among many trade union leaders. Of course, there was always active opposition among industry and commerce groups and their corporate law firms. Fortunately, the OSHA legislation passed and President Nixon signed it into law. But it was not long before OSHA became a favorite whipping boy for reactionary politicians on the industry take. With its tiny budget, and surrounded by hostile elements in Congress and the business world, OSHA could scarcely begin fulfilling its charge. Still, with the occasional leadership of people like Eula Bingham, OSHA helped steer the country toward significant successes in reducing mortality and morbidity on the job.

Despite an unconscionable number of opportunities lost, OSHA stands as an example of successful government regulation even discounting automation–reducing exposures to risk. Workplace fatalities from trauma have been halved since passage of the OSHA, even though the total workforce has increased by almost 60 percent. In the mining sector, regulated by the Mine Safety and Health Administration, the fatality rate is approximately one quarter of that during the preregulatory era. In construction, fatalities are down 80 percent and injuries have decreased by 40 percent.

These improvements are a testament to how even a modest degree of political will can translate into thousands of lives saved every year.

Nearly 6,000 workers still die in the United States every year from traumatic injuries. The death toll from occupational diseases, easier for industry to ignore because the diseases frequently manifest after a worker has left the job voluntarily or involuntarily and because causation from the silent violence of toxins is less obvious, is far higher. At least 50,000 to 60,000 American workers, as many as 100,000 by some respectable estimates, die from occupational disease every year. Millions suffer every year from serious workplace injuries. The cost to the nation, the financial burden upon bereaved families, and the societal losses associated with workers dying early in their productive lives—totals well over $100 billion annually, according to the National Safety Council. This doesn't even count the pain and suffering involved.

Human costs cannot be reduced to numbers. Mike Cade, who continues to work at Equilon's Puget Sound refinery, where his brother Ted was killed, is still haunted by the explosion that took his brother's life.

"In the morning, it's kind of that depression, you don't want to get up. It's a fight to leave the bed; it's a fight to leave the room; it's a fight to leave the house," Mike Cade told the *Seattle Times*. "At night, I still have the nightmares. It's a lot of waking up with the bed moved a couple feet and me all drenched," Cade said. "Luckily, I don't remember most of them."

Since the explosion, equipment was installed allowing workers to stand two hundred feet away when performing the dangerous operation that led to Ted Cade's death. That and other safety reforms following the disaster may prevent other families from suffering the horrors that Mike Cade and Ted's widow and children must now endure.

As this example highlights, much of the national toll of work-related death, disease, and suffering could be prevented, if only employers were forced to take preventative action—to follow the basic nostrum, "Better Safe Than Sorry." OSHA has not been given the requisite funding, authority, and political backing to protect American workers, and things have gotten progressively worse over time. This includes during the Clinton administration, which through cowardice rather than hostility, diminished enforcement levels even from the preceding Bush administration. The current Bush administration takes a hostile approach toward OSHA, seeking, through a variety of means, to weaken the lifesaving agency even further.

The agency's tiny budget—less than $500 million a year—is far less than it needs to do its job. One former agency chief, Charles

Jeffress, estimates that, for the agency to adequately monitor the American workplace, it would need a budget at least 20 times as much as Congress has allotted it.

There are six million workplaces in the United States. There are 2,000 job safety inspectors. In some states where a state agency rather than the feds has responsibility for workplace inspection, an average job site will be visited less than once every two hundred years.

When an employer is caught violating workplace safety rules—often as a result of a retrospective review following an accident—the penalties are shamefully trivial. The average OSHA penalty for a willful violation of the workplace safety laws (an instance where an employer had knowledge of a hazard likely to cause death or serious harm but failed to comply with the law) is $27,000. The maximum penalty is $70,000. That's for knowingly putting an employee's life at risk.

Compare that penalty to the proposed $500,000 fine for each time a radio or television station broadcasts an indecency. That tells you a little about the lack of priority placed on saving workers' lives.

According to Drs. Sidney Wolfe and Peter Lurie, for over ten years, there has been no new occupational health standard for a toxic chemical issued by OSHA.

About a million people in the United States annually lose time from work due to repetitive motion, or musculoskeletal, injuries. These are the kind of injuries that come from typing on computer keyboards, jumping on and off a delivery truck many times a day, or running goods over scanners as a check-out clerk. If you've ever suffered one of these injuries, or know someone who has, you know they can be excruciating.

OSHA first promised to develop a rule to address repetitive stress in 1990, when Elizabeth Dole was Secretary of Labor. Under Bill Clinton, OSHA was slow to move on the rule. By the mid-1990s, Republicans in Congress blocked OSHA from adopting a rule. Clinton finally put a rule into effect in post-election November 2000, but it was rescinded by President Bush. Fifteen years after being promised relief, workers are still without a regulatory rule to protect them from repetitive motion injuries.

The modest rule that was briefly in place required employers to identify hazards and fix them to reduce—not eliminate—the problem. It's what any responsible employer would do anyway. If the rule were in place, it would probably spare a half million such injuries a year.

Or, consider the government's failure to limit exposure to hexavalent chromium, a carcinogenic chemical used in producing stainless steel, chrome plating, and pigments. For more than two decades, the government has known of the chemical's toxicity, which roughly doubles the lung cancer risk of the hundreds of thousands of workers exposed to it over time. In 1993, Public Citizen's Health Research Group and the Oil, Chemical, and Atomic Workers Union petitioned OSHA to issue a regulatory standard to reduce permissible exposure levels. More than a decade later, and despite a lawsuit, OSHA has done nothing. Thousands of hexavalent chromium-exposed workers will die as a result.

The story is the same for other life-saving and harm-reduction regulations that OSHA refuses to issue.

Progress in the Workplace

Despite the overall record of retreat and defeat, there have been some positive gains by unions and community groups in recent years.

With the minimum wage falling in real terms and unionization rates declining steadily, ACORN and other groups have led communities around the country to rally behind living wage ordinances. These ordinances require employers to pay not just the minimum wage, but a living wage—often defined as enough for a family of four to get by on. The ordinances typically apply to employers receiving government contracts, but sometimes require all employers in the jurisdiction to satisfy living wage requirements. More than seventy communities have adopted such laws, which get to the heart of what an economy is supposed to be: a means to enable people to support themselves at an acceptable standard of living.

While most unions still do not invest sufficient resources in organizing, an increasing number are doing so. One of the most impressive organizing efforts in recent years was the Justice for Janitors campaign of the Service Employees International Union (SEIU). This campaign organized almost entirely immigrants, traditionally a difficult group to organize because of their vulnerability to employer pressure and fear of government repression. Over the past several decades, the janitorial services industry has grown rapidly. Most large building owners outsource their work. When unions tried to organize workers at a particular company—a difficult challenge, because they would be spread among many different buildings—the firms would frequently fire and intimidate the workers leading the effort. If the unions succeeded, the firms would go out of business and reopen as a nonunion shop. The innovation of the Justice for Janitors campaign was to switch attention from the janitorial firms and simply demand that major buildings employ unionized janitors. With this change in focus and an aggressive worker-community coalition campaign that featured colorful protests and civil disobedience, tens of thousands of janitors were able to join unions.

The AFL-CIO has brought some new blood and energy into the labor movement through its union summer and college intern programs. These internship programs have been a synergistic success. As much as the students have helped the programs with organizing and research efforts, the internships have been of benefit to the students. Many have graduated from these programs and gone on to full-time work for some of the more progressive unions. Hundreds of college students have been involved in the nitty-gritty of union organizing campaigns. They come to see the challenges posed by oppressive employers who intimidate their vulnerable workforce as a matter of course. Many bridge class divides as students (many from relatively privileged backgrounds) and have witnessed and learned about everyday hardships experienced by working families. Inspired by their summer work, students have offered critical solidarity to union campaigns on their own campuses and led campaigns to demand that their universities stop using sweatshops to make official university apparel.

Some smaller unions have also demonstrated how to effectively represent workers. The United Electrical Workers has a long tradition of engaging and educating their workers and have become real advocates for progressive change both in and out of the workplace. The union's leadership leads by example, turning over frequently and accepting modest salaries commensurate with what their members earn.

The California Nurses Association (CNA) has strengthened their bargaining leverage and improved health care by advocating for patient rights. In recent years it has successfully lobbied several California bills into laws to protect consumers. The nurses' union highlights the abuses of HMOs and does careful analysis of the health care industry's profiteering and its pay packages for top bosses. CNA refuses to accept workplace changes that will compromise care, demanding adequate staffing ratios for patients in hospitals. In defending the general principle of patient care as well as nurses' particular interests, the CNA has shown nurses that they can best uphold their professional ethics by supporting the union. As a result, the union's membership has grown rapidly.

What these examples show is that, for all the immense power corporations have accumulated, for all their success in tilting the playing field of employer-employee relations, creative and aggressive campaigning can still yield results—improving wages and benefits, making jobs and workplaces more fulfilling, and directing the economy in a more humane direction. Corporations have succeeded in holding workers down by creating more levers of power. Organized labor has tapped the surface of a deep well of potential new tools to empower workers. To take just one example, it's past time for organized labor to invest in radio, television, and cable communications properties.

"American workers aren't going to sit still if things continue to come apart," prophesized the late Tony Mazzocchi, founder of the Labor Party and a former top official in the Oil, Chemical, and Atomic Workers. "If you look at the history of American workers, you'd think they're in a sleepy lagoon, and then all of a sudden there is an explosion."

CORPORATE CRIME
AND VIOLENCE
Without Shame

I t's not unusual for a politician to return a political contribution after finding out that it comes from a disreputable source. So what does it say that the two major political parties received $9.3 million from convicted criminals during the 2002 election cycle and didn't blink an eye? Without shame, they just pocketed the cash.

What does it say? It says that the money came from criminals who are themselves without shame: corporate criminals. It says that despite all of the publicity surrounding the most recent corporate crime wave, we still see such violations as less violent or abusive than street crime: while the latter is evil, the former is just business as usual.

After all, the two parties would never consider accepting cash from street thugs, muggers, and crooks. But corporate thugs, muggers, and crooks? No problem.

According to *Corporate Crime Reporter*, thirty-one major convicted corporations gave the $9.3 million to the two political parties in the 2002 election cycle. Archer Daniels Midland (ADM) tops the list. In 1996, ADM pled guilty to one of the largest antitrust crimes ever. The company was convicted of engaging in conspiracies to fix prices, eliminate competition, and allocate sales in the lysine and citric acid markets worldwide. ADM paid a $100 million criminal fine—at the time, the largest criminal antitrust fine ever.

ADM then gave $1.7 million to Democrats and Republicans during the 2002 election cycle.

In May 2004, Warner-Lambert, a unit of Pfizer Inc., pled guilty and paid more than $430 million to resolve criminal charges and civil liabilities in connection with its Parke-Davis division's illegal and fraudulent promotion of unapproved uses for one of its drugs products.

Pfizer, the pharmaceutical giant, is the maker of Lipitor, Viagra, and Zoloft. In 1999, Pfizer pled guilty to fixing prices in the food additives industry. The company paid $20 million in fines. During the 2002 election year cycle, Pfizer gave $1.1 million to the Democrats and Republicans. Chevron was convicted in 1992 of environmental crimes and paid a $6.5 million criminal fine. Chevron gave $875,400 to both parties during the 2002 election cycle. And both political parties said thank you and looked the other way.

How can that be? How can our two major political parties knowingly deposit money from guilty corporate criminals that do real damage to average Americans and not be ashamed? It happens because of a failure of our institutions—educational, political, civic, and media—to tackle a problem that strikes at the heart of our democracy—the double standard.

Corporate Attack on Law and Order

A case in point is the recent major financial frauds that dominated the headlines over the past few years and cost investors trillions of dollars. These crimes resulted directly from a calculated decades-long effort by big business and its lobbyists in Washington to compromise, weaken, or effectively dismantle the policing agencies and institutions—the regulatory agencies, the lawyers, the accountants, the civil justice system, and the banks. Inside the beltway, this dismantling is affectionately known as *deregulation*.

Once the law and the police were emasculated, an immoral and unethical managerial class ignored the tattered constraints that remained, cooking the books and setting up a market crash that would wipe out the pension funds and savings of millions of innocent investors and workers.

According to William Lerach's seminal article, "The Chickens Have Come Home to Roost," the 1990s attack on corporate crime police was led by the Big Five accounting firms (now, with the demise of convicted criminal Arthur Andersen, the Big Four), the securities industry, high-tech firms, and their law firms and lobbyists in Washington. They were driven by bad memories from the 1980s, when trial lawyers representing securities fraud victims and federal prosecutors, including former U.S. Attorney Rudolph Giuliani, held Wall Street cheats like Michael Milken accountable by demanding multimillion dollar settlements and federal prosecutions.

Determined to escape accountability and seeking revenge for these mild efforts at justice in the 1980s, Big Business launched its attack on and in the courts and in Congress in the 1990s. The Supreme Court weighed in on the side of the crooks with two major rulings. First, the Court held that the federal racketeering statute doesn't apply to securities fraud. Next, it held that professionals like lawyers, accountants, and bankers who knowingly aid and abet a securities fraud artist are *not liable* under federal securities law.

Then, in 1995, Congress, in its questionable wisdom, passed a law making it more difficult for victims of securities fraud to recover from the crooks. The Private Securities Litigation Reform Act established a difficult standard of proof, imposed a freeze on plaintiffs' ability to discover evidence until much later in the legal process, and replaced joint and several liability with proportionate liability.

In 1999 at the behest of the securities industry, Congress and President Clinton repealed the Glass-Steagall law, which for six decades had separated the business of commercial banking from investment banking to prevent conflicts that contributed to the financial disarray of the 1930s.

At the same time, Republican and Democratic presidents put corporate lawyers and executives at the helm of the Securities and Exchange Commission (SEC), arguably the top corporate crime beat in the country. President Clinton named Arthur Levitt, a Wall Street executive who, despite his reputation as a reformer, sided with the securities industry in its hour of need and helped push through the 1995 law limiting investor protections.

President Bush named Harvey Pitt, the accounting industry's lawyer, to succeed Levitt. True to form, upon taking office Pitt said he wanted the SEC to have a "gentler" relationship with his former client, the accounting industry. (This same Harvey Pitt, according to *Forbes* magazine, gave the following advice at an October 2000 seminar for in-house counsel: Chief financial officers whose e-mails detail cozy conversations with analysts about earnings estimates should "destroy" the incriminating messages "because somebody is going to find this, and it will probably be the SEC when they investigate." The destruction should stop "when you hear about an inquiry ramping up.")

Like Schoolyard Marble Games

In testimony to Congress and through articles in major newspapers, citizen, consumer, and investor groups warned that history was about to repeat itself, that naming corporate lawyers to police their own would destroy the legal structure that had kept the corporate chieftains in check and would result in a wave of corporate crime that would rival the 1930s.

In January 2000, I wrote in the *Progressive* magazine about the newly passed bill to gut Glass Steagall and the Bank Holding Company Act:

> Never underestimate the ability of Congress to repeat its mistakes. A decade ago, after it gambled and lost on deregulation, Congress was forced to launch a $500 billion taxpayer-financed bailout of the savings and loan industry. Congress has just rolled the deregulation dice again. This time, the outcome may be even more costly. The current gamble, which President Clinton signed into law on November 12 to the enthusiastic applause of Congressional leaders, makes the savings and loan schemes of the 1980s look like schoolyard marble games.

Warren Buffett, the conservative Omaha investor, also saw the wave of corporate frauds coming. In 1999, Buffett wrote:

> In recent years, probity has eroded. Many major corporations still play things straight, but a significant and growing number of otherwise high-grade managers—CEOs you would be happy to have as spouses for your children or as trustees under your will—have come to the view that it's OK to manipulate earnings to satisfy what they believe are Wall Street's desires. Indeed, many CEOs think this kind of manipulation is not only OK, but actually their duty. These managers start with the assumption, all too common, that their job at all times is to encourage the highest stock price possible (a premise with which we adamantly disagree). To pump the price, they strive, admirably, for operational excellence. But when operations don't produce the hoped-for result, these CEOs resort to unadmirable accounting stratagems. These either manufacture the desired "earnings" or set the stage for them in the future.

Fortune magazine predicted the same. In an August 1999 article, "Lies, Damned Lies and Managed Earnings," *Fortune*'s Carol Loomis wrote that the "eruption of accounting frauds . . . keeps suggesting that beneath corporate America's uncannily disciplined march of profits during this decade lie great expanses of accounting rot, just waiting to be revealed."

Exposure of these frauds began with corporate restatements of earnings—the most watched indicator of corporate fraud. The numbers of restatements, complied by the Huron Consulting Group, rose steadily from 158 in 1998 to 233 in 2000 to 270 in 2001, and 330 in 2002.

In many of the cases, the details of the frauds were exposed by investors, by reporters, by former executives. For example, a group of investors caught the WorldCom fiasco early, but a politically connected judge dismissed their complaint in 2001. A year later, WorldCom collapsed in the largest bankruptcy in American history. In July 2002, one month after the WorldCom collapse, *Forbes* magazine ran an article titled "Asleep at the Switch" that described the debacle:

> WorldCom book-cooking was laid out chapter, line and verse in a shareholder suit over a year ago. Sadly, a judge with knotty political ties tossed it out as directors, auditors, regulators—and the press—snoozed. WorldCom's board of directors, shocked by word in late June that WorldCom had buried $3.8 billion in costs in one of the biggest accounting frauds in history, had good reason not to be shocked at all. Over a year ago a raft of former employees gave statements outlining a scandalous litany of misdeeds deliberately understating costs, hiding bad debt, backdating contracts to book orders earlier than accounting rules allow.

According to *Forbes,* the shareholder complaint "was backed by one hundred interviews with former WorldCom employees and related parties."

"The allegations were startling in their breadth and detail," *Forbes* reporter Neil Weinberg wrote. "A former New York sales rep told of WorldCom's cutting bandwidth prices in half for client Aubrey

G. Lanston & Co., then booking the order twice—once at the old rate and once at the new one. A Tulsa, Oklahoma, quality-assurance analyst said WorldCom's balance sheet listed assets that included receivables as much as seven years past due. A billing specialist in Hilliard, Ohio said the company held off paying suppliers to delay recognizing expenses and to boost profits."

The judge who dismissed the case? U.S. District Court Judge William H. Barbour Jr., a first cousin and former law partner of Haley Barbour, former Republican National Committee chairman and now governor of Mississippi.

The pattern exhibited in the WorldCom case was repeated over and over again: "alleged" fraudulent activity, predicted and documented in the mainstream press, and preventable with law and law enforcement tools at our disposal. The result: huge sums lost to investors. Thousands of jobs displaced or lost. Pension funds wiped out.

Let's take a quick tour of some of the damage:

- *Adelphia Communications Corp.:* Prosecutors alleged that the founding fathers of the cable company and other executives used the company as their own private piggy bank. Prosecutors are seeking forfeiture of $2.5 billion and seeking to put the bosses in prison.
- *Enron Corp.:* Federal officials say the energy giant created off-the-books partnerships and employed "aggressive accounting methods" to hide debt and inflate the firm's bottom line. The company's accounting firm, Arthur Andersen, was convicted of destroying documents and forced out of business. Michael Kopper, the former managing director, pled guilty to money laundering and wire fraud. Former CFO Andrew Fastow pled guilty to fraud. Enron, once the nation's seventh biggest company on paper, collapsed, throwing thousands out of work and costing investors, pensioners and employees an estimated $100 billion.

- *HealthSouth Corp.:* Federal officials say that the hospital company's executives inflated earnings by $3.8 billion and $4.6 billion to meet Wall Street expectations. Fifteen former HealthSouth executives have been convicted. The founder and former chair and CEO of the company, Richard Scrushy, has been indicted, has pled not guilty, and awaits trial.

- *Rite Aid:* Federal officials alleged that the company inflated its net income by $1.6 billion. To cover up the alleged fraud, company officials destroyed some documents and fabricated others, the prosecution alleged. Several former executives pled guilty. The company's former CEO Martin Grass pled guilty, was fined $3.5 million, and will spend up to eight years in prison. Franklin Brown, the former general counsel and vice chairman, was found guilty of obstruction, witness tampering, and lying to federal investigators.

- *Tyco:* The company admits to booking $2 billion in erroneous accounts. Federal prosecutors charged that the former CEO L. Dennis Kozlowski and the former CFO Mark Swartz stole $170 million from the company and used questionable accounting to hide the illegalities. After a six-month trial, a New York state judge declared a mistrial. State prosecutors say they will try the two men again. Mark Belnick, the company's former general counsel, is charged with falsifying records to cover up improper loans.

- *WorldCom:* Federal officials alleged that a massive fraud hid more than $11 billion in cost and inflated profits. The company filed for bankruptcy. The company changed its name to MCI. WorldCom's former CEO, Bernard Ebbers, has been charged with many counts of fraud, and awaits trial. WorldCom's former CFO, Scott Sullivan, pled guilty and is cooperating with the ongoing federal investigation.

Interestingly, the banks and brokerage firms following these and other failing companies knew something was up but didn't blow the whistle. They, along with the law firms and accountants, were conflicted out of an independent judgment. They made money and looked the other way.

In June 2002, Weiss Ratings released a study that found that among the fifty brokerage firms covering companies filing for bankruptcy that year, forty-seven continued to recommend that investors buy or hold shares in the failing companies even as they were filing for Chapter 11. Lehman Brothers maintained six buy ratings on failing companies, while Salomon Smith Barney maintained eight hold ratings up through the date the companies filed for bankruptcy. Also sticking with buy ratings on failing companies until the very end were Bank of America Securities, Bear Stearns, CIBC World Markets, Dresdner Kleinwort Wasserstein, Goldman Sachs, and Prudential Securities.

"This analysis shows that Wall Street's record is far worse than previously believed," says Martin D. Weiss, chair of the independent ratings firm Weiss Ratings. "Even when there was abundant evidence that companies were on the verge of bankruptcy, over 90 percent of the latest ratings issued by brokerage firms continued to tell investors to hold their shares or buy more."

Merrill Lynch was caught recommending stocks in failing companies to the regular Joe investors, while accurately telling investment banking clients that the stocks were "crap" and "junk." New York Attorney General Eliot Spitzer exposed some e-mails from Merrill Lynch analysts and forced the company to pay $100 million.

A handful of other big Wall Street banks settled similar cases, paying fines barely worth a day's revenues, and the executives got away. But not Martha Stewart. The executives engaged in wrongdoing on a scale far greater than what she has been convicted of doing.

The Cost of Corporate Crime

Every year, the Federal Bureau of Investigation (FBI) releases an annual report titled "Crime in the United States."

The report should more accurately be titled "Street Crime in the United States," since it surveys primarily crimes like murder, manslaughter, robbery, assault, burglary, and arson. Last year, I wrote to Attorney General Ashcroft asking that the Justice Department produce a parallel report on corporate crime, documenting the financial and accounting frauds and the environmental, workplace safety, consumer products, and food safety crimes that kill, injure, and sicken millions of Americans every year.

It's clear why the attorney general chooses not to produce such a report. It would galvanize public opinion to support the local, state, and federal corporate crime police—a threatening prospect to an attorney general and president so closely allied with big business interests.

Without such a comprehensive annual report, we are left to rely on outside evidence as to the nature and scope of the problem. But such evidence suffices to establish, without question, that corporate crime and violence inflict far more damage on society than all street crime combined.

In 2002, the FBI estimated that the nation's total loss from robbery, burglary, larceny-theft, motor vehicle theft, and arson was a not insignificant $18 billion. Let's compare that to just one segment of corporate fraud: health care fraud. The General Accounting Office puts health care billing fraud at $150 billion, but Malcolm Sparrow, a professor at Harvard and author of the authoritative *License to Steal: Why Fraud Plagues America's Health Care System,* says fraud could account for as much as 30 percent of all health care expenditures. Last year, health care expenditures were $1.6 trillion. A Dartmouth study estimated that about a third of health care is useless, redundant, or harmful.

And that's just health care fraud.

The savings and loan fraud, which former Attorney General Dick Thornburgh called "the biggest white collar swindle in history," cost us anywhere from $300 billion to $500 billion. Then you have the lesser frauds: auto repair fraud, $40 billion a year; securities fraud, $15 billion a year before the recent crime wave hit; and on down the list.

Corporate crime is about more than just money. It's also about inflicting physical injuries and even the taking of innocent human life.

In 2002, the FBI documented 16,204 homicides in the United States. Compare that to the more than 55,000 deaths on the job or from occupational diseases, the 420,000 who died from promoted tobacco-induced disease, the 10,000 who die every year from illnesses caused by asbestos, the 65,000 deaths from air pollution, and the 80,000 people who lose their lives from medical incompetence in hospitals annually.

In 1995, Ralph Estes, a professor emeritus of accounting at American University, took a comprehensive look at what he called the social costs that corporations externalize onto workers, consumers, and the environment. This is another way of looking at the costs of corporate crime, both prosecuted and not. Estes totaled private and government estimates of these various costs, including: pollution $307.8 billion; defense contract overcharges $25.9 billion; price-fixing, monopolies, deceptive advertising $1.16 trillion; unsafe vehicles $135.8 billion; workplace injuries and accidents $141.6 billion; death from workplace cancer $274.7 billion. He came up with a total cost of $3 trillion. He calls this "the public cost of private corporations." Many of these costs in turn generate economic demand for goods and services—health care, insurance, repairs, and so on.

Every once in a while, corporate crime explodes into the headlines in a spectacular fashion:

- In 1989, the Exxon Valdez oil tanker hit a reef in Prince William Sound, Alaska, and spilled 11 million gallons of crude oil onto 1,500 miles of Alaskan shoreline, killing birds and fish, and destroying the way of life of thousands of Native Americans. In March 1991, the company pled guilty to environmental felonies and was fined $125 million. Alaskans sued Exxon and were awarded $287 million in compensatory damages and $5 billion in punitive damages. Exxon has been appealing the award ever since. In the latest decision, a judge earlier this year put the punitive damage award at $4.5 billion—but Exxon promises to appeal that decision.

- In 1984, a Union Carbide pesticide factory in Bhopal, India, released 90,000 pounds of the chemical methyl isocyanate. The resulting toxic cloud killed several thousand people and injured hundreds of thousands. Union Carbide (now a wholly-owned subsidiary of Dow Chemical) and its former CEO, Warren Andersen, still face manslaughter charges in Bhopal.

- Eighty years ago, clean, quiet, and efficient inner and outer city rail systems dotted the U.S. landscape. They were eliminated in the 1930s and 1940s to make way for dirty and noisy gasoline-powered automobiles and buses. The city rail systems were destroyed by the very companies that would most benefit from destruction of inner city rail—oil, tire, and automobile companies, led by General Motors. By 1949, GM had helped destroy major metropolitan electric trolley systems in forty-five cities, including New York, Philadelphia, Baltimore, St. Louis, Oakland, Salt Lake City, and Los Angeles.

  In 1949, a federal grand jury in Chicago indicted GM, Standard Oil of California, and Firestone, among others, of criminally conspiring to replace electric transportation with gas- and diesel-powered buses and to monopolize the sale of buses and related products to transportation companies around the country. GM and the other convicted companies were fined only $5,000 each, for what some analysts called the economic crime of the century. Everyday people continue to pay the price for clogged highway traffic unrelieved by adequate modern transit systems on these old trolley-rail rights of way.

Corporate Homicide: "A Simple Lack of Guts and Political Will"

Despite these convictions, for the most part, the drip, drip, drip of intentional, serious corporate wrongdoing that takes one life at a time, or steals one pension plan at a time, remains either underprosecuted or not prosecuted at all—because of either the failure of the law or the failure of law enforcement.

Let's look at corporate homicide, for example. For most of the 16,000 street murders in the United States, a criminal homicide prosecution results. Tens of thousands of Americans die every year due to corporate criminal recklessness, yet you can count the annual corporate criminal prosecutions every year on your fingers.

Why so few? Lack of political and prosecutorial will.

In July 2003, in a state courtroom in Wilmington, Delaware, attorneys for Motiva Enterprises (a joint venture company between Saudi Aramco and Royal Dutch Shell) entered a plea of no contest—the equivalent of a guilty plea—to one felony count of criminally negligent homicide and six misdemeanor counts of assault in the third degree. The charges arose out of an explosion and fire at the company's Delaware City facility in 2001 that resulted in the death of boilermaker Jeffrey Davis and injuries to six other workers. Delaware Attorney General M. Jane Brady said the "company did not take their responsibilities to the plant workers or the community seriously, and disregarded the potential consequences of their decision-making."

Of the thousands of Americans killed on the job every year, how many are deserving of a homicide prosecution to bring a modicum of justice to their families and loved ones? Surely more than the tiny handful whose cases are currently tried every year in the United States.

Homicide prosecutions are for the most part state law prosecutions. When a tough, principled state prosecutor comes along, corporate homicide prosecutions are sure to follow. But tough, principled prosecutors are few and far between. The last homicide prosecution brought against a major American corporation was in 1980, when a Republican prosecutor in northern Indiana charged Ford Motor Co. with homicide for the deaths of three teenage girls who were incinerated when their Ford Pinto was rear-ended—the a gas tank collapsed and spilled fuel, starting the fire that caused their deaths. The prosecutor alleged that Ford knew it was marketing a defective product. But Ford brought in a top-flight criminal defense lawyer, who, together with a local lawyer who was a friend of the judge, secured a not guilty verdict after convincing the judge to keep key evidence out of the jury room.

In January 2003, the *New York Times* ran a series of articles exposing McWane, Inc., a privately held company based in Birmingham, Alabama, and one of the world's largest manufacturers of cast-iron sewer and water pipe. The *Times'* investigation determined that McWane is one of the most dangerous employers in America. Since 1995, at least 4,600 injuries have been recorded in McWane foundries, hundreds of them serious. Nine workers have been killed. McWane plants, which employ about 5,000 workers, have been cited for more than 400 federal health and safety violations.

One McWane worker, Frank Wagner, was killed in an industrial explosion in upstate New York that, according to a team of state prosecutors, resulted from reckless criminal conduct by his employer. "The evidence compels us to act," the prosecution team wrote in a confidential memorandum to then state attorney general, Dennis C. Vacco, in 1996.

According to the *Times,* the team of prosecutors urged Vacco to ask a grand jury to indict McWane and its managers on manslaughter and other charges. But Vacco never sought a criminal indictment against the company. The company did eventually plead guilty to a state hazardous waste felony and paid $500,000, but it was not held accountable for Mr. Wagner's death.

According to the *Times* report, three of the nine workers killed at McWane facilities since 1995 died as a result of wanton violations of federal safety standards. But referrals to the Justice Department for criminal prosecution of fatalities resulting from federal safety crimes are considered a waste of time. Why? Because under federal law, causing the death of a worker by willfully violating safety rules is a misdemeanor carrying a maximum prison term of six months. (Harassing a wild burro on federal lands, apparently considered a more serious crime, is punishable by a year in prison.) As a result, according to the *Times*, McWane viewed the burden of regulatory fines "as far less onerous than the cost of fully complying with safety and environmental rules."

"At the time of Mr. Wagner's death, company budget documents show McWane calculated down to the penny per ton the cost of OSHA and environmental fines, along with raw materials," the *Times* reported.

According to the *Times*, Wagner's death is similar to at least one hundred deaths of Americans every year—the results not of accidents, but of intentional wrongdoing or indifference. These are acts deserving of homicide prosecutions. "They happened because a boss removed a safety device to speed up production, or because a company ignored explicit safety warnings, or because a worker was denied proper protective gear," the *Times* reported.

The investigation found that from 1982 to 2002, OSHA investigated 1,242 of these horror stories, instances in which the agency itself concluded that workers had died because of their employer's "willful" safety violations.

Yet in 93 percent of those cases, OSHA declined to seek prosecution. "A simple lack of guts and political will," John T. Phillips, a former regional OSHA administrator in Kansas City and Boston told the *Times*. "You try to reason why something is criminal, and it never flies."

The same for tobacco. Ira Robbins, a professor of law at American University in Washington, D.C., argues that the time is ripe to bring a homicide prosecution against tobacco executives.

"Government should not ignore the criminal aspects of what the tobacco companies were doing," Robbins said last year. "In fact, a good argument can be made that, over time, tobacco company executives consciously disregarded the substantial and unjustifiable risk that people might be killed. If this could be proven, then it would come under the classic definition of involuntary manslaughter."

As Robbins observes, to gain a second-degree murder conviction, a prosecutor must show "the conscious disregard of a substantial and unjustifiable risk that death would occur under circumstances manifesting extreme indifference to the value of human life." Professor Robbins argues that a 1,400-page summary of evidence against the tobacco companies filed in the Justice Department's civil racketeering case against these companies lays the groundwork for homicide charges. The Justice Department is seeking to recover $289 billion from tobacco companies.

The Department alleges that in 1953 the tobacco companies launched a decades-long "fraudulent scheme to deceive the public about the dangers of smoking and discredit scientific and medical evidence that smoking was a cause of disease."

How about the petrochemical industry? In 2001, Bill Moyers ran an exposé of the chemical industry and how it killed hundreds of workers on the front lines, "how the chemical companies, through their silence and inertia, subjected at least two generations of workers to excessive levels of a potent carcinogen, vinyl chloride, that targets the liver, brain, lungs, and blood-forming organs."

Dan Ross died at age 46 of a rare brain cancer. According to Moyers, Ross was convinced that his job was killing him, and he died not knowing how right he was. The documentary shows his widow, Elaine Ross, who vows to her dying husband that she would "never, ever let the chemical industry forget who he was—never." She joins up with Louisiana trial attorney Billy Baggett, who through legal discovery amasses thousands of internal company documents. The documents formed the basis of a twelve-part series by then *Houston Chronicle* reporter Jim Morris ("In Strictest Confidence") that ran from June 1998 to December 1998.

Morris and Moyers reported on a 1959 Dow Chemical memo showing that vinyl chloride exposure at 500 mg "is going to produce rather appreciable injury when inhaled seven hours a day, five days a week for an extended period." The memo says, "As you can appreciate, this opinion is not ready for dissemination yet and I would appreciate it if you would hold it in confidence but use it as you see fit in your own operations."

Then there is the 1973 Ethyl Corp. memo claiming that results on rat tests "certainly indicate a positive carcinogenic effect." And the 1971 Union Carbide internal memo that voices a general worry about the political climate in the United States and warns that: "a campaign by Mr. R. Nader and others could force an industrial upheaval via new laws or strict interpretation of pollution and occupational health laws."

Yes, big corporations know that their workplace hazards are taking the lives of workers. They also know how to create a political climate to avoid being brought to justice. But they ought to be criminally prosecuted. The evidence is there. What's needed is the will to enforce the law.

Facing Down the Corporate Crime Lobby

Facing down the corporate crime lobby presents a formidable task. For one thing, Washington, D.C., and the state capitals are corporate-occupied territory. Corporate lobbyists, corporate PACs, white-collar criminal defense attorneys, corporate propaganda tanks, public relations firms, their apologists at law schools—all work in conjunction to create a climate of leniency for corporate criminals.

First, the brain trust lays down a foundation of amorality. Frank Easterbrook and Daniel Fischel are University of Chicago law professors—Easterbrook is also a federal judge—who believe that nothing, not even law and order, should stand in the way of making money. Twenty years ago, writing in the *Michigan Law Review,* Easterbrook and Fischel stated that "managers not only may but also should violate the rules when it is profitable to do so."

The Chicago School considers such corporate crimes as fraud, corruption, pollution, price-fixing, occupational disease, and bribery "externalities" and claims that fines for such "externalities" should be considered "costs of doing business." Others, like George Mason University Law Professor Jeffrey Parker argue that corporate crime does not, indeed cannot, exist.

"Crime exists only in the mind of an individual," Parker argues. "Since a corporation has no mind, it can commit no crime."

Parker argues that a since a corporation is not a person, it should not be treated like one in the criminal law arena. (Very well, Professor, should the Supreme Court revoke the legal fiction of the corporation as person, and all the rights and privileges that follow, including the First Amendment right to speak and associate, the Fourth Amendment right to privacy, and the Fourteenth Amendment right to equal protection?) Parker argues that "there is no legitimate function of corporate criminal liability that cannot be served equally as well, if not better, by civil enforcement." (How about shaming and deterring wrongdoers and sending a serious message through criminal prosecution? Civil fines can't do that very effectively.)

Milton Friedman says the only moral imperative for a corporate executive is to make as much money for the corporate owners as he or she can. Management guru Peter Drucker concurs: "If you find an executive who wants to take on social responsibilities, fire him.

Fast." And William Niskanen, chair of the libertarian Cato Institute, says that he would not invest in a company that pioneered in corporate responsibility.

John Braithwaite, one of the world's foremost corporate criminologists, says that the Friedman, Parker, Drucker, Niskanen position amounts to an argument that corporations are not part of the moral community—it is a "rationalization to insulate corporate actors from shaming by the wider community."

While the brain trust works from the outside to create a legal system that insulates the corporate actors from shaming by the wider community, the corporate defense attorneys work the system from the inside to the same ends. The corporate criminal justice system has been compromised by an imbalance of power and resources.

Opening just a few windows on this world will give you an idea:

- The Environmental Crimes Section of the Department of Justice is responsible for criminally prosecuting all environmental crimes in the country. It has only thirty full-time lawyers.
- The Securities Fraud Task Force of the U.S. Attorney's office in Manhattan has just twenty-five lawyers on its staff. The results are predictable. According to a recent article in *Fortune* magazine in March 2002, "Enough Is Enough: White-Collar Criminals: They Lie They Cheat They Steal and They've Been Getting Away With It for Too Long," in the ten years from 1992 to 2001, SEC enforcement attorneys referred 609 cases to the Justice Department for possible criminal charges. Federal prosecutors decided what to do on 525 of the cases—declining to prosecute 64 percent of them. Of those they did pursue, the feds obtained guilty verdicts in 76 percent. But even then, 40 percent of the convicted white-collar crooks—most of them from smaller corporations—didn't spend a day in jail. Only eighty-seven did.

When these or any of the other small, specialized prosecutorial offices bring a charge against a major American corporation, they are overwhelmed by a corporate law firm with hundreds of lawyers and paralegals.

Take the exceptionally unique prosecution of Royal Caribbean Cruise Lines. It is a testament to the federal prosecutors in that case that the company was eventually convicted of criminally polluting the nation's oceans. Despite overwhelming evidence leading to that conviction, the company was determined to beat the rap.

To defend itself, Royal Caribbean hired Judson Starr and Jerry Block, both of whom served as head of the Justice Department's Environmental Crimes Section, and former Attorney General Benjamin Civiletti. Also representing Royal Caribbean were former federal prosecutors Kenneth C. Bass III and Norman Moscowitz. Donald Carr of Winthrop & Stimson also joined the defense team. As experts on international law issues, the lawyers hired former Attorney General Eliot Richardson, University of Virginia law professor John Norton Moore, former State Department officials Terry Leitzell and Bernard Oxman, and four retired senior admirals.

As the case proceeded to trial, the company engaged in a massive public relations campaign, taking out ads during the Super Bowl, putting a former Environmental Protection Agency administrator on its board of directors, and donating thousands of dollars to environmental groups.

Federal prosecutors overcame this legal and public relations barrage and convicted the company in July 1999 on twenty-one counts. The company paid a record $18 million criminal fine for dumping waste oil and hazardous chemicals into the ocean and lying to the Coast Guard about it.

But it is this display of corporate crime defense prowess that makes prosecutors think twice about proceeding against a major company. Increasingly, prosecutors go after lower-level executives instead. Even so, scores of major American corporations like Royal Caribbean have been criminally prosecuted and sanctioned in recent years, which tells us something about the extent of corporate crime. *Corporate Crime Reporter*'s list of the Top 100 Corporate Criminals of the 1990s ranks these corporate criminals by amount of the criminal fine.

Last year *Corporate Crime Reporter* also published its report on the top 100 False Claims Act settlements. The federal False Claims Act is a remarkable law that says to citizens of the United States: If you have information about corporations that are defrauding the federal government, come forward, tell federal prosecutors about it, and if federal prosecutors can verify your claim, they will join with you and sue the corporation to recover the amount of money that the corporation defrauded from the United States. If you can prove your case, and the government recovers the defrauded money, then you, ordinary citizen, will get a share of the recovery—anywhere from 15 percent to 30 percent. And the law is working. Since 1986, when strengthening amendments to the False Claims Act were passed into law, the government has recovered $12 billion in taxpayer monies from corporate crooks—and more than a few whistleblowers have became millionaires as a result.

There are enforcement actions the public doesn't hear about. Bob Bennett, one of the nation's premiere white-collar crime defense lawyers, says that "90 percent of the work I do never sees the public light of day." Bennett and his colleagues burn the midnight oils to keep their clients out of the public spotlight—cutting special deals, giving up corporate executives to save the corporation from criminal prosecution, seeking civil settlements where criminal prosecutions are warranted. After all, for big corporations, reputation is everything.

Take corporate bribery. In the late 1970s, the Securities and Exchange Commission asked corporations to come forward and disclose bribes and other improper payments overseas. More than four hundred major companies did so, and the revelations led to the passage of the Foreign Corrupt Practices Act, which prohibits U.S. companies from bribing overseas.

Corporate lawyers handling foreign bribery cases report a sharp increase in business in the past couple of years. Some businessmen say it is impossible to do business in China without paying bribes. But where are the criminal prosecutions for bribery? They are few and far between.

Homer Moyer Jr., a partner at the corporate defense firm of Miller & Chevalier, likens his practice of defending corporations against charges of bribery to an "iceberg."

"Very little of this practice is publicly visible," Moyer said. "Many of these cases are resolved informally, without publication of consent decrees—many are just dismissed." When an enforcement action results, information that is made publicly available is often sketchy because defense counsels "negotiate what information can be released," Moyer said.

Only a handful of bribery charges are brought every year by the Justice Department's understaffed Fraud Section—a dozen in 2002—and the charges rarely carry criminal sanctions.

It took a lawsuit to unearth a secret settlement practice at the Office of Foreign Assets Control (OFAC) of the U.S. Treasury. OFAC enforces the laws governing doing business with designated enemies of the United States. Big banks and other financial institutions had a sweet deal with OFAC: OFAC would bring an enforcement action against the banks for doing business with, say, Libya. The bank would settle the case, and OFAC would agree not to publicize it. Hundreds of enforcement actions against major American corporations never saw the light of day.

Ira Raphaelson, a defense attorney at O'Melveny & Myers, told reporters last year about how he settled a criminal case brought by the Justice Department against a corporate client of his, and the press never caught wind of it because there was an agreement not to publicize the case. Raphaelson said that there have always been "side deals" between the government and defense attorneys not to publicize a case:

> There are settled criminal cases that the government and the defense attorneys agree not to talk about in public. There always have been these side deals. If there is a prosecution that is a bad prosecution that is settled, and I have a side deal with the prosecutors not to talk about the prosecution, I'm not going to talk about it. In my case, the government put out no press release. There was no publicity to the case.

Lanny Breuer, a partner at Covington & Burling, concurs about the existence of a secret settlement practice. "There is this kind of practice of keeping information about criminal cases out of the press," Breuer said.

Even when prosecutors overcome all odds, and successfully bring a criminal prosecution, and the prosecution is publicized, so the world knows that it happened, there is a price to pay for the imbalance of power.

Take the case of Ball Park Franks. Bil Mar Foods is a unit of the Chicago-based giant Sara Lee Corporation, the maker of pound cakes, cheesecakes, pies, muffins, L'Eggs, Hanes, Playtex, and Wonderbra products. Bil Mar makes hot dogs—Ball Park franks hot dogs.

In July 2001, Sara Lee pled guilty to two misdemeanor counts in connection with a listeriosis outbreak that led to the deaths of at least twenty-one consumers who ate Ball Park Franks hot dogs and other meat products. One hundred people were seriously injured. The company paid a $200,000 fine. Close examination of the evidence shows that a felony charge was warranted but federal prosecutors were overpowered by lawyers for Sara Lee; in particular, the Chicago firm of Jenner & Block, led by former Chicago U.S. Attorney Anton Valukas.

Think of it—twenty-one dead and only two misdemeanors and a $200,000 fine. To announce the slap-on-the-wrist plea agreement, federal prosecutors and Sara Lee issued a joint press release. It was perhaps the first joint press release with a convicted criminal defendant in Justice Department history. Imagine the Justice Department issuing a joint press release with a convicted terrorist or child molester. They would not. They could not.

Rigging the System

Larry Thompson is not the kind of lawyer who should have been heading up a Corporate Fraud Task Force. Thompson, a former corporate lawyer, knows the ins and out of corporate wrongdoing. Before his Senate confirmation as deputy attorney general, Thompson sat on the board of Providian Financial Corp. a credit-card company that paid more than $400 million to settle allegations of consumer and securities fraud. He was also chair of the company's audit and compliance committee.

According to the *Washington Post,* "Providian was one of the biggest credit-card companies in the so-called subprime market, which targets people with low incomes and bad credit histories." In 2001, the company settled charges that it inflated its financial results by charging excessive fees and engaging in other practices that state and federal regulators said broke consumer protection rules.

As head of the President's Corporate Fraud Task Force, appointed by George W. Bush, Thompson told reporters that he wanted to hold corporations accountable for the criminal culture and conduct they promote. Instead, he helped rig the system so that corporations have a way to get out of a criminal jam. In a memo issued under his name in January 2003 (known in defense circles as "the Thompson memo"), Thompson opened a loophole for corporations to escape punishment for criminal behavior.

The memo, titled "Federal Prosecution of Business Organizations," gives prosecutors discretion to grant corporations immunity from prosecution in exchange for cooperation. These immunity agreements, known as deferred prosecution agreements, or pretrial diversion, were previously reserved for minor street crimes and never intended for major corporate crimes. The U.S. Attorneys' Manual explicitly states that a major objective of pretrial diversion is to "save prosecutive and judicial resources for concentration on major cases."

Thompson's memo was followed by a rash of deferred prosecution agreements in cases involving large corporations, including a settlement with a Puerto Rican bank on money-laundering charges and a Pittsburgh bank on securities charges. Corporate defense attorneys are seizing on these agreements with the Justice Department so as to avoid any publicity.

"This is a favorable change for companies," Alan Vinegrad, a partner at Covington & Burling in New York, told *Corporate Crime Reporter* last year. "The memo now explicitly says that pretrial diversion, which had been reserved for small, individual, minor crimes, is now available for corporations." Vinegrad said that while there have been a handful of publicized pretrial diversion cases, the Justice Department can cut these kind of deals with companies without filing a public document—and therefore without any publicity to the case.

When in Doubt, Shred It

Much of the history of corporate crime and violence in this country has never seen the light of day because of a simple dictate widely followed in corporate boardrooms: When in doubt, shred it.

In 2002, Arthur Andersen was indicted for obstructing justice. Federal officials alleged that on October 23, 2001, Andersen partners assigned to the Enron audit launched "a wholesale destruction of documents" at Andersen's offices in Houston, Texas.

"Andersen personnel were called to urgent and mandatory meetings," the indictment alleged. "Instead of being advised to preserve documentation so as to assist Enron and the SEC, Andersen employees on the Enron management team were instructed by Andersen partners and others to destroy immediately documentation relating to Enron, and told to work overtime if necessary to accomplish the destruction."

During the next few weeks "an unparalleled initiative was undertaken to shred physical documentation and delete computer files," according to the indictment. "Tons of paper relating to the Enron audit were promptly shredded as part of the orchestrated document destruction," the indictment alleges. "The shredder at the Andersen office at the Enron building was used virtually constantly and, to handle the overload, dozens of large trunks filled with Enron documents were sent to Andersen's main Houston office to be shredded. A systematic effort was also undertaken and carried out to purge the computer hard-drives and e-mail system of Enron-related files."

Andersen was convicted by a jury in Texas and forced out of business. But who is to say that many sizeable American corporation could not be convicted of a similar crime?

Again, the former chair of the SEC, Harvey Pitt, was notorious for giving advice to his fellow defense lawyers on when and how to destroy incriminating documents. For example, in a 1994 article in the *Cardozo Law Review* titled "When Bad Things Happen to Good Companies: A Crisis Management Primer," Pitt wrote: "Ask executives and employees to imagine all their documents in the hands of a zealous regulator or on the front page of the *New York Times*. . . . Each company should have a system for determining the retention and destruction of documents. Obviously, once a subpoena has been issued, or is about to be issued, any existing document destruction policies should be brought to an immediate halt."

In a 1980 law review article, "Document Retention and Destruction: Practical, Legal and Ethical Considerations," former SEC enforcement chief John Fedders took this advice one step further.

"On occasion, counsel will be shown a document which could expose the corporation to liability if it became available to adverse parties," Fedders wrote. "If the document is not yet scheduled for destruction under the terms of the program, management may advocate a waiver of the program to allow the document to be promptly destroyed."

This sort of advice has been followed. For example, in April 2002 an Australian judge found that British American Tobacco (BAT) engaged in a massive document-destruction scheme intentionally designed to thwart smokers or former smokers from bringing suit against the company. After the conclusion of one plaintiff's case and before the beginning of another, BAT's chief counsel told an associate, "now is a good opportunity to dispose of documents if we no longer need to keep them. That should be done outside the legal department." Thousands of the 30,000 documents were then destroyed, along with electronic versions of the documents, summaries, indices, and ratings.

"The decision to destroy all such lists and records, can only have been a deliberate tactic designed to hide information as to what was destroyed," the judge wrote.

Crack Down on Corporate Crime

In response to corporate crime waves, the government usually passes a series of meek reforms (like the Sarbanes Oxley law of 2002). Over the years, our citizen groups have introduced numerous proposals to crack down on corporate crime, including: the FBI creation of an annual Corporate Crime in the United States report; tripling the budgets of the federal corporate crime police; adopting three-strikes-and-you're-out policies for corporate criminals; banning corporate criminals from government contracts; expanding the False Claims Act to include environmental and securities fraud areas; and creative sentencing alternatives, such as sentencing fit coal mine executives, convicted of violating safety laws resulting in casualties, to working with the miners in the mines.

Some of the shrewdest observers of corporate crime come from that former penal colony, Australia. John Braithwaite, who has written many books on corporate crime, argues that "if we are serious about controlling corporate crime, the first priority should be to create a culture in which corporate crime is not tolerated." He believes that "the moral educative functions of corporate criminal law are best achieved with heavy reliance on adverse publicity as a social control mechanism."

"The policy instruments for harnessing shame against corporate offenders include adverse publicity orders as a formal sanction, the calling of press conferences following corporate convictions, encouraging consumer activism and investigative journalism," he writes.

Braithwaite's prescription would take us in the opposite direction we've been heading in recent years with the Thompson memo, deferred prosecution agreements, and secret settlements. It would move us away from a criminal justice system massaged by the corporate crime lobby to limit adverse publicity.

What is needed is political leadership uncompromised by corporate influence, leadership that will not just talk the talk on corporate crime enforcement, but deliver justice to the American people. For too long people have suffered at the hands of big corporations that defraud consumers; pollute our air, water, and soil; bribe our public officials, injure and destroy the health of workers, and steal from our governments.

Creating a culture in which corporate crime is not tolerated in word, law, or deed is long overdue.

Crack Down on Corporate Crime
(citizenworks.org)

1. *Track the Extent and Cost of Corporate Crime.* Establish a public online corporate crime database at the Department of Justice. The FBI should also produce an annual corporate and white-collar crime report as an analogue to its "Crime in the United States" report, which focuses on street crime.

2. *Increase Corporate Crime Prosecution Budgets.* Both the Securities and Exchange Commission and especially the Department of Justice's corporate crime division have been chronically underfunded. Without proper resources, it is difficult to apply the rule of law to corporate criminals. As a result, government prosecutors and regulators are forced to settle for weak fines and ignore many more violators entirely.

3. *Ban Corporate Criminals from Government Contracts.* Enact a tough, serious debarment statute that would deny federal business to serious and/or repeat corporate lawbreakers. These standards should apply to corporate contracts in Iraq. The federal government spends $265 billion a year on goods and services. Let's make sure taxpayer money isn't supporting corporate criminals.

4. *Crack down on Corporate Tax Avoidance.* Punish corporate tax escapees by closing the offshore reincorporation loophole and banning government contracts and subsidies for companies that relocate their headquarters to an offshore tax haven. Give the IRS more power and resources to go after corporate tax cheats. Require publicly traded corporations to make their tax returns public.

5. *Restore the Rights of Defrauded Investors.* Repeal self-styled securities "reform" laws that block defrauded investors from seeking restitution, such as the Private Securities Litigation

(Continued)

Reform Act of 1995, which allowed the aiders and abettors of massive corporate crime (e.g., accountants and lawyers) to escape civil liability.

6. *Democratize Corporate Governance.* Grant shareholders the right to democratically nominate and elect the corporate board of directors by opening up proxy access to minority shareholders and introducing cumulative voting and competitive elections. Require shareholders to approve all major business decisions, including executive compensation. Shareholders, after all, are the owners.

7. *Rein in Excessive Executive Pay.* Require shareholder authorization of top executive compensation packages at each annual shareholder meeting. Require that stock options, which now account for about half of executive compensation, be counted on financial statements as an expense (which they are). Eliminate tax deductions for compensation above twenty-five times the compensation received by the lowest paid worker in a corporation, as business guru Peter Drucker has suggested.

8. *Regulate Derivatives Trading.* Regulate all over the-counter financial instruments, including derivatives, so that they are subject to the same or equivalent audit and reporting requirements as other financial instruments traded on the stock exchanges. Rules should be enacted regarding collateral-margin, reporting and dealer licensing in order to maintain regulatory parity and ensure that markets are transparent and problems can be detected before they become a crisis.

9. *Expand Disclosure.* Enact corporate sunshine laws that force corporations to provide better information about their records on the environment, human rights, worker safety, and taxes, as well as their criminal and civil litigation records.

10. *End Conflicts of Interest on Wall Street.* Re-enact structural reforms that separate commercial and investment banking services and prevent other conflicts of interest among financial entities, such as those that have dominated big banks in recent years.

11. *Fix the Pension System.* Corporations must be held more responsible for the retirement security of their employees. At a minimum we need to give workers a voice on the pension board; not require workers to stuff their 401 (k) plans with company stock; and give workers a right to vote for their 401 (k) stock. In addition, an Office of Participant Advocacy should be created in the Department of Labor to monitor pension plans.

12. *Foster a National Discussion on Corporate Power.* Establish a Congressional Commission on Corporate Power to explore various legal and economic proposals that would rein in unaccountable giant corporations. The Commission should seek ways to improve upon the current state corporate chartering system through federal chartering of global corporations and propose ways to correct the evasive legal status of corporations, such as being treated as "persons" under our Constitution. The Commission should be led by a congressionally appointed expert on corporate and constitutional law, and should hold public citizen hearings in at least ten cities.

CORPORATISM
UBER ALLES

The evolving multinational corporatism is a gigantic control machine. Calibrated with thousands of antennae, feedback mechanisms tell its brain how far it can go in taking control until it meets resistance from countervailing forces. These forces have been disappearing or declining for three decades, creating vacuums and advantages quickly filled by these ever-larger companies and their coordinated trade associations. Remarkably attuned to controlling markets and properties, to seeking lower cost venues by externalizing responsibilities, the big corporation is largely oblivious to those past restraints that moderated its excesses and enhanced its successes. Its determination to abolish these external restraints powers forward. Unified internally by the singular yardstick of sales and profits, this conglomerate drives relentlessly to push away all boundaries to its domination. Obviously, it does not always succeed. Like older bull elephants losing to younger challengers, corporations rise, remain, decline, fall, but unlike elephants, they merge and even mutate into other lines of commerce. However, taken together, global companies possess a common personality that must strive to co-opt or subjugate governments, oppose or weaken trade unions, close off avenues for remedy by others and always, always find ways to concentrate more power in their hands. Control comes to them naturally—it falls under their definitions of self-interest.

Maximum expediency is the corporation's mantra. Nothing reveals this more than the willingness of these behemoths to turn on the very economic ideology that legitimizes them—capitalism. Big business is in the advanced stage of destroying the very capitalism that gives it ideological cover. Consider the following assumptions of a capitalistic system:

1. Owners are supposed to control what they own. For a century, big business has split ownership (shareholders) from control, which is in the hands of the officers of the corporation and its rubber-stamp board of directors. Investors have been disenfranchised and told to sell their shares if they don't like the way management is running or ruining their business. Nowadays, with crooked accounting, inflated profits, and executive self-dealing, it gets harder for even large institutional investors to learn the truth. As Robert Monks says: "Putting owners in charge of what they own is of course the purest form of capitalism."

2. Under capitalism, businesses are supposed to sink or swim, which is still very true for small business. But, larger industries and companies often become "too big to fail." They demand that Uncle Sam serve as their all-purpose protector, providing a variety of public guarantees and emergency bailouts. Some wildly mis-run firms such as Enron are allowed to fail and go bankrupt. By and large, however, in industry after industry where two or three companies dominate or warn of a domino effect on their industry, as with a large bank, Washington, D.C., becomes their guarantor.

3. Capitalism is supposed to exhibit a consensual freedom of contract—a distinct advance over feudal society. Yet, the great majority of contracts for credit, insurance, software, housing, health, employment, products, repairs and other

services are standard-form, printed contracts, presented by sellers on a take-it-or-leave-it, noncompetitive basis.

4. Capitalism requires a framework of law and order. Adam Smith, John Locke, Frederick Hayek, and Milton Friedman all understood this necessity. Rules of economic fair play are needed to prevent mayhem, fraud, deception, and predatory practices. Easily the most powerful influence over most of government are the large industries that receive privileges and immunities. Only those caught in positions of extreme dereliction, like Enron, ever have reason to expect more than a transferable slap on the wrist for violating legal mandates.

5. Capitalist enterprises are expected to compete on an even playing field. Corporate lobbyists, starting with their abundant cash for political campaigns, have developed a "corporate state" where government lavishes many subsidies on big business while denying comparable benefits to individuals and family businesses. We have a government of big business, by big business, and for big business.

In summary, *corporate socialism*—the privatization of profit and the socialization of risks and misconduct—is displacing capitalist canons. This worsening condition prevents an adaptable capitalism, served by equal justice under law, from delivering higher standards of living. Civic and political movements must call for a decent separation of corporation and state. Otherwise invasive commercial imperatives will erode the civic and spiritual values of our democratic society.

Corporate executives, as a class, have pulled off nothing short of a coup d'etat by seizing power from shareholders—the real owners. It is remarkable how the corporate owners lost their rights to effectively control what they own. That means the ability to nominate their own board of directors and to have real elections to decide who will run the company. The staggering compensation plans for CEOs rubber stamped by a selected board of compliant directors has led to inflating profits, downloading debt, and other crooked accounting. The purpose, always, is to increase stock prices to make the bosses' stock options more valuable. All too often top executives end up jeopardizing their own companies. "Surveying continuing record executive pay," *Fortune* headlined in its May 3, 2004 issue, "the average CEO in 2002 earned 282 times what the average worker did. In 1982, the ratio was 42 to one."

Robert Monks, whose experience with corporate board membership activity is extraordinary, has listed "six major inappropriate powers giving rise to serious conflicts of interest by corporate management." He concludes, "Market capitalism cannot fulfill the requirements of allocating resources efficiently if shareholders—individual, institutional and beneficial—accept de facto disenfranchisement of their powers, leaving important decisions almost wholly to senior corporate managements with conflicting interests."

To be sure, shareholders, as owners, with the authority to approve or disapprove the payment packages of their top managers, would have stopped cold these vast excesses in greed, and in Warren Buffetts' judgment, that would have in turn stopped the cooking of the books at the heart of the recent corporate crime wave. Again, a fish rots from the head down.

Humanitarian Yardsticks

Given what large companies often do to their owners and to capitalism, it is no surprise that they damage our political economy in asking to be deregulated, undertaxed, and subsidized. Start with the control of the yardsticks by which progress is measured. Economic indicators, except for unemployment data that are understated, are not measures of the well-being of children, women, and men in the society. Imagine Alan Greenspan going to Congress for his regular state of the economy testimony before the Joint Economic Committee.

Mr. Greenspan is customarily given indicators that are based on bloodless aggregate data—such as inventory levels, investment flows, interest charged to businesses, profits, inflationary signs, deficits. It is mostly about the gross domestic product (GDP)—a peculiar but dominant yardstick of economic growth. But the GDP hides more than it reveals. It ignores distributional benefits of economic activity—who gets the benefits and who doesn't. So I wonder what it would be like if just once Chairman Greenspan testified on economics as if people matter—to use E. F. Schumacher's felicitous phrase. Perhaps, he would start in the following way:

> Mr. Chairman and distinguished members of the Joint Economic Committee, I am here today to declare that the state of our economy is not good. The recent 5 to 8 percent quarterly increases in the GDP rate are accurate but misleading. Most of the gains are going to the wealthy classes. Unemployment is increasing, underemployment is increasing, jobless Americans who have given up on finding a job are increasing and thereby no longer counted as unemployed. Child poverty is growing and if you add "near poverty" as a classification it becomes a national disgrace. In California, fully 45 percent of all children are either "poor" or "near poor." This is unacceptable in such a wealthy country. The number of those without health insurance continues to climb, now over 45 million people. The underinsured population is growing as copayments, deductibles, exemptions, and other insurance trapdoors lead to inadequate coverage. Consumer debt continues to set records, beset as it is with such high consumer credit interest rates even though I have kept the federal funds rate at near forty-year lows. Law enforcement for consumer protection would amuse my old mentor, Ayn Rand, for it scarcely exists. Consumers are being defrauded and overcharged in the tens of billions of dollars yearly. Most times they are not even aware of these heists, as in the computerized billing frauds and abuses in the health care industry, not to mention auto repair rackets, predatory lending, credit card and

bank charges, adulterated food, and medical quackery. Notwithstanding consistent economic growth, a majority of workers is still falling behind in inflation-adjusted wages and, our data show, there is an additional incomparability with peak wage years such as 1972 and 1973. Namely, today's workers must spend more money commuting to and from work and other work-related family costs are much larger. Daycare can cost a worker $500 a month alone.

Affordable housing continues to be elusive for over five million working families. Housing prices are in a period of irrational exuberance. It qualifies as a "bubble" and makes it more difficult for the Federal Reserve to raise interest rates when other economic factors such as inflationary trends call for such increases.

We are commencing a project to refocus GDP figures from a human perspective. For example, child malnutrition and hunger are not incorporated indicators in our assessments of the economy's health. Buying a Nintendo game for a child jiggles the GDP but a parent spending quality time with a child is not an economic activity. Some of these nonmonetary intangibles cannot be calculated because they are not for sale. We cannot deal with not-for-sale inputs such as volunteerism. But we should do a better job in providing you with information on changes in distributional effects of aggregate economic activity on real people. Corporate crime and natural resource depletion indicators should detract from the GDP but we have no database available from the Justice Department and the EPA. I say should because people lose money or health due to corporate crime. But so elastic is our economy that corporate crime may generate considerable economic activity simply from law enforcement with all the expenditures for prosecution and especially for defense. Other trends like workplace casualties, auto crash injuries, and medical malpractice deaths should be subtracting from the GDP but instead are viewed as contributing to it by increasing demands for goods and services. Troubling.

I once was asked by your colleagues whether I was concerned about the nation's trade deficit. I replied, Mr. Chairman, only if it persists. Well, twenty-eight straight years of growing trade deficits merits the word *persistent*. The buying more abroad than we are selling trend boggles my free trade mind enough to leave some options open for future revisions.

Well, Mr. Chairman, I trust that I did not confuse you and your colleagues too much or at least as much as I have confused myself. You see, all my professional life I have been a quantitative economist and these preliminary soundings in my testimony have given me a case of cognitive dissonance. But it sure beats just believing. More next time. Thank you.

If Chairman Greenspan gave testimony like this, it would produce seismic waves among the corporate crowd. For they use similar quantitative yardsticks. Exxon did not subtract from its own GDP the Exxon Valdez oil spill disaster in Alaska. It instead deducted it as an expense and probably made it up in the following months when gasoline prices spiked on the West Coast as a reaction to the tanker's large leak. Nor is depleting minerals considered for subtraction under customary GDP accounting practices. As Herman Daly has noted, "growth in GDP, so-called economic growth, has for some countries literally become uneconomic growth, because it increases unmeasured costs faster than it increases measured benefits. Consequently, many policies justified mainly by their contribution to GDP growth, such as global economic integration, lose their rationale. Maybe that is why the World Bank lost interest in correcting the national accounts."

The dominance of essentially corporate yardsticks for evaluating our economy distracts and obscures the true economic condition of the people and the nation's assets. It is a sensational controlling process because it affects what is and what is not publicly discussed. It misdirects what's considered important for societal priorities. Only when people declare independence from the games being played and demand accurate descriptions of reality will yardsticks begin to measure the people's welfare. Before labor unions were formed, there was little attention paid to the horrible working conditions and pay. There was even less study or statistics about these conditions. Workers were expendable and replaceable. Until the use of the automatic coupler, it was cheaper for the railroads to put workers between the freight cars to couple them and be crushed to death in the thousands than to establish safer practices. As organized labor became more influential in the economy and the councils of government, all working people learned more about their aggregate condition because the government felt obliged to collect these statistics.

In understanding the webs of control that big business is always extending over its subjects, we should realize how they have outpaced the traditional checks and balances. Indeed, we are lunching off those past reforms and allowing them to depreciate—namely, union organizations, federal and state regulation, judicial actions, democratization of credit for community-based entrepreneurship, large farm cooperatives, social safety nets, and heightened community standards and organizations that keep up with ever new corporate outrages and technological hazards.

While traditional restraints have atrophied or been subject to active corporate attrition, the globals have concentrated power and wealth in new and more remote ways. Many top executives are always testing the likelihood of opposition in order to push the envelope. In 1940, the compensation of a CEO in a large U.S. company was twelve times that of the average worker in that same company. They would never have dared to push the shareholders, much less their unions, to give themselves a multiple of forty or eighty times. In 2000, according to *BusinessWeek,* their successors dared. They reached a pay multiple of nearly 531 times! That is not only expansion of CEO power, but given what Buffett observed was its effect on our economy, it was a large expansion of their abuses of power.

Growing Inbalances

The same testing of the waters has been going on against the labor unions. An unequal two-tier system—one for present workers and the other for all new workers—would not have been proposed by management in the 1950s or 1960s. Now it is a concession by unions in various industries, along with more co-payments and deductibles in company health insurance plans. The ease with which factories can be shipped overseas or white-collar jobs outsourced has given big bargaining chips to companies either with unions or, as is mostly the case, without unions where workers may be thinking of forming one. Globalization depresses worker wages and other legitimate demands and is doing so at an accelerating pace. Accountants, legal researchers, radiologists, engineers, and computer programmers are among an army of occupational categories whose practitioners are at risk of being sent abroad. More and more, there is this feeling among transnational companies that they can get away with almost anything—from where they choose to pay or not pay taxes. Their brazen schemes become hydra-headed with collateral demands for packages of subsidies for locating or building their structures in a given community. One that went right through the window was the way Microsoft and General Electric pulled the plug on some New Jersey taxes. In a move of wondrous effrontery, they demanded from then Governor Christie Todd Whitman a subsidy package for locating their MSNBC headquarters and three hundred workers in that state. Included in this bundle of goodies was a refund to Microsoft-General Electric's joint venture for the equivalent of all the taxes paid by those workers to the state of New Jersey. The corporate attorneys who figured out this recycling apparently were not inhibited by their knowledge that their corporate clients were among the most profitable companies in the world. I cannot imagine this occurring thirty years ago nor the current municipal and county moves to use taxpayer monies to build sports arenas for billionaires. Any company demanding such largesse years ago would have been laughed out of town. In those days, real capitalists used their own or their friends' investment funds.

Such severely growing imbalances of power illustrate both corporate supremacy and the growing vassaldom of public officials. These subsidies for big time sports entertainment are not popular with a majority of taxpayers of either conservative or liberal background. Nor do people like the use of eminent domain to destroy homes, churches, schools, or hospitals for a company's installation when it could be located nearby. Some of the condemned land is ultimately used for a mere parking lot or not used at all. Promises by the company of certain levels of employment and the like in return are not binding and can be broken at any time. Fortunately, there is a brewing revolt reflecting itself through unlikely coalitions between conservatives and liberals. Rejections have resulted when voter referenda are permitted.

The political economy, not just the economy, is being turned over to these global powers, including the most sensitive government and security secrets and data through their corporate contracts with federal departments. What have they been delivering with all that power? Isn't responsibility supposed to accompany great power? Well, let's look further at the record.

They have been pushing commercialism into every unwanted corner of American life. More and more, these companies have been breaking faith with their retirees' pensions and health insurance. They are increasing demands for complete immunity or indemnity from Congress wherever they cannot break the tort system from holding them accountable. Over the past generation, with varying degrees of success, tobacco companies, the weapons industry, HMOs, the airline companies, the nuclear and chemical companies, the cruise companies, biomaterials producers, and insurance companies have all tried to evade the all-American proposition that bad or reckless behavior has legal consequences. Ultimately, they have taught the country that the law is for sale in our legislatures.

Big companies win big victories over the people, but not always, so they have a contingency plan. Quit the country. This used to mean mostly making use of very permissive national havens, as do shipping companies carrying the flags of Panama or Liberia. Today, fleeing U.S. jurisdiction is much more sophisticated, for free-loading companies that receive the benefits of the United States.

Enter the new kind of international trade agreements so cleverly designed as not to be restricted to trade. NAFTA and the World Trade Organization (WTO) are international systems of autocratic governance. They are brilliantly suited to the long-held desire of mega-corporations to go around pesky domestic regulations into any arena they want to call their own. These agreements, enforceable upon their signatory nations, reverse priorities of social progress by subordinating worker, consumer, and environmental priorities to the supremacy of international commerce. Recall that when social justice advanced in our country, it was because commercial interests were subordinated to the higher human need. Lawmakers and the laws told the auto companies that their bottom line will adjust to improved motor vehicle safety and not the reverse. They told the polluters that their profits must take into account the toxic harm their operations inflict on innocent human beings. Over the decades, civic values over commercial values improved life in numerous countries where this priority could work. When allowed to operate, the tide of democracy does lift all boats including the yachts of big business executives and the property of their companies.

A genuinely democratic society is good for good business but it is properly bad for bad business. Democracies expand economies, standards of living, and enhance corporate profits in the aggregate far more than authoritarian regimes do. When business plutocrats get whatever they want in the form of monopolies, concessions, little taxation, subsidies, and military protection at the sacrifice of citizens, everybody suffers including many businesses. Let's make a comparison between countries roughly of equal size and resources—Brazil and the United States. The different levels of democratic development produce starkly different levels of economic output. The GDP of California alone is much larger than the GDP of Brazil which has over five times the population.

Let us review the process by which this unpopular trade autocracy was imposed on unwilling Americans (as polls showed). Such unpopularity mystified many observers, given the avalanche of corporate, media, and government propaganda behind passage of these trade deals in the Congress from 1992 to 1995. George H. W. Bush sent the proposed NAFTA treaty with Canada and Mexico to Congress and William J. Clinton did the same with the WTO treaty. Both presidents employed the anti-democratic "fast track" procedure, one that Congress had agreed to adopt. This meant that Congress would have a certain set time either to pass or reject these hundreds of pages without any amendments being permitted. I do not believe that voters send their Senators and Representatives to the Congress so that they can tie their own hands and not exercise their judgments in the form of amendments. In any event, autocratic procedures lead to autocratic outcomes and the two treaties passed. But they were characterized as trade agreements and not treaties (which is what Harvard constitutional law scholar Lawrence Tribe thought they were). Treaties require a two-thirds majority to pass in the Senate. So their names were changed to trade agreements, which needed a simple majority vote.

No American is permitted to have the legal standing to challenge this legerdemain in federal court.

While intensively opposing the WTO treaty by visiting many congressional offices, there was no indication that any legislator or staffer I met had ever read the several hundred pages. They had a year to do so. Their salary checks do not bounce. These treaties represented the greatest surrender of local, state, and national sovereignty in our history. One would think it was time for a little reading of the entire text, not just orating from decidedly slanted memos prepared by the U.S. Trade Representative's office located near the White House or the innumerable business associations and law firms serving global industry and commerce. This abdication amazed us as we related one disturbing provision after another about which they were not aware. So we had an idea. We challenged any member of Congress to read the entire treaty and answer ten simple questions in public. Senator Hank Brown (Rep. Colorado) called and accepted the challenge. He agreed to reserve the Senate Foreign Relations Committee room for the questioning. I called my friend, Richard N. Goodwin, who was being portrayed as a congressional investigator in the movie *Quiz Show,* to come down from Massachusetts and ask the questions which by then had lengthened to twelve. Senator Brown sat in the witness chair encircled by television cameras, radio mikes, and reporters. I sat with Richard Goodwin where the Senators usually sit during a hearing. One by one Goodwin asked the questions. One by one Senator Brown answered them correctly. He had really done his homework. We congratulated him on his perfect score. Then the Senator said he had something else to say. He said he was a free trader and he had voted for NAFTA, but after he read through the WTO agreement, he was appalled by the various anti-democratic sections and decided to vote against approval when it came to the Senate floor. Which he did. His was an exemplary performance but no other member of Congress emulated his dedication. His example had no influence on his colleagues. None changed their vote and the WTO was approved, but not without considerable dissent. It was a sobering episode that taught people about the many slovenly puppets masquerading as denizens of "the world's greatest deliberative body."

THE PRIORITIES
OF INSTITUTIONAL
INSANITY

He came as a penniless youth of fifteen from Syria, put himself through college and Washington University (St. Louis) medical school and settled in Elk City, Oklahoma. In 1929, Dr. Michael Shadid opened the first cooperatively owned hospital in America, which served the impoverished farmers and their families. Dr. Shadid pioneered prepaid group medicine and, against the ferocious opposition of medical societies, spread the doctrine of cooperative medicine all over the United States and Canada. Twenty-five hundred farmers owned their own hospital in Elk City providing medical and health care, both preventative and curative. Their prepayment was a fraction of what they would pay under the usual fee-for-service medicine. Following this inspired, politically astute physician came the prepaid group practice of medicine at Puget Sound and Kaiser Permanente on the West Coast. Imagine controlling your own health care! Fee-for-service held on for most of the century until, in the 1970s, the federal government started promoting Health Maintenance Organizations (HMOs) on a large scale.

The dream began turning into a nightmare as smaller non-profit HMOs were replaced by ever-larger for-profit HMOs, hospital chains, and the perennial health insurance company giants. Today, our country is under the yoke of corporate medicine dominating the Washington landscape. It ties the hands and judgment of physicians and nurses, secures and often defrauds the government of huge amounts of taxpayer dollars and, in contrast to nonprofits, delivers poorer, more rationed, more expensive, less accessible, choiceless health care. Obscenely compensated executives contrive to undermine Medicare with your own tax dollars. The picture is not pretty and costs are spinning out of control. A Dartmouth study estimates that almost a third of the health care sub-economy of $1.6 trillion this year goes to either duplicate or useless care or makes matters worse!

You've probably read, or viewed on television, the many exposés of this industry, its denial of care, its overbilling, its rip-off of Uncle Sam, its large monetary settlements with the Justice Department. The benefits go mostly to the CEOs worth hundreds of millions of dollars each, according to the data provided by the California Nurses Association. HMO overhead and profits as a percent of premium ranged from 14 percent for Pacificare to 33 percent for Cigna in 1999. With big money, ruthless organization, and lobbying, they prevail over superior non-profit health care services that are non-profit. The latter do not have organized consumer-patient groups to seek and bargain for the best arrangements. Instead, large employer groups, which could be more aggressive and in some recent instances have asserted themselves, routinely deliver groups of employees to these HMOs that have managed through mergers to reduce the level of competition in geographical areas.

One third of all Americans are either uninsured or underinsured. This is the case despite our country spending much more money per capita on health care as does Canada, France, Switzerland, and Sweden, whose universal systems cover everybody in their countries and produce better health outcomes. We're paying as taxpayers, workers, and consumers and still tens of millions of people have no health insurance. That number has been increasing year after year.

The unwritten rule beneath the monetized minds of the HMOs, for-profit hospitals, and the drug companies is "Pay or Die." And die the poor do. The Institute of Medicine of the National Academies estimates that about 18,000 Americans die every year because they cannot afford to pay for diagnosis, treatment, or cures. That is 1,500 people a month! What about the preventable sickness, the pain, the family disruption? Add to this human toll the medical malpractice, the medical mistakes, the over-prescription of drugs and their adverse effects, the assembly-line pace of pressured physicians and under-staffed nurses, the drug company bribes and kickbacks to many physicians, and it spells mayhem—a silent form of preventable violence, far greater than many more publicized trauma and disease totals in other sectors.

Years ago, I suggested to a group of psychologists that they expand their research into the mental health or outright insanity of organizations, both corporate and government. They could find fertile ground studying the drug companies for kleptomania, General Motors for endless resistance to being toilet-trained out of its gaseous emissions, the HMOs for attention-deficit disorder. They laughed, but I was serious. Were humans to behave this way, they would be viewed as manifestly deviant.

Jamie Court, whose book *Making a Killing: HMOs and the Threat to Your Health,* was not just about data, and the aggregate statistics. He documented the travails of many real people—the consequences of profiteering run amuck. There was five-month-old Chad Aitken who was given vaccine shots that caused a reaction. When his mother called their HMO for assistance, she was told, incorrectly, that her insurance had lapsed and was refused care. Chad died. David Goodrich was diagnosed with stomach cancer but was unable to get HMO approval for recommended treatment. He finally started therapy with his physicians anyway. By then it was too late. He died leaving his wife Teresa, a kindergarten teacher, with $750,000 in medical bills. No wonder nearly half of all personal bankruptcies in this country involve illness or medical debts.

Suffering the Consequences

One of Jamie Court's many poignant cases comes from the Olsen family. Two-year-old Steven Olsen fell on a twig that punctured his cheek and sinus. A few days later, he developed a fever and his parents took him twice to the urgent care physician. They were told not to be concerned. Steven was lethargic. On the third visit, the little boy was admitted to the HMO-approved hospital where Mrs. Kathy Olsen asked the medical staff to do a CT scan. Since the hospital's contract with the HMO specified that money spent on patients like Steven come out of hospital funds or the monthly per-patient fee paid them from their HMO, there was a tendency to ration care. They told the Olsens that a scan was unnecessary. Three days later, Steven fell into a coma due to a brain abscess that could have been detected easily by a scan. Steven became blind and has cerebral palsy. He and his parents face a lifetime of expensive tests and treatments along with around-the-clock care, pain, anguish, and immense costs.

When I met Steven and his parents—who were waiting to see their Senator Diane Feinstein (D-California) but had to settle for a staffer—I recalled that HMOs were originally promoted as being keen on prevention. Maybe that belief was premised on a nonprofit HMO. Perverse incentives and awful consequences come from the rampant profit motives of today's commercial HMOs. These HMOs rake off tens of billions of dollars from consumers and taxpayers, yet deliver no health care themselves. These corporations just regulate more and more doctors and nurses and pay for more and more politicians to let them continue their harmful practices. They are indeed a profitable bureaucracy piling up expenses, restricting medical judgments and corporatizing the practice of medicine, just as if their profits are the first and foremost priority. While the American Medical Association was living in the past by rejecting a universal health insurance system, they discovered that in the 1990s more and more of their members fell into a spider's web of private corporate government—HMO style—and lost their professional independence. In reaction, thousands of interns, residents, and other physicians, to defend themselves, are doing the formerly unthinkable—organizing or joining unions.

Physicians are moving toward support of a single-payer, universally accessible and affordable health care system. Polls show the public is already there, even with the massive daily propaganda by the corporations to slander the concept, which is really only a fuller version of Medicare with built-in protections from commercial looting. A very recent survey of physicians in Massachusetts shows about two-thirds favor a single-payer system that preserves choice of doctor and hospital, unlike the current HMO restrictiveness.

Over eleven thousand doctors have already signed on to the Physicians for a National Health Program (NHP) which was drafted by a broad panel of experienced practitioners and professors of medicine. In their book *Bleeding the Patient—The Consequences of Corporate Health Care,* describing both the necessity and the practicality of the NHP, Drs. David Himmelstein, Steffie Woolhandler, and Ida Hellander write,

> Non-profit national health insurance can expand coverage, improve care, and limit costs by slashing health care bureaucracy and outrageous profits. Our resources for care—hospitals, clinics, high-tech machinery—are already plentiful, your personnel ready and willing and our current spending levels are sufficient. . . . Overall, the average American would pay no more for health care under the NHP than they do at present.

The difference is that the coverage would be universal, comprehensive and without co-payments, deductibles, and the other maddening fine print of exclusions and denial of remedies for the patients. Health outcomes would be better also, as the authors demonstrate: "The experience of many nations—that spend less and get more health care—proves that national health insurance works." These are nations where workers are paid as much or more than in the United States—as in Sweden, Switzerland, and Germany.

Only in America

Visitors from these and other countries like France, Italy, and Holland can scarcely believe how American workers (who work longer hours than they do) have to endure what they in their countries take for granted.

In the world's richest country, three-quarters of the millions of uninsured are children or working adults. Long-term health care is not available to their elderly relatives unless they pay directly or demonstrate that they have no assets. Despite the economic boom of the 1990s, eight million more Americans were uninsured at the end of the decade. Workers have to accept paying a higher share of their premiums through co-payments and deductibles—a major issue in union-management negotiations. The elderly are forced to increase their out-of-pocket costs. Americans go into bankruptcy because they cannot pay their medical bills. Thousands of Americans die every year because they cannot afford health care. Large numbers of other people delay prenatal care or do not see a doctor after discovering a breast lump or chest pain because they cannot pay for the service. Seriously ill patients ask to die because they do not want to burden their families with more bills. Other uninsured citizens are forced to choose between medical care, drugs or food, rent or heat. European visitors shake their heads in disbelief. They give another meaning to the phrase "Only in America." The system is not working.

We really don't have to take this anymore. Already, half of health care in this country is now paid for by taxpayers (Medicare; Medicaid; federal, state, and municipal employee plans; etc.), as well as a large portion of the medical research and support of medical schools and teaching hospitals. Take the $1.6 trillion (and mounting) that will be spent every year (nearly $6,000 per person already, on the average) and shift it to health care—preventative and treatment—for the people and away from the canyons of corporate greed and looting of taxpayers, replete with costly bureaucracies, billing fraud and denials of care.

Here is what the NHP would comprise. Every person receives a health care card assuring payment for all needed care. There would be complete free choice of doctor and hospital. Physicians and hospitals would remain independent and nonprofit and negotiate fees and budgets with NHP. There would be far less billing fraud and paperwork (in Canada patients rarely see a bill) for health care providers, patients, and their beleaguered families. There would be far less bureaucratic interference in day-to-day clinical practice. We would learn both from the successes and the mistakes of other nations with universal coverage. I would add that patients would be able to join their own fully staffed consumer watchdog associations through simple voluntary dues check-offs. No longer would the health care system have profit incentives that ignore working with patients for safe workplaces and environments, good diets, exercise, and cessation of addictions. The NHP is both health care, prevention, and a payments system.

My guess is that if the various national groups (unions, church groups, civic organizations) that support the NHP would deploy 1,000 full-time, experienced organizers in the needed congressional districts and states, together with their own additional mobilizations, the present 25 percent of the Congress now in favor of universal health care would grow to a majority in months, not years. Organization and coordination are all that NHP lacks because the general public registers majority support already. Think about it: An oligarchy, with a corporate-dominated government demands the future expenditure of trillions of dollars against projected stateless terrorism. But, it refuses, decade after decade, to put in place a health care and health care payment system to save hundreds of thousands of American lives and prevent larger numbers of injuries and diseases certain to occur year after year. This behavior is not sane. It fits the clinical definition of insanity by deliberately leaving fellow Americans defenseless, having to pay or die, pay or get sicker, pay or stay disabled. No fire department or neighbor would refuse to put out a house fire if the owner was delinquent on her property taxes.

Let's make this point another way. Put yourself in the place of your members of Congress. The Centers for Disease Control (CDC), a federal agency, has been warning of a coming pandemic from East Asia that could be as devastating as the 1919 influenza epidemic that took almost a million American lives. Infectious disease specialists at the CDC say such a pandemic is overdue. Each year a flu strain is announced and a vaccine is prepared. Often the strain has a Chinese name because the same sequence repeats itself again and again. Ducks or chickens get the flu, give it to the pigs on farms in China. Then it passes to farmers and the virus is off and running to North America and around the world. CDC has about five full-time infectious disease specialists stationed in China to work on early alerts, lab testing, and other indicators with the Chinese authorities. CDC knows that there are not enough specialists there or here, not enough facilities there or here, not enough research and vaccine production capabilities there or here. We are not ready, put simply, for a viral attack that could take more American lives than did World War II. So you are sitting in a congressional chair. You hear that David Kay has returned to Washington, D.C., empty handed after managing 1,500 U.S. inspectors for Saddam's weapons of mass destruction on a budget of $500 million. The entire budget of the CDC is $7.2 billion. Kay was on a mission to vindicate George W. Bush's political reputation and failed. But neither

Congress nor George W. Bush appear ready to grapple with saving untold American lives by forestalling the human devastation from a pandemic. Is this sane?

But, then, even in the realm of stateless terrorism, sanity is in short supply. During the early 1970s, during the hijacks of commercial passenger aircraft to Cuba, our aviation safety group began urging the FAA, the airlines, and the aircraft manufacturers to harden cockpit doors and strengthen their latches. Some foreign airlines have done so. Three decades passed and all three of these decision makers could not be bothered. Year after year, they ignored the advice of airline security specialists. It was too expensive, or not necessary. As airline regulator, the permissive FAA has long had what close observers call a "tombstone" mentality. That is, the FAA, at best, acts after crashes point to a problem long known, but ignored. Well, the families of 9/11 victims have learned about the FAA's tombstone mentality the hard way. Finally, on a leisurely schedule, the airlines are now equipping their planes with cockpit doors that would keep hijackers from turning the aircrafts into giant, lethal, fuel-loaded missiles. Were these airline organizations in government and business acting sanely? Can anyone say these are unrealistic priorities? Storekeepers shutter their shops in high crime neighborhoods.

The concentration of greed and power breeds institutional insanity as a matter of course and misdirection. It is driving America backward into the future.

Military vs. Civilian Investment

I wonder how Seymour Melman feels these days. For over half a century, this Columbia University professor of industrial engineering has been meticulously connecting the massive overspending and waste in our military budget with the de-industrializing of the United States and the draining of public investment in public works—repairing the crucial physical capital of America. He sees the permanent war economy weakening the civilian economy and draining the scientific and engineering talent it needs. This results in the loss, he believes, of millions of good paying jobs.

Melman cites the "Report Card for America's Infrastructure" that was issued in 2002 by the American Society of Civil Engineers (asce.org/reportcard). One and a third trillion dollars, the Engineers say, is needed just for repair of twelve categories of public works. These include schools, drinking water systems, solid waste, sewage systems, airports, dams, navigable waterways, public transit, bridges, and roads. Melman's knowledge of U.S. industry is legendary. The federal government's military spending crowds out civil manufacturing whose products repair and modernize America's infrastructure, he states. Unsurprisingly, not one U.S. company submitted a bid in 2002 for supplying a new fleet of subway cars for New York City—a contract worth $3 to $4 billion.

Other studies have shown that a billion dollars in civilian investment creates considerably more jobs than a billion dollars in a military weapons system. Melman questions why thirteen years after the fall of the Soviet Union, this military budget continues to expand the massive redundancy and costliness of weapons systems such as the next wave of fighter planes, missiles, submarines, and aircraft carriers. He sees our domestic economic needs being strip-mined right down to libraries, fire and police departments, sanitation departments, schools, health care, and services for elderly people.

In a more detailed manner than President Eisenhower's famous comparison of the cost of weaponry to civilian needs, Melman shows what we could have by way of domestic public investment if we tame our military expenditures. Jobs in public works in our country are usually good paying jobs in local communities improving public services. Such jobs cannot be outsourced to China. The manufacturing base to supply these public works projects would be expanded with a similar expansion in employment. Melman does not subscribe to the thesis that we can have a prosperous economy without a strong manufacturing foundation and its multiplier effects. He characterized our present economic system not as capitalism but as state capitalism fusing big business with big government.

As an aside, now in his mid-eighties, Melman does his own research and has just written a new book. When I asked him who researched his finding that in the fall 2002 L.L. Bean catalog, 92 out of the 100 products offered were imported, he replied, "I did."

Now, if there is ever a consensus about any jobs programs, investing in public works or infrastructure wins the prize. In communities around the country, support comes from the construction industry; trade unions and workers; the local mayors; the banks; insurance companies; sellers of fuel, food, and real estate; and local chambers of commerce. One could go on and on. Yet, apart from highway funds, the allocations are woefully small. Just ask our only struggling passenger train system—AMTRAK—which can scarcely get the $1.5 billion it needs for capital improvements and operating needs each year. In contrast, the missile defense system took $9.1 billion this year and over $140 billion since Reagan's folly got underway. Moreover, according to Professor Theodore Postel and other scientists, the system is unworkable because, among other reasons, it is very easy to decoy.

The Growing Gap

So, if just about everyone back home favors such repair and modernization, why isn't it happening? The easy answer is that the military industrial complex is much more organized and entrenched in Washington, D.C. Right off, a major public works program faces the charge that our country would be plunged into a deficit it cannot afford. That is the usual argument. Well, George W. Bush inherited a surplus. What did he and his supporters in Congress do? They pushed through, over an anemic Democratic Party opposition, two large tax cuts, mostly for the wealthy, that will cost far more than the American Society of Civil Engineers' estimate of $1.3 trillion, upgraded in 2003 to $1.6 trillion. Blocking such tax cuts could have led to community rehabilitations. Now, there is a massive deficit, as far as the forecast can predict from tax cuts, justified by President Bush as a way to expand the economy. These tax savings are not going to public investment infrastructure. Nor do rich people who already have far more than they spend rush into the market to spend their newly received mega-tax savings. Last year, Bernard Rapoport, founder of the American Income Life Insurance Company, called me and said: "Ralph, what am I going to do with another $150,000 a year? I've got more money than I can spend. Bush is talking economic nonsense."

Making connections between how the super-rich and corporations rig the tax system in their favor requires dedication—how they make sure that the IRS has neither the mandate nor budget to audit their schemes needs a further effort of enquiry. We must learn how their lobbyists and PACs go beyond the ways they've already legalized to shift the tax burden to lesser-endowed humans whose children inherit the deficits and interest payments. With this effort and knowledge, we can turn this Great American Rip-Off into a Great American Political Issue before elections.

One sensible and surprising institution involves very rich people like Warren Buffett, George Soros, Paul Volcker, and William Gates Sr. Responsible Wealth has over 1,000 rich members opposed to the repeal of the estate tax—a refreshing transcendence of their own economic interest. Gates is so passionate about the reasons and morality behind the estate tax that, in addition to lobbying Congress, he co-authored with Chuck Collins the book *Wealth and Our Commonwealth: Why America Should Tax Accumulated Fortunes.*

The bookstores have many fine investigative books on tax loopholes, tax breaks, tax shelters, tax havens, and the scurrilous greed of tax escapes, whether super-rich or large companies. Among the best recently are *The Cheating of America* by Charles Lewis and Bill Allison and *Perfectly Legal* by David Cay Johnston. These books help us understand what is going on. Understanding the complex web of connections is essential. Otherwise, people will not see what they are losing where they live, work, and play in the cruel trade-off between consummate greed and public need.

Enter John O. Fox, who after thirty-six years as a Washington tax lawyer quit and moved to western Massachusetts (an exciting civic region). There he has pioneered, teaching undergraduates at Mt. Holyoke College, a course on U.S. tax policy. Fox is on a mission. His new book is titled *10 Tax Questions the Candidates Don't Want You to Ask*. Among them are: "Would you limit the home mortgage interest deduction so that it subsidized the purpose of one basic home, and would you redirect some of the tax savings to help qualified renters purchase a basic home? Would you stop giving tax breaks for much higher pension contributions for highly paid employees (managers) than for rank-and-file employees? Should Congress prohibit pension plans from depriving employees of their pensions after they have been employed for at least three years?"

John O. Fox, despite his many years in the grim world of corporate tax law, is idealistic. Given the insipid, stagnant, sloganized, debateless campaign culture, how can reporters, much less voters, get a foot in the door of the bubble that encloses the candidates and their microphones? What does he think that we live in—the Lincoln-Douglas era when debates continued for hours before large standing audiences?

Let us start evaluating our institutions—local, state, national, and international—by the same yardsticks that we judge people. Depersonalization runs rampant and thereby runs away from familiar frameworks of accountabilities. Let's stop the institutional insanity!

FOREIGN POLICY FOLLIES

The shortcomings of America's political leaders do not stop at our borders. The conduct of foreign policy is equally shortsighted and more undemocratic.

When the president beats the drums of war, the dictatorial side of American politics begins to rear its ugly head. Forget democratic processes, congressional and judicial restraints, media challenge, and the facts. All of that goes out the door. It's the president, stupid—plus the clique that surrounds him and the vested interests that reflexively support him. Dissenting Americans may hold rallies in the streets, but their voice is drowned out by the bully pulpit.

The invasion and occupation of Iraq, and the resulting quagmire, is Bush's most egregious foreign policy folly, but reflects a broader dynamic. Listen to retired General Wesley Clark's stinging indictment of the administration: "President Bush plays politics with national security. Cowboy talk. The administration is a threat to domestic liberty."

But Clark was a Democratic candidate for president. So let's listen to Michael Kinsley, the respected columnist who has written for *Time* and the *Washington Post,* and is now editorial and opinion editor for the *Los Angeles Times.* In March 2003, Kinsley wrote that "in terms of the power he now claims, George W. Bush is now the closest thing in a long time to dictator of the world." An unelected dictator at that.

Bush a dictator? You'd never know it from the words he uses most often—"freedom," "liberty," "our way of life." You'd never know it from public opinion polls, which respond favorably to an un-challenged jingoism. The politics of fear sells. Cold war politics sold. The war on terrorism sells. But it's a very expensive sale for the American people. Even with the Soviet Union long gone, America's military budget amounts to half the operating federal budget. While vast resources and specialized skills are sucked into developing and producing redundant and exotic weapons of mass destruction, America's economy suffers and its infrastructure crumbles.

As the majority of workers fall behind, Bush has appointed himself ruler of Baghdad and, with the complicity of a fawning Congress, is draining billions of dollars away from rebuilding America's public works—schools, clinics, transit systems, and the rest of our crumbling infrastructure.

How does Bush sell America on this diversion of funds and focus? With the politics of fear. He, John Ashcroft, and company openly tout the state of permanent war.

Are there no limits to their hubris? The same Bush regime that applies rigid cost-benefit analysis to deny overdue government health and safety standards for American consumers, workers, and the environment sends astronomical budgets to Congress for the war on stateless terrorism. Bush's own Office of Management and Budget throws its hands up and observes that the usual controls and restraints are nowhere in sight. To appropriate runaway spending in the name of homeland security, the powers-that-be need only scream one word: Terrorism!

If you ask the Bushies how much this effort will cost, they recite a convenient mantra: "whatever it takes to protect the American people." In fact, trillions of dollars annually would not suffice to fully secure our ports, endless border crossings by trucks and other vehicles, the rail system, petrochemical and nuclear plants, drinking water systems, shipments of toxic gases, dams, airports and airplanes, and so forth. So "whatever it takes" is actually a prescription for unlimited spending.

Much of the war on terrorism involves domestic guards and snoops. The word "terrorism," endlessly repeated by the president and his associates, takes on an Orwellian quality as a mind-closer, a silencer, an invitation to Big Brother and Bigger Government to run roughshod over a free people who in the past fought real wars without losing their liberties or composure.

A country with numerous and highly complex vulnerable targets cannot be fully secured against determined, suicidal, well-financed and equipped attackers. That obviously doesn't mean we shouldn't take prudent measures to reduce risks, but our allocation of funds must be made realistically, rather than just throwing money at the problem. Domestic security specialists know that we are spending unwisely, but they are not about to blow the whistle. As one expert told me, these specialists do not speak out because they wish to get on the gravy train, gathering lucrative contracts.

Then there's the great unmentionable. If you listen to Bush, Cheney, Rumsfeld, and crew, well-financed suicidal al Qaeda cells are all over the country. If so, why haven't any of them struck since September 11? No politician dares to raise this issue, though it's on the minds of many puzzled Americans. As General Douglas McArthur advised in 1957, and General Wesley Clark much more recently, it is legitimate to ask whether our government has exaggerated these risks facing us, especially when such exaggeration serves political purposes—stifling dissent, sending government largesse to corporate friends, and deflecting attention from pressing domestic needs.

George Bush willingly moves us toward a garrison state, an American Sparta, through the politics of fear. We're experiencing a wave of militarism resulting in invasive domestic intelligence gathering and disinvestment in civilian economies. The tone of the president becomes increasingly imperial and even un-American. As he once told his National Security Council, "I do not need to explain why I say things. That's the interesting thing about being the President . . . I don't feel like I owe anybody an explanation."

The president has implied that he occupies his current role by virtue of divine providence. His messianic complex makes him as closed-minded as any president in history. Not only is he immune from self-doubt, but he fails to listen to the citizenry prior to making momentous decisions. In the months leading up to the invasion of Iraq on March 20, 2003, Bush didn't meet with a single citizens' group opposed to the war. In the weeks leading up to the war, thirteen organizations—including clergy, veterans, former intelligence officials, labor, business, students—representing millions of Americans wrote Bush to request a meeting. He declined to meet with a single delegation of these patriotic Americans and didn't even answer their letters.

Bush's authoritarian tendencies preceded the march to Baghdad. First he demanded an unconstitutional grant of authority from Congress in the form of an open-ended war resolution. Our King George doesn't lose sleep over constitutional nuance, especially when members of Congress willingly yield their authority to make war to an eager president.

Next, Bush incessantly focused the public on the evils of Saddam Hussein (a U.S. ally from 1979–1990), specifically how his weapons of mass destruction and ties to al Queda posed a mortal threat to America. The administration's voice was so loud and authoritative, and the media so compliant, that all other voices—of challenge, correction, and dissent—were drowned out.

And so Bush plunged the nation into war based on fabrications and deceptions, notwithstanding notes of caution and disagreement from inside the Pentagon, the CIA, and the State Department. This was a war launched by chicken hawks, counter to the best judgment of battle-tested army officers inside and outside the government.

In retrospect, it seems clear that there were no weapons of mass destruction except those possessed by the invading countries. It also seems clear that Saddam Hussein was a tottering dictator "supported" by a dilapidated army unwilling to fight for him and surrounded by far more powerful hostile nations (Israel, Iran, and Turkey). The notion that this man posed a mortal threat to the strongest nation in the world fails the giggles test.

Bush's war arguably meets the threshold for invoking impeachment proceedings under Article II, Section 4 of the Constitution. But not a chance with today's compliant, complicit Congress. Not a chance in an environment that considers dissent unpatriotic. An environment in which the media neglects its role as watchdog.

Some brave Americans did speak out against the war, or at least expressed grave reservations. How much coverage did they receive on television or in other mass media? This will go down as a disgraceful chapter in the history of journalism. The media were mostly cheerleaders—uncritical of the leader, dismissive of dissenters, indifferent to their obligation to search for truth and hold officialdom's feet to the fire, and grateful to the spike in ratings occasioned by the build-up and eventual war. MSNBC, or, in reality, owner General Electric, fired Phil Donahue at least in part for his willingness to criticize the White House war effort.

In the end, the media felt betrayed. David Kay, Bush's chief arms inspector in Iraq, returned in February 2004 after 1,500 inspectors scoured the country, and summed up his findings in a sentence: "We were wrong" about Iraq's weapons of mass destruction. Only then did the media respond with fury at having been duped. Too little, too late. A democratic society needs media to do their job prospectively, not after an unnecessary and pre-emptive war.

What about the leaders of the legal profession, the national and state bar associations, people presumably devoted to the rule of law? You might expect them to speak out. Don't be silly! Apart from select criticisms of enforcement of the Patriot Act, the organized bar has neglected its role as sentinels for our democratic processes. Few lawyers, law school deans, and state attorney generals have met their professional obligations. (There were a few shining exceptions, such as law professors David Cole and Philip Heyman.)

If there was precious little organized resistance to the Bush war from outside government, the situation was even worse within government. The system of checks and balances requires three vigilant branches, but Congress has disgraced itself from virtually the beginning of the Bush administration, assisting an extraordinary shift of power to the executive branch.

In October 2001, a panicked Congress passed the Patriot Act, giving the Bush administration unprecedented powers over individuals suspected (and in some cases not even suspected) of crimes. Two years later, Congress gave the president a virtual blank check to wage a costly war.

In these respects, and others, the war on terrorism has important parallels to the Cold War. Domestically, the latter was characterized by relentless focus on a bipolar world largely dictated by the iron triangle of giant defense companies, Congress, and the military leadership, mutually reinforced with campaign contributions, lucrative contracts, new weaponry, and bureaucratic positions.

A foreign policy responsive to the iron triangle produced some perverse results. The United States overthrew any number of governments viewed as too congenial to similiar reforms that our own ancestors fought for—land reform, workers rights, and neutrality toward foreign countries. We replaced such governments with brutal puppet regimes. We also used our armed forces to protect the interests of the oil, timber, mining, and agribusiness industries.

Actually, such policies long proceeded the Cold War. No one articulated it more clearly or candidly than Marine General Smedley

Butler, whose provocative eyewitness accounts rarely made their way into our history books:

> I spent 33 years in the Marines, most of my time being a high-class muscle man for big business, for Wall Street and the bankers. In short, I was a racketeer for Capitalism.
>
> I helped make Mexico, especially Tampico, safe for American oil interests in 1914. I helped make Haiti and Cuba a decent place for the National City Bank boys to collect revenues in.
>
> I helped in the raping of half a dozen Central American republics for the benefit of Wall Street. The record of racketeering is long. I helped purify Nicaragua for the international banking house of Brown Brothers in 1909–1912. I brought light to the Dominican Republic for American Sugar interests in 1916. In China I helped to see to it that Standard Oil went its way unmolested.

"War is a racket," Butler wrote, noting that it tends to enrich a select few. Not the ones on the front lines. "How many of the war millionaires shouldered a rifle?" he asked rhetorically. "How many of them dug a trench?"

Butler devoted a chapter of his long-ignored book, *War Is a Racket,* to naming corporate profiteers. He also recounted the propaganda used to shame young men into joining the armed forces, noting that war propagandists stopped at nothing: "even God was brought into it." The net result? "Newly placed gravestones. Mangled bodies. Shattered minds. Broken hearts and homes. Economic instability."

Does this all sound familiar? The September 11 attack gave rise to a corporate profiteering spree, including a demand for subsidies, bailouts, waivers from regulators, tort immunity, and other evasions of responsibility. Before the bodies were even recovered from the ruins of the World Trade Center, the *Wall Street Journal* was editorializing that its corporate patrons should seize the moment.

Foreign policy amounts to more than national defense, and national defense amounts to more than a mega-business opportunity for weapons and other contractors. All too often, corporate sales priorities have driven defense priorities, leading to militarization of foreign policy.

Consider the 1990's "peace and prosperity" decade, possibly the greatest blown opportunity of the twentieth century. In 1990, the Soviet Union collapsed in a bloodless implosion. Suddenly we faced the prospect of an enormous "peace dividend," an opportunity for massive savings or newly directed expenditures since the main reason for our exorbitant military budget had disappeared.

Not so fast, said the military-industrial complex, there must be another major enemy out there—maybe Communist China, or a resurgent Russia, or some emerging nation developing nuclear weapons. We allegedly needed to prepare for the unknown, hence went full-speed ahead with billions for missile defense technology. In the battle for budget allocations, what chance did the "repair America" brigades have against the military-industrial complex? More B-2 bombers or repaired schools? F-22s or expansion of modern health clinics? More nuclear submarines or upgraded drinking water systems? We know who won those battles. And after 9/11, it was no contest.

As the perceived threat shifted from the Soviet Union to stateless terrorism, the weapons systems in the pipeline from the Cold War days moved toward procurement. On top of that is the chemical, biological, surveillance, detection, intelligence budgets to deal with the al Qaeda menace. Everything is added, almost nothing displaced.

We are constantly told by politicians and the anti-terrorist industry that 9/11 "changed everything." This sentiment suggests the lack of proportionality of our new permanent war. It's also a sentiment that must make Osama bin Laden ecstatic. Bin Laden wanted to strike fear in America. He did so, and then watched as the first response to this fear was a crackdown on anyone with a Muslim or Arab name or visage. Thousands were detained or arrested or jailed on the flimsiest of suspicions, opening the Bush administration up to the charge of hypocrisy when we challenge Islamic nations about due process violations. All of this created more contempt for America among young people throughout the Middle East, no doubt helping the recruiting efforts of our enemies.

Bin Laden must have delighted in attempting to push America toward becoming a police state and sowing discord among us. He must have been thrilled by red and orange alerts, inconvenience at airports, all kinds of excessive expenditures damaging our economy. And bin Laden must have taken perverse delight in press reports that Bush believes he was put on this earth by God to win the war on terrorism. Bin Laden met his counterpart when it comes to a messianic impulse. If he wished to inspire a clash of civilizations, he apparently found a willing collaborator in Bush.

As all this suggests, America's response to 9/11 was not only disproportionate but also counterproductive. Recently on ABC's *Nightline,* a Washington think tank fellow said something sensible: "When you are fighting terrorism, you want to do it in a way that does not produce more of it." Are we doing that?

Terrorism takes many forms, as in the Sudan, as in the Rwanda rampage that claimed 800,000 lives, the state terrorism of dictators, the added terrorism of hunger, disease, sex slavery, and man-made environmental disasters. With no major state enemy left, what can we do to prevent and diminish these various forms of terrorism, as well as deter more suicidal attacks from fundamentalists? Perhaps we need to redefine national security, redirect our mission, reconsider our relations with other countries.

Starting with the Israeli-Palestinian conflict. Whether cause or pretext, this conflict gives rise to widespread animosity against the United States, the chief ally and supplier of economic and military aid to Israel. The outlines of a peaceful resolution are known and supported by a majority of Israelis and Palestinians—a two-state solution creating a viable, independent Palestinian nation with its capital in East Jerusalem and in charge of its own air, water, land, and boundaries. Compensation of Palestinians for lost property, and the return of some refugees to Israel to rejoin their relatives are issues warranting negotiation.

To make peace a reality, the United States must connect with the peace movement in Israel. The "refuseniks"—veteran Israeli officers and soldiers of the Israel Defense Forces (over 1,300 of them)—have rejected duty in the Occupied Territories. Their declaration states: "We shall not continue to fight beyond the 1967 borders in order to dominate, expel, starve, and humiliate an entire people." (For their entire statement, see www.seruv.org.il.) PEACE NOW has been pushing the Israeli government to seek peace through negotiations and mutual compromise. In a recent call-to-action, PEACE NOW said, "A small minority of settlers has taken over the government and country. The disengagement plan has failed—and the government of Sharon and Lapid are not offering any alternative options for an end to the conflict!" Within the Knesset, leaders of the Meretz Party have been very critical of Sharon's policies. MK Yossi Sarid (a leader of the Meretz Party), referring to Sharon said, "You don't have the right to destroy Menachem Begin's life work, and his establishment of peace with Egypt, and you don't have the right to destroy the labors of Yitzhak Rabin's life, and his forging of peace with Jordan." Rabbi Michael Lerner, founder of Tikkun, is an outspoken critic of occupations by both Israel and the United States. Rabbi Lerner said, "The Bush/Sharon axis of occupation has little chance of bringing lasting peace, but they may bring temporary electoral advantages, even as they erode the moral authority of two countries which could have been beacons of hope and instead have become symbols of insensitivity and arrogance."

Unfortunately, our government has supported the Sharon govern-ment, which remains dominated by those who believe that Israel can achieve a military solution to the conflict. America cannot effectively mediate peace unless it is seen as pro-Palestinian as well as pro-Israeli. We can start by recognizing that there is far greater freedom inside Is-rael than in America to discuss candidly the conditions of the conflict.

Thomas Friedman of the *New York Times* has observed, inter-viewed, and thought about how to break the cycle of violence in this conflict between a massively more powerful Israel and its Palestinian adversaries, both of whom he has criticized.

On February 5, 2004, his column evidenced his frustration with the governments of Israel and the United States:

> Mr. Sharon has the Palestinian leader Yasir Arafat under house ar-rest in his office in Ramallah, and he's had George Bush under house arrest in the Oval Office. Mr. Sharon has Mr. Arafat sur-rounded by tanks, and Mr. Bush surrounded by Jewish and Chris-tian pro-Israel lobbyists, by a vice president, Dick Cheney, who's ready to do whatever Mr. Sharon dictates, and by political handlers telling the president not to put any pressure on Israel in an election year—all conspiring to make sure the president does nothing.

A second task for a redirected national security strategy involves arms control—reduction or elimination of nuclear weapons and other weapons of mass destruction. This requires choosing between encouraging the lucrative private export of arms (the current posi-tion) or seeking the systematic diminution of such lethal trafficking.

There's been much good work in this area, both by the Arms Con-trol unit of the Defense Department and by various private prominent scientists and disarmament experts. There have also been setbacks, in-cluding the Bush administration's rejection of the ABM Treaty and the Clinton administration's rejection of treaties abolishing landmines and prohibiting the trafficking in small arms.

The goals of Mid-East peace and worldwide disarmament would both benefit from a shift toward more multilateralism. We must work with friends and neighbors to address all the problems of this tormented world—settling conflicts, heading off human and ecological disasters, early detection of epidemics, spreading peaceful scientific and technological advances, and making available proven solutions to all areas of the world.

An energized and serious media is indispensable. Our media traffic in the trivial, devoting thousands of prime-time hours to the trials and tribulations of Madonna, Michael Jackson, O. J. Simpson, Tanya Harding, and the like. But how many Americans have heard of the annual Human Development Report of the United Nations Development Program? This report makes a great case for global optimism, demonstrating the availability of inexpensive life-saving measures. For far less than we spend on gambling, or cosmetics, and cigarettes, the world could have health, clean drinking water, and schooling. We are sorely in need of what William James called the "moral equivalent of war." We should declare war on worldwide misery and deprivation, and contribute to raising the quality of life for billions of people worldwide.

In the 1940s, 1950s, and 1960s, the innovative thinker and architect Buckminster Fuller used to astonish audiences with a detailed explanation of how world poverty could be ended with an annual expenditure equivalent to one month's spending on weapons. Billions of devastated lives later, Fuller's plan remains unfulfilled.

The late James Grant, one of America's unsung heroes and the head of UNICEF, helped save millions of young lives by negotiating entry into countries where deadly diseases could be easily prevented. My Princeton class of 1955 formed a global tuberculosis project to call attention to the relative ease with which this destroyer of two million lives a year could be combated.

Slowly but surely, the World Health Organization, prodded by various private and public foundations, has been highlighting the need for a multinational assault on global infectious diseases such as tuberculosis, AIDS, and malaria. At long last, Western Economists recognize what rural villages have known forever—disease undermines economic development. Fighting disease is justified on economic as well as human grounds.

Democracy is also good for economic development, but only if done properly. Today, spreading democracy has become a mantra for plutocratic propaganda and a justification for unwise actions like the invasion of Iraq. If the Bush administration wants to spread democracy, it doesn't have to do so with tanks and missiles. We can nurture democratic growth in the Third World by assisting institutions already in place. In some cases, we have done the reverse. For example, over the decades, Washington has reduced the very modest contributions to the American University of Cairo and the American University of Beirut, even though these universities are rare success stories in a troubled region.

Power without accountability is a bad formula, and a commonplace one in the conduct of foreign policy. Our government spends billions for blunders, and no one is forced to resign. Our government violates our own laws and international laws, and reporters never ask, "What is the legal authority for this operation?" Our government props up brutal regimes and turns millions of people against us, and justifies such actions with a slogan—fighting communism, or a war on terrorism, or a war on drugs.

The foreign policy and intelligence agencies operate in secrecy and rarely have to explain themselves, even to each other. (The 9/11 Commission provides a welcome exception, but received a chilly reception from the Bush administration.) Federal Judge Damon Keith wrote, "democracy dies behind closed doors." The U.S. Constitution requires publication of the government budget, but when an American citizen challenged the secrecy of the CIA budget in federal court, the case was dismissed. The judge said that this taxpayer had no legal standing to bring the action. Then who does have standing—the attorney general? Don't hold your breath waiting for the attorney general to sue his own president.

There's an impressive catalog of actions taken by our government and shrouded in secrecy: illegal spending, government overthrows, corporate tax havens, sovereignty-shredding trade agreements, circumventing our courts and agencies, taking nuclear waste from other countries, and allowing advanced weaponry and data to be sold by companies to oppressive regimes. Often such actions remain unknown and unchallenged. (A few years ago, the General Accounting Office explained that the sprawling Pentagon budget is unauditable. A one-day news story, long forgotten.)

In 2000, Chalmers Johnson, a professor and former naval officer, wrote a book called *Blowback* and defined the word, invented for internal use by the CIA, as follows: "the unintended consequences of policies that were kept secret from the American people." Johnson explains that the actions of terrorists, drug lords, rogue states, and arms merchants "often turn out to be blowback from earlier American operations." Johnson's book is devoted to instances of blowback and their cumulative impact. These boomerangs, he writes, "hollowed out our domestic manufacturing and bred a military establishment that is today close to being beyond civilian control."

Our government acts in our name. When it resorts to violence or bribery abroad, or supports crude force on ordinary people to benefit repressive regimes and global corporations, the American people should know about it. When billions of our taxpayer dollars go to the International Monetary Fund (IMF) and workers worldwide get their wages and services cut and taxes raised because of "structural adjustments" imposed by the IMF, Americans are entitled to be in the loop.

In his book *Fortress America,* William Grieder asks a fundamental question: "Are the armed forces deployed in behalf of U.S.-based multinationals or U.S. citizens?" Grieder believes that our national defense policy does not serve the interests of our citizenry, but there is no debate on this subject. He claims the American people are "open to more dramatic changes in national defense than a status quo Washington imagines. They await a real debate."

We wait and we wait. But citizens have an obligation to at least try and learn what our government is doing abroad, *especially* since our government acts in our name. Apart from ethnic groups interested in the "old country," Americans pay far too little attention to foreign policy. This is regrettable. Americans have too much goodness and too much talent not to play a more fundamental role than that of passive spectator. America's foreign policy might not consist of a succession of follies if it were conducted and monitored more democratically.

GLOBALIZATION

I n approving the far-reaching, powerful WTO and smaller international trade agreements, such as NAFTA, the U.S. Congress,
like the governments of other nations, has accepted harsh legal
limitations on what domestic policies it may pursue and thus ceded
much of its capacity to protect citizens. This new governing system is
designed to exert control over minute details in the lives of the majority of the world's people. This system is structured not to enhance
the well-being of human beings, but rather the well-being of the
world's largest corporations and financial institutions.

Unlike members of Congress, Big Business knew what the WTO
agreements contained. That's because corporate lobbyists helped draft
them. Big Business has crafted these agreements to circumvent national and local governmental democratic processes, to undermine
citizens' ability to force effective regulation of corporate activity, and
to lock in rules that enable corporations to shut plants in one country
and move elsewhere, even to a country under the thumb of a repressive regime, with virtually no restrictions.

Under these trade deals, U.S. and other nations' laws, whether
federal, state, or local, must comply with the special business-friendly
rules of the trade agreements. Laws to protect consumers, or to ensure that products are not made with child labor, or to safeguard the
environment—all such laws risk being decreed impermissible "non-
tariff trade barriers" under the tricky rules of trade agreements.

Secret tribunals established by the trade agreements render binding judgment on U.S. and other national laws. If the secret tribunals declare an American consumer protection law, say, to be in violation of WTO, NAFTA, or some other agreement, the United States has a choice: change the law or pay fines or accept sanctions to maintain it. The potential sanctions are so severe that governments now regularly repeal laws, or even withdraw them from consideration, lest they be challenged at the WTO or another trade body.

These are thus pull-down agreements: They pull down our accumulated victories and achievements in the areas of wages and hours, union organizing, food safety protection, consumer safeguards, and protections for our natural environment, among others, and have a chilling effect on future advances. For example:

- The WTO ruled that the United States must revise the gasoline cleanliness rules adopted to implement the Clean Air Act. The oil companies had tried to block these rules in U.S. courts and failed. But a successful challenge to the rules at the WTO by Venezuela led the U.S. Environmental Protection Agency to adopt replacement regulations, rules that the agency itself had previously rejected as unenforceable.
- In 1997, Massachusetts passed a law saying that it would not do business with companies doing business in Burma, which is governed by a vicious military dictatorship. The European Union challenged the law at the WTO, saying Massachusetts did not have the right to refuse to contract with European companies based on where they did business. Shortly thereafter, Maryland considered a similar law for companies doing business in Nigeria, then also ruled by brutal dictatorship. The bill was unexpectedly defeated, after the U.S. State Department—which feared it would spark another WTO challenge—testified against it. (The Massachusetts law was ultimately overturned by the

U.S. Supreme Court, as an interference with Congress's power to regulate foreign commerce.)

- Laws that prohibit the import of goods made with child labor (several of which been proposed by Iowa Senator Tom Harkin) are flat-out illegal under the WTO whose rules say an importing country cannot be concerned with the process by which an imported product is manufactured, except in the case of prison labor.

- The United States, operating at the behest of the biotech industry, has announced its intention to file a WTO challenge to a European de facto moratorium on approval of genetically modified crops. The United States says, correctly, that WTO rules require countries to accept food products unless they can prove them unsafe with a high degree of scientific certainty. The Europeans' position—one that should be adopted in the United States—is that they do not want to expose consumers to biotech foods until they are shown to be safe. But this application of the Precautionary Principle asks that proof of safety be supplied by the entity introducing a new product. As such, it conflicts with the WTO's corporate-friendly rules.

  The threatened action on biotech foods follows an earlier case at the WTO, where the United States successfully challenged a European ban on the import of hormone-treated beef. To preserve this consumer protection measure, Europe must now pay an annual fine to the United States.

- The WTO requires countries to adopt the pesticide and food safety standards maintained by an industry-dominated international organization based in Rome, called the Codex Alimentarius. Codex standards permit higher residues of many dangerous chemicals on foods than do U.S. rules, meaning these food safety rules could be ruled in violation of WTO mandates.

- In their important book, *Whose Trade Organization?*, Lori Wallach and Patrick Woodall report: "At its 1999 meeting, the

Codex approved maximum residue levels for the pesticide methyl parathion that did not take into account the impact of the level on children, as is required by U.S. law. Two months after Codex made the methyl parathion determination the U.S. EPA banned the use of the chemical on fruits and vegetables because of the risk it posed to children. As a result, the U.S. regulation is now exposed to challenge under the WTO . . . because it provides greater protection than the WTO-recognized international standard."

Perhaps nothing has shifted as much power to multinational corporations as the investment chapter of NAFTA, known as Chapter 11. Chapter 11 contains two key features: First, it provides an array of strong protections against government action or regulation that might affect foreign investors. One gift to corporations is a prohibition on "expropriation," or actions "tantamount" to expropriation, except for public purpose and with fair market value compensation. In theory, expropriation would seem to apply only in cases where a government exercised eminent domain, such as taking over a factory. But in NAFTA, the definition is far, far more expansive. The second key feature of Chapter 11 is that it permits investors to bring suit for compensation directly against governments that have allegedly infringed on their investment rights.

NAFTA's Chapter 11 has provided the basis for a number of eyebrow-raising cases. In the largest Chapter 11 suit yet brought against the United States, in 1999 the Canadian corporation Methanex sued the U.S. government for $970 million because of a California executive order phasing out the sale of a Methanex product. Methanex claims that California's phase-out of methyl tertiary butyl ether (MTBE), a gasoline additive, violates the company's special investor rights granted under NAFTA because the California policy limits the corporation's ability to sell MTBE. MTBE poisons groundwater.

Methanex says that instead of banning MTBE, California should enforce rules prohibiting improper disposal. This case is pending.

The MTBE case is reminiscent of a 1998 case brought against Canada by the U.S.-based Ethyl Corporation. In that case, Ethyl sued Canada for $250 million after Canada banned the gasoline additive methylcyclopentadienyl manganese tricarbonyl (MMT) because of health risks. The state of California had banned MMT and the U.S. Environmental Protection Agency was working on a similar regulation. Ethyl claimed the Canadian ban violated NAFTA because it "expropriated" future profits and damaged Ethyl's reputation. After learning that the NAFTA tribunal was likely to rule against its position, the Canadian government revoked the ban, paid Ethyl $13 million for lost profits, and, as part of a settlement with Ethyl, agreed to issue a public statement declaring that there was no evidence that MMT posed health or environmental risks.

In another pending case, the U.S.-based United Parcel Service (UPS) is pursuing a NAFTA Chapter 11 case against Canada for $100 million, arguing that the Canadian postal service's involvement in the courier business infringes upon the profitability of UPS operations. Canada Post is a government-owned corporation that does not receive public subsidies. Nevertheless, in this case, the first NAFTA investor-to-state case against a public service, UPS claims that by integrating the delivery of letter, package, and courier services, Canada Post has cross-subsidized its courier business in breach of NAFTA rules. For example, UPS argues that permitting consumers to drop off courier packages in Canada Post mailboxes unfairly advantages Canada Post as against other courier services.

Yes, you read this right. According to UPS, to comply with NAFTA, Canada Post should have separate boxes to drop off courier packages, picked up by nonpostal worker personnel, taken to separate facilities, processed by workers who don't handle the regular mail, and delivered by personnel not associated with the regular mail. This case is still pending. The United States, Canada, and Mexico should amend NAFTA, if they chose not to repeal it entirely, by revoking this notorious Chapter 11 immediately.

The Ravages of Corporate Globalization on America

The pull-down effect is imposed through other means, as well. U.S. corporations long ago learned how to pit states against each other in "a race to the bottom" to profit from whatever state would offer lower wages, pollution standards, and taxes. In the world of corporate globalization, companies pit countries against each other. When one city, state, or country works to ensure that corporations pay their fair share of taxes, provide their employees a decent standard of living, or limit pollution, they are typically met with the refrain: "You can't burden us like that. If you do, we won't be able to compete. We'll have to close down and move to a country that offers us a more hospitable climate."

Complying with the much too modest standards of the international global warming treaty would "harm U.S. competitiveness," alleges a leading U.S. business-backed study on global warming. Cutting greenhouse gas emissions would be "suicidal for competitiveness," British industry told the U.K. government in January 2004. In the face of such warnings, and the implicit threat that jobs will move elsewhere, governments are reluctant, to say the least, to act. As a result, the rich countries have moved at a snail's pace to confront global warming, probably one of the greatest looming threats to planetary well-being.

Frequently, the threats by industry to close or move factories are a bluff. But often they are not, especially when it comes to the matter of wages. Two parallel developments are proceeding at a stunning pace:

U.S. manufacturers are closing factories, in large part either because they can't compete with low-wage competitors in China or elsewhere. And large multinationals like General Electric are themselves shifting operations from the United States to low-wage havens abroad.

In significant part due to the ravages of corporate globalization, the United States has lost more than two million manufacturing jobs since 2001. The much-pruned but still vital manufacturing centers of the Midwest have been devastated, whole communities ripped apart by plant closings.

For example, Galesburg, Illinois, a town of 34,000, is dealing with the pain of the closure of a Maytag refrigerator manufacturing plant. The factory employed 1,600 in good-paying jobs, and provided jobs to one-in-twelve adults in the local workforce, according to the *Chicago Tribune.* Maytag said it had no choice but to move its factory to Mexico, so it could match the lower production costs of Whirlpool and General Electric, which have already shifted much of their manufacturing out of the United States. On the day of the closing announcement, Diana Stephenson, who worked at the plant for twenty-eight years, told the *Chicago Tribune:* "I never saw chins drop so far, with men and women crying. Everybody that talked to me was worried about their children and their future."

More than half-a-million U.S. workers have been certified under one narrow government retraining program as having lost their jobs due to NAFTA. And notwithstanding predictions from NAFTA's backers to the contrary, these job losses have not been offset by new jobs in facilities manufacturing for export to Mexico. Of course, it's not exactly clear that NAFTA's corporate backers ever believed these rationalizations for entering into the agreement.

Corporate globalization provides big companies seemingly endless routes to escape the civilizing effects of citizen controls and imposed obligations—like taxes. Business has long been masterful at devising loopholes and shelters to avoid paying taxes, of course, but globalization has significantly enhanced their escape capacities.

In a particularly brazen move, more than two dozen major U.S. corporations have reincorporated offshore in order to lower their tax rate. The reincorporated companies don't close their U.S. headquarters; they simply engage in the paper transaction of filing incorporation papers in a tax haven country. One Ernst & Young tax partner put it plainly to the *New York Times:* "We are working through a lot of companies who feel that . . . just the improvement on earnings is powerful enough that maybe the patriotism issue needs to take a back seat."

But the reincorporation gambit is small potatoes compared to the more exotic offshore tax shelters used by Halliburton and others. Employing such devices as tax payment deferrals, income stripping, and parking intangibles offshore, multinationals manipulate their assets and income to avoid billions in taxes. Montana Senator Max Baucus, ranking minority member on the Senate Finance Committee estimates that offshore tax shelters cost the public treasury $70 billion a year. Then there's the transfer-pricing maneuver, by which companies manipulate internal transactions between subsidiaries to shift income to the subsidiaries located in lower tax national jurisdictions. North Dakota Senator Byron Dorgan estimates the annual cost of transfer pricing at more than $50 billion.

Corporate Globalization Ravages the Third World

The damage done to the United States by corporate globalization pales in comparison to the violence inflicted on the Third World. With weaker governments and frail civic institutions, most of the Third World is far less able to counterbalance the growing power of multinational corporations. Consider the following snapshots from around the world.

HIV/AIDS—Drug Availability

HIV/AIDS now ranks as perhaps the worst pandemic in the history of the world. More than forty million people worldwide are HIV-positive. For all but a few, an HIV diagnosis is a preventable death sentence.

Existing treatments, which enable many people with HIV/AIDS in the United States and other industrialized countries to live relatively healthy lives, are unavailable to 98 percent to 99 percent of the people in developing countries.

Life-saving HIV/AIDS drug cocktails cost more than $10,000 a year in the United States and other rich countries. Until recently, that was the price throughout the developing world and even in Africa— where the epidemic has hit worst and where per capita income is typically little more than a dollar a day. The drugs cost so much not because they are expensive to manufacture, but because the brand-name companies have patent monopolies that prevent price-lowering competition.

Manufacturers in India, where drug patents will not come into force until 2005, are able to make AIDS drug cocktails for as little as $140 per person per year—less than 2 percent of the price companies like GlaxoSmithKline, Bristol-Myers Squibb, Merck, and Boehringer Ingelheim were charging just a few years ago. Once the Indian companies entered the market and offered dramatic discounts, the brand-name companies started lowering their prices—but they still typically charge four or more times the generic price.

Under the terms of the WTO's intellectual property agreement, all developing countries must provide patents on pharmaceuticals. However, there are safeguards that permit any country to authorize generic competition for pharmaceuticals or other products while they stay on patent. For years, the Clinton administration told countries it was unacceptable to use these safeguards, but that policy changed after protest by citizen groups like the Consumer Project on Technology and AIDS activist organizations Health GAP and ACT UP.

Still, the U.S. Trade Representative, who effectively works as an arm of the drug companies, is coercing developing countries into entering new trade agreements, Such agreements protect the monopolies of brand-name drug companies. Countries in the WTO will not be allowed to exercise their own safety standards. In addition, drug companies themselves lobby and threaten governments in developing countries. Often such countries suppress the generic cheaper competition that could save millions of dollars and help control HIV/AIDS. This ghastly economic imperialism epitomizes the immorality of monopoly power.

Smoking—Merchants of Death

With sales declining in increasingly health-conscious richer countries, the Big Tobacco companies have pinned their future on expanding into the developing world and the former Eastern bloc. Some companies feature marketing and advertising campaigns that deceptively tie smoking with youthful rebellion, Western notions of freedom and sophistication, and hipness—and thereby work to addict children to a lifetime of smoking. Shamefully, many of their ads feature pop music or sports stars. The tobacco merchants of disease increasingly target women and girls, who often have far lower smoking rates than males.

After the U.S. government forced open markets in Asia-to-U.S. cigarette imports in the 1980s and 1990s, overall smoking rates increased by 10 percent, according to the World Bank. In the year after the South Korean market opened, smoking rates among teenaged girls quintupled. The tobacco industry is a grim reaper in waiting. Globally, the World Health Organization predicts that tobacco use will kill ten million people a year by 2025, with 70 percent of these deaths in developing countries. The numbers are unfathomable.

When countries try to enact appropriate health regulations, they may find themselves facing threats under trade agreements. For example, tobacco companies have argued that having to put large warnings on cigarette packs violates their guaranteed trademark rights. They have even suggested that such requirements in Canada are tantamount to an expropriation under NAFTA's Chapter 11.

Structural Adjustments

The International Monetary Fund (IMF) and World Bank, two institutions that have little if any direct affect on the U.S. economy, exercise decisive and destructive influence over the economies of much of the developing world.

Based in Washington, D.C., the IMF provides loans to developing countries with balance of payment difficulties, helping them pay debts to foreign creditors. Private lenders and other public lenders generally will not lend to troubled economies unless they have a loan agreement with the IMF. The IMF, whose decision making is controlled by the rich countries, in particular the United States, makes its loans on the condition that borrowing countries agree to a set of maniacal edicts known as "structural adjustment." Imagine all the other ways that taxpayer dollars, given to the IMF, could be used to truly help people in less developed countries. Over the past two decades, the World Bank, which also makes loans for infrastructure and other projects in developing countries, has joined the IMF in making loans for structural adjustment. The results have been devastating.

In the two regions with the most structural adjustment experience, per capita income has stagnated (Latin America) or plummeted (Africa). Structural adjustment policies call for the sell-off of government-owned enterprises and services—including functions such as tax collection that are fundamentally government responsibilities—

to private owners, often foreign investors. Privatization is typically associated with layoffs and pay cuts for workers in the privatized enterprises, and often the giveaway of valuable assets to privileged insiders. That's how Russia and Mexico corruptly became home to such a high number of the world's billionaires.

Many IMF and World Bank loans call for the imposition of "user fees"—charges for the use of government-provided services like schools, health clinics, and clean drinking water. For impoverished people, even modest charges may effectively deny access to services. When the World Bank mandated that Kenya impose charges of $2.15 for sexually transmitted disease clinic services, attendance fell 35 percent for men and 60 percent for women. Similar results have been seen throughout the developing world.

Under structural adjustment programs, countries open up their economy to unregulated imports, and undertake a variety of measures to promote exports. Removing protections for local industry and agriculture has an even harsher impact than in rich countries. In Mozambique, for example, the IMF and World Bank ordered the removal of an export tax on cashew nuts. The result: 10,000 adults, mostly women, lost their jobs in cashew nut-processing factories. Most of the processing work shifted to India, where child laborers shell the nuts at home. In Mexico, since adoption of NAFTA, more than a million corn farmers have been driven off the land, unable to compete with cheap U.S. imports produced on highly mechanized farms.

The relentless focus by structural adjustment orders on exports comes at the expense of production for domestic needs. In the rural sector, the export orientation is often associated with the displacement of poor people who grow food for their own consumption as their land is taken over by large plantation owners (who benefit from government assistance) growing crops for foreign markets.

Oil Equates to Destruction

For years, Nigeria was ruled by one of the world's most brutal and corrupt dictatorships. Oil revenue kept the dictatorship afloat. Multinational oil companies like Shell and Chevron pumped the black gold from the oil-rich Nigeria Delta. When the Ogoni people, who live in the Delta, protested the dictatorship and the oil-drilling operations despoiling their land, the military responded with a crackdown. It executed the Ogonis eloquent leader, Ken Saro-Wiwa, and other Ogoni leaders.

No thanks to the oil companies, a fed-up populace managed to usher in a transition from Nigeria's dictatorship to a struggling democratic regime. But oil drilling remains destructive in Nigeria. The Ogoni and other ethnic groups have suffered as their land, air, and water have been despoiled by the oil companies, through flaring of gas, repeated spills, poor pipeline placement, and unlined toxic waste pits.

Unfortunately, the Nigerian case is typical of oil company operations in developing countries. The oil giants have a record of coddling dictators, trashing the environment, and wrecking local communities dependent on now-polluted streams and no-longer fertile lands.

In Burma, for example, Unocal and other companies are building a gas pipeline to Thailand. Funds from that project—which activists claim benefited from slave labor employed by the government—are propping up Burma's military junta. In Ecuador, tens of thousands of indigenous people charge that Texaco's operations destroyed the streams and natural environment they depend on for survival. In Chad, Exxon-Mobil is leading a consortium developing an oil project that threatens ecologically vulnerable areas and is projected to lead to the spread of HIV/AIDS (via new roads, migration, and increased prostitution). The Chad government spent $4.5 million of its first oil-related revenues on weapons; the government had promised to spend the money on poverty alleviation. In Indonesia, people living in Aceh Province, in North Sumatra, charge that Mobil Oil contracted with the Indonesian military to provide security for a natural gas project, and that the military units committed widespread human rights violations.

Plundering Our Neighbors

Corporate globalization has ushered in an era of unprecedented wealth and income inequality. Corporate and financial plunder of developing countries—and the transfer of money from the masses to a narrow elite in almost all countries, rich and poor—has led to a shameful concentration of wealth and privilege.

Global inequalities now reach staggering levels. The four hundred highest income earners in the United States make as much money in a year as the entire population of twenty African nations—more than 300 million people. The richest three hundred and fifty people in the world hold more wealth than the bottom three billion.

Again these income and wealth inequalities translate into far-reaching social inequalities. For example, a person born in a high-income country can expect to live half as long again as someone born in a less-developed country. A person in a less-developed country is twenty-five times more likely to die from tuberculosis than someone in a high-income country.

Confronting Corporate Globalization

As overwhelming as the odds seem of curbing corporate globalization and directing the global economy in a more humane and ecologically sustainable direction, citizens across the planet have achieved major victories against entrenched corporate power. That's one reason corporate globalizers prefer to negotiate trade and investment agreements in secret, behind closed doors, away from public scrutiny, preferably with no public awareness whatsoever.

Just a few years ago, the World Trade Organization was a little known global agency, and most people wouldn't know it from the World Tourism Organization (a small U.N. agency). That changed in Seattle in 1999. There, following on years of organizing from groups like Public Citizen and dozens of church groups and worker organizations, tens of thousands of people went to the streets to protest the WTO's corporate orientation. The inspiring street protests, combined with an empowered grouping of African governments, undermined the efforts of rich countries to expand WTO powers to further benefit multinationals. Such efforts have mostly stalled ever since.

A year earlier, an international network of civic organizations thwarted a U.S.-European attempt to craft an international investment agreement, known as the Multilateral Agreement on Investment (MAI). The MAI would have taken NAFTA's Chapter 11 to a global scale. But activists obtained a copy of the draft agreement, which was being negotiated in secret, posted it on the Internet, and developed careful and detailed analyses that showed how far-reaching the agreement would be. The deal couldn't survive public scrutiny, and it soon crumbled.

Civic groups have become especially adept at campaigning against particular corporate abuses, achieving numerous victories. The anti-sweatshop campaigns on campuses have forced universities to take responsibility for how apparel displaying their logos is made. Campaigns targeting shoe and apparel makers such as Nike and the Gap have highlighted working conditions in places where the subcontractors produce for these firms. The firms have been forced to accept at least some responsibility for improving conditions. The Burma solidarity campaign has pressured almost every major company except the oil corporations to end their investments in Burma and cut off trade with the country.

Other victories abound. The campaign for access to essential medicines has completely changed the framework for global patent issues. It has helped drop the price of AIDS drugs by more than 98 percent. It has shaped international opinion that public health needs must not be subordinated to commercial interests.

A small Colombian indigenous group, the U'wa, networked with supporters worldwide to defeat plans by Occidental Petroleum to drill for oil in their historic lands. Among other tactics, the U'wa threatened to commit collective suicide if Occidental carried out its drilling plans. Citizen campaigns all over the world have dashed the dreams of the nuclear power industry to spread its dangerous technology. No new nuclear power plants have been built in the United States in decades and Germany is now undertaking a long-term phase-out of nuclear power.

Thanks to the work of Results, Essential Action, and other groups, the U.S. Congress passed legislation requiring the U.S. representatives to the IMF and World Bank to oppose loans from those institutions that included user fees for basic health care and education. The institutions haven't come fully around, but the World Bank has backed off from supporting school fees. As a result, 1.5 million additional children—mostly girls—are now enrolled in school in Tanzania.

Citizen campaigns have also succeeded in crafting a people-centered globalization, which is starting to lift health, safety, and environmental standards rather than dragging them down WTO-style. For example, driven by tobacco-control citizen groups, countries adopted the world's first public health treaty in 2003. The Framework Convention on Tobacco Control calls for a comprehensive ban on tobacco advertising, promotion, and sponsorship (with an exception for countries, such as the United States, which deem such a ban unconstitutional), large health warnings, and measures to confront widespread smuggling of tobacco products.

Environmental groups have successfully lobbied and campaigned for a range of important environmental agreements, among them a ban on the export of hazardous waste. Before the treaty was adopted, waste brokers simply dumped rich countries' wastes in poor nations.

Meanwhile, in every country, citizens are banding together to create people-controlled institutions, outside of the control of the multinational corporate predators, that meet human needs.

The Grameen Bank in Bangladesh specializes in micro-credit—small loans at reasonable interest rates to enable people to become entrepreneurs and escape the grip of local loan sharks. The success of the Grameen Bank has sparked global interest in micro-credit, which is helping develop local economies throughout the developing world.

As Michael Barratt Brown documents in *Africa's Choices,* successful cooperative and other small-scale economic development projects—frequently led by women—are proliferating throughout Africa. He points to everything from goat and sheep projects in Niger to soap-making cooperatives in Tanzania.

In Brazil, the rural association of landless workers known as the MST has specialized in self-help land redistribution. In a country with one of the most unequal income and wealth distributions in the world, large landowners leave fertile land untilled while thousands and thousand of poor rural workers have no land whatsoever. The MST organizes peaceful takeovers of the unused land, parceling it out to the poor who will use it.

These civic efforts to counter corporate globalization are united by the vision of a political economy oriented to satisfying people's needs rather than corporate imperatives. It emphasizes the importance of orienting local economies first to meet local needs, especially in the area of food production. For reasons of environmental sustainability and corporate accountability, it favors, in the phrase of economist Herman Daly, "balanced trade" and short supply lines—meaning purchases and sales should be made locally before regionally, regionally before nationally, nationally before globally.

No one denies the importance of trade, but societies need to focus their attention on fostering community-oriented production. Such smaller scale operations are more flexible and adaptable to local demands and environmentally sustainable production methods. They are also more susceptible to democratic control and foster businesses less likely to migrate and more likely to coincide with community interests.

The citizen movements argue that basic services like health and education should be provided as a matter of right, not based on the ability to pay. They want to protect the global commons—the seas, the atmosphere, shared knowledge—away from corporate privatization. But there remains a huge role for the marketplace, especially as it involves locally controlled, more democratic, and smaller scale enterprises, as opposed to oligopolistic corporations. The citizen campaigns want to decentralize economic power, which is why land reform is so essential in developing countries; and they want to facilitate citizens joining together into organizations—like labor unions—that can offset concentrated corporate power. They want to contain unlimited capital mobility, so that absentee corporations and financial institutions do not maintain the veto power over economic policies exacted by threats from business to leave the jurisdiction unless government capitulates to their demands.

Their emphasis on local economies notwithstanding, the civic movements embrace globalization—just not the corporate-dominated variety. They seek pull-up agreements, such as human rights treaties that set a fundamental standard for civilized behavior; the tobacco control agreement that requires members to meet minimum requirements to protect health; and the treaties that establish thresholds of environmental protection—as opposed to the pull-down model of the WTO and NAFTA.

At stake is the very basis of democracy and accountable decision-making that is the necessary undergirding of any citizen struggle for just distribution of wealth and adequate health, safety, and environmental protections. The corporate alternative is an economic model of supranational limitations on any nation's legal ability to put human well being before commercial activity. Corporate globalization seeks to eliminate democratic accountability over matters as intimate as the safety of our food or the conservation of our land, water, and other resources. This fetishization of profit creates grotesque inequalities and has terrible consequences for planetary ecology.

As economist Herman Daly warned in his January 1994 "Farewell to the World Bank," the push to eliminate the nation-state's capacity to regulate commerce "is to wound fatally the major unit of community capable of carrying out any policies for the common good. . . . Cosmopolitan globalism weakens national boundaries and the power of national and subnational communities, while strengthening the relative power of transnational corporations."

More and more people are coming to see the triumph of such a perverse corporatist mentality as intolerable. By banding together in existing and new organizations; by forming networks, enterprises, and cooperative ventures; we build momentum for a just world.

STAND FOR JUSTICE

Half of democracy is about just showing up—informed people showing up to vote, to rallies, marches, demonstrations, to give testimony, attend action meetings for schools, to partake in community protection, advance civil rights, improve health care, and work for peace. But most people don't show up, even though it doesn't take all that much time or money and there is no one to stop them. Politicians pander to us with slogans, flatter us for doing nothing about their behavior. Do we need to lull ourselves with shrugging cynicism or other rationalizations for apathy? Too much can go wrong for our country if we don't apply some "tough love" and get our friends and neighbors going. So much goodness, well-being, fulfillment, and foresight are ours for the asking if we dedicate our values in those directions.

Democracy does take some work. Democracy does take a no-excuses attitude, a positive refusal to become discouraged. The reverse option is to continue losing more and more control over most everything that matters to us outside or inside the home. Don't you want to have a voice in the matters that affect the living conditions of you and your family? Injustice hurts and shuts you out. Justice helps and lets you in.

The first step is to decide how much time we're going to devote to what irks us. Here again is a loss of control—"I just don't know where the time has gone," or "I just don't have the time." We're pulled in all directions by the time-takers—waiting on the phone for a simple answer; stuck in bumper-to-bumper commuter traffic; taking things to be repaired; negotiating suburban sprawl; ferrying kids and going to appointments; trying to figure out our bills, which seem to be in code; and above all, having to work longer and longer on the job or jobs to pay those bills. Americans work on average longer than French workers who have a shorter work week, longer paid vacations, childcare, paid sick leave, and health insurance.

The good news is that time can be managed and liberated for what we decide is important. You have probably formed some distinct impressions about Congress, enough perhaps to turn you off in dismay or disgust, though you may like your own Representative. You've heard story after story of how many of these politicians—not all—grovel to raise campaign cash, called "legalized bribery" by David Brinkley. How many elected officials wallow in cowardliness when they should be standing tall, how many are always alert to raising their pay and expanding their benefits, and perfecting their charming ways of sweet-talking the public? How many push for one-party redistricts? There are 535 members of Congress (435 Representatives and 100 Senators). Only ten or so put their voting record on the web in a clear retrievable fashion. The rest have declined all such requests by voters and citizen groups.

Now suppose one early summer evening, a person knocked on your door and introduced himself this way: "Hi, I'm your new neighbor. Just wanted you to know that I spend over 20 percent of your income, can raise your taxes while lowering taxes on corporations and the wealthy, can send your children off to war, and can let special commercial interests gouge and harm you and your family. See you later."

What would you do? Express umbrage at his interruption that is preventing you from watching a rerun of *Cheers*? Or would you say,

"Hey, come back here, you mean something to me, so I better mean something to you!" That person is your member of Congress.

Presently, about 1,500 large corporations control or block most of the votes of most members of Congress on very important matters. It is not beyond the realm of realization to look forward to a time when a few million modestly organized Americans, representing the values of much greater numbers of their fellow Americans, turn the national legislature into a Congress of the people, by the people, and for the people.

The most effective way to begin this process is to cut the reins of commercial campaign contributions that presently restrain members of Congress and direct them toward further concentration of greed and power in ever fewer hands. "Campaign finance reform" has to be one of the most dull and yet most important phrases in our language. It was Thomas Jefferson who said that "of all the mischiefs, none is so afflicting and fatal to every honest hope as the corruption of the legislature." Two hundred years later, Senator Robert C. Byrd (Dem-WV) said, "It is Money! Money! Money! Not ideas, not principles, but money that reigns supreme in American politics!" All along, a hefty majority of the people have wanted some kind of campaign finance reform and many nonvoters cite the corruption of dirty money in elections as a reason why they do not vote.

Still, the dull phrase is utterly too vague to bring home the intimate and cruel effects on people's lives. As Will Rogers quipped, "Congress is the best money can buy." For years, I've seen the way cash register politics works against you. Hundreds of drug industry lobbyists prowl the halls of Congress. Their industry PACS contribute tens of millions of dollars to key legislators, and you pay higher prices for medicines and medical devices. Your tax dollars fund new drug development that the National Institutes of Health gives away to drug companies, which charge you staggering prices for new medicines they received free. You pay.

HMOs and large hospital chains send checks to Congress and our country continues to be the only western democracy without universal health insurance. Nothing is done by our government about tens of thousands of deaths and hundreds of thousands of serious injuries from medical malpractice in hospitals. Little effort is devoted to law enforcement against the looting of Medicare and Medicaid using unscrupulous over-billings and phantom services that total tens of billions of dollars yearly. You pay.

Auto manufacturers and their dealers have locked up with lucre those members of the House and Senate who block improved auto safety, fuel efficiency and pollution standards. You pay. The oil, gas, coal, and nuclear industries spread their dollars around Congress and between the political parties. In return, they deny you solar energy and an energy efficient economy, make you subsidize them with your taxes, get us embroiled in overseas turmoil, and expose you to their continued toxic pollutants. You pay.

The giant military weapons companies work Capitol Hill with a commercial intensity second to none. The result is redundant and immensely wasteful munitions, planes, ships, and missiles, most of which come in way above budget. Your tax dollars subsidize sales of many such weapons to repressive regimes abroad. You can't get community programs—such as education, clinics, public transit, drinking water upgrades, public libraries—funded because military budgets are rapacious. You pay. Uncle Sam is turned into one giant corporate welfare paymaster for the Molochs of Big Business. And we pay because we are not organized to have a say for our country's future and a say for our own or our children's well-being.

So the few decide for the many and, not surprisingly, the few put themselves first. Nothing new here. When the people are not organized to transmit and reflect their demands on a regular basis, the organized few prevail. Mass media exposés of the nexus between money, lobbyists, and members of Congress engaged in wrongdoing may produce temporary squirming, but then it is back to normal. For the very people charged with maintaining political law and order are indebted to this dirty money system, and they're not likely to self-prosecute or change the system.

The book *End Legalized Bribery* by retired member of Congress from Hawaii, Cecil Heftel, has on its cover a picture of Bill Clinton and Newt Gingrich shaking hands at a "town hall" meeting in New Hampshire on June 11, 1995. At the event, a citizen, Frank MacConnell, asked them if they would form a blue-ribbon panel to produce a plan to reform the nation's campaign finance system. With the national broadcast media looking on, both men quickly agreed. Heftel burnishes the words THEY LIED under the picture, because nothing came of that handclasp. Heftel then devotes a hundred and thirty-five readable pages to laying the basis for his Clean Money Campaign Reform with free access to television and radio time for those ballot qualified candidates who agree to receive public monies, and avoid all private money except small contributions to demonstrate some popular support and serious intent.

This little book offers a galvanizing narration of the outrages corporate lobbyists inflict on regular Americans, conducting what reporters Jeffery Birnbaum and Alan Murray, writing for the *Wall Street Journal,* called a nightly sale with the members of Congress as the merchandise. As I read it, I recalled previous sterling denunciations of the dirty money system corroding our democratic processes written in the 1980s and 1990s by Elizabeth Drew, Philip Stern, Brooks Jackson, Donald L. Barlett, and James B. Steele. Nonetheless, the money race continued to worsen, with more politicians dialing for the same business dollars with frenzied diligence. When you ask the members of Congress about the monetized life they lead, most express disgust with the "whole rotten system," as one put it. Yet, they are the legislators who can do something major to stop what a congressional staffer called "the rat race of rot and roll."

When corruption is so institutionalized that it becomes a way of life, though sometimes distasteful to its predators (some of whom feel they are being shaken down) and to its practitioners, many voters just shrug their shoulders in resignation and conclude that "the system is rigged." Well, not quite. Senator William Proxmire (D-Wisc.) was elected again and again without asking for any campaign contributions. He would spend a few hundred dollars just for postage to mail back unsolicited donations that dribbled into his campaign office. Of course, it helped that he would literally walk all over the state of Wisconsin, hold more hearings than almost anyone, listen to the people, watchdog government waste, and vote in a progressive manner.

Proxmire is long retired and his example is not around to set the standard of proper behavior that is possible when you represent the people first. Heftel quotes Thomas Paine who wrote, "A long habit of not thinking a thing wrong gives it a superficial appearance of right." Certainly, Senator Mitch McConnell (R-KY) thinks that money is free speech and that not nearly enough is spent on campaigns. According to McConnell, campaigns should go unregulated except for the stipulation that donations be disclosed. He neglects the fact that money can suppress the speech of those who don't have enough of it even to compete on a level playing field, or to attract more media and respectable poll numbers. These gravitate to those with the most money so that small starts based on character, integrity, and honesty, as Heftel points out, do not have a chance to have a chance. He points out that public financing costing "$6.50 per citizen per year is all it would take to own our democracy." He also notes that "two or three dollars would do the trick for state elections." The present seaminess costs citizens hundreds of billions of dollars a year—the cost of neglected health, injuries, fraud, crime, and aggravation.

I have always been fascinated by the intense interest and time that people invest in their hobbies. As a youngster, I poured hours into collecting stamps and playing chess. Years later, I wondered why the joys of civic activity are not seen by more people as a kind of hobby. One day I opened the *New York Times* to read that a bird with a Western European habitat had been sighted in a New Jersey marsh. The exciting news spread to birdwatchers all over the mid-Atlantic region and they responded by getting in their cars, boarding trains, buses, and planes to the Garden State for the rare opportunity to catch a glimpse of their intrepid feathered friend. What if, I mused in a moment of fantasy, the bird took off, flew south and alighted on the Capital dome of the Congress, pursued by legions of birdwatchers? They might take time to enjoy a brief stint at "Congress watching." Certainly, we need that.

Several hundred Congress Watchers in each congressional district—well-linked, marshalling the votes, statements, financing, and other activities of their senators and representatives for astute diffusion among the 500,000 or so residents of each congressional district—would do wonders for responsive politics. Holding vibrant accountability sessions between citizens and their members of Congress, attended by the media, would keep legislators' feet on the ground and their pockets clean. Easy slogans would go out the windows before the probes and proposals of their informed constituents. Participants in this watchdog club could inform their neighbors what a little public investment of their time can produce, how it can replace the private investment of the corporate lobbyists that have turned Congress into a bustling bazaar of giveaways to those who are paying the pipers. Ending what Heftel called a system of campaign finance laws that promotes "begging, bribery, and extortion" will attract much better and more honest candidates for public office who want to get things done and do not want to get their hands dirty by demanding money that carries a quid pro quo. As the grassroots strength of the Congress Watchers increases, you'd see changes in the legislators' record and attentiveness to subjects and directions that the big boys of business do not welcome. Watching the muscle of the people turn the Congress in their direction would be a lot of fun, an exercise in the politics of joy and justice.

All the above may still not arouse you because it doesn't connect with your temperament. Let me try another approach. Once upon a time there were mothers who lost their children in car crashes due to drunk drivers. One day in 1980, Candace Lightner lost her teenage daughter to a drunk driver. She got mad, real mad. Mad enough, she says, to seek justice and revenge. So she started MADD, or Mothers Against Drunk Driving, which took off like a rocket. Nationwide, thousands of other mothers joined her to pass or toughen laws against drunk driving and get them enforced. Mothers who lost their beloved children did not have to be tutored in motivation. They had their un-relenting grief to propel them to action. All over America, relatives of victims swing into action after tragedies stemming from defective products, dozing truck drivers, street crime, contaminated blood, tox-ics around homes, E-coli contaminated meat.

If you are not driven to action by tragedy, yet another approach is available. Ask yourself what really sparks your indignation among the assortment of injustices you view on television, hear on radio, or read in newspapers and magazines? Let one example make this point. Whether you stood for or against the invasion and occupation of Iraq, compare the way the Bush government treats the men and women on active duty with the way it treats Halliburton and other corporate prof-iteers from this war. Reservists and National Guard members find that their incomes are lower, some far lower. Lower-rank enlistees need food stamps. Their self-employed businesses are shaky or crumbling in their absence. The National Consumer Law Center reports in its study "In Harm's Way—at Home" that "scores of consumer-abusing busi-nesses directly target this country's active-duty military men and women daily." Some in the National Guard are so hard-pressed that they have lost their homes or had their furniture repossessed. Barbara

Ehrenreich writes that charities have started to "help families on U.S military bases, like the church-based Feed the Children, which delivers free food and personal items to families at twelve bases."

Many of the troops in a volunteer army come from the ranks of the working poor. The poor have always fought the wars, starting with George Washington's army. While George W. Bush is busy transferring more wealth to the super rich using tax cuts and corporate welfare, the children of military personnel receive less funding for their base schools. Veterans' disability benefits are subtracted from the military retirement pay of soldiers.

Enraging veterans further, Bush's 2005 budget asks Congress to increase veterans' drug co-payments and institute an "enrollment fee" that veterans' groups believe will drive about 200,000 veterans out of the VA system and discourage many more from enrolling. This is the same shameless chicken hawk, George W. Bush, who frequently takes Air Force One to military bases in the United States to pose with soldiers for one photo opportunity after another to feed to a compliant media. However, the "pause and run" photo opportunist has refused to go to Dover, Delaware to pay his respects to the returning dead, those who gave their young lives to his illegal, fabricated war in the quicksands and alleys of Iraq. No news photographers or camera teams are allowed at the Dover base by this administration. Old and new veterans are beginning to filter out Bush flattery and flag-waving to cut to the core of what Bush is doing to them in the hard reality of programs and budget cuts while far greater government deficits are registered to reduce taxes for big companies and the rich. How's your dander when you learn about what Bush does in contrast to what he says? Ready to show up?

If you're poor, you may feel too busy dealing every day with your travails to think about showing up. Well, prepare to be poorer every day. Earlier, I mentioned that your minimum wage buys three dollars less (adjusted for inflation) then the minimum wage did in 1968.

Sounds like too many poor Americans are falling behind . . . every day. Have you heard of ACORN (the Association of Community Organizations for Reform Now, www.acorn.org)? It is a citizen action group composed of low- and moderate-income people. In November 2000, they issued a report called "Separate and Unequal" on predatory lending in America—something that was criminal through the 1960s before most of the state usury laws were repealed in the 1970s under pressure from the financial industries.

The world of predatory lending among lower income minorities and poor Whites is little known to the rest of America. Signing on the dotted line of such a fine-print contract is routine for the down and out so that the law itself becomes an instrument of oppression used by the loan sharks. Although the variety of gouging and deception takes different forms depending on the type of case and place involved. ACORN reports about the (often Wall Street-financed) predatory lenders going to work on Mason and Josie, "an elderly African American couple who have excellent credit and whose primary source of income is Mason's veteran's benefits. Their mortgage was at a 7 percent interest rate when a broker convinced them to consolidate some credit cards into the mortgage." The new mortgage for $99,000 carried an interest rate of 8.4 percent and the broker added a second mortgage for $17,000 at an interest rate of 13 percent. The first mortgage built in nearly $6,000 in broker and third-party fees. Both loans included prepayment penalties. Then the broker applied a series of confusing payment schedules so that his customers were not aware that both loans required balloon payments after 15 years. ACORN concludes that "after making monthly payments of nearly $950 over the next fifteen years, Mason and Josie will face a balloon payment for $93,000."

ACORN and other neighborhood groups become more effective when more of the residents in the areas they are defending become active participants. This leads to a central point in civic action. A large percentage of the causes you may decide to advance are already the mission of existing local, state, national, or international nonprofit advocacy organizations that will welcome you with open arms. Their web sites are easy to locate. There are manuals and books on organizing, advocating, and strategies that work. Why reinvent the wheel when your engagement can make existing ones move faster and better?

Sometimes, there are no precursors. The massacre of September 11, 2001, was without precedent and the grief-stricken families of the fallen had to start from scratch to secure an independent investigation. While President Bush focused on the television airwaves toward Afghanistan, the families began organizing to discover what went on in our government that failed to prevent the attacks on that fateful day. Washington officialdom was initially not interested. The White House was cool to a proposed independent investigative commission. A small number of families, led by four widows, became increasingly persistent and the mass media conveyed their determination. The politicians always have trouble saying NO to the bereaved, which is one reason they do not like to have them testify in Congress. The bereaved speak from their hearts and minds; their only proxies are their conscience and their quest for truth.

For months they knocked on congressional doors, took their case to officials in the executive branch, located outside allies and refused to take NO for an answer. They cited commissions created to investigate previous calamities in American history. Finally, President Bush relented and appointed five Republican and five Democratic members to the National Commission on Terrorist Attacks upon the United States. The Commission will make its final report at the end of July 2004, after a series of highly publicized public hearings and private sessions in search of the facts and the most effective recommendations. In the audience, carefully monitoring the proceedings, were the families of 9/11, secure in their belief that had they not stood for justice, there would have been no such commission. Our country owes them an immeasurable debt of gratitude.

Now, it is time to hear from the families of other lost sons and daughters, the families of the maimed—those without legs or arms, the blind and seriously ill, who fill the wards of Walter Reed Army Hospital and other military hospitals. Some of these bereaved Americans hold George W. Bush responsible for an illegal, unnecessary war in Iraq based on fabrications and deceptions. Who can forget seeing the weeping father from Baltimore wailing, "President Bush, you took my only son." A war unlike other wars, launched against the public opposition of retired generals and admirals, former intelligence and diplomatic officials, now free to speak out. A war against the private advice of many inside the CIA, the U.S. Army and the State Department, below the level of Bush's compliant political appointees.

The "glory" of war always precedes its reality. And a war intended to be a political distraction from problems at home, a political chilling of the president's opposition, and a source for oil and gas resources, given to the president's corporate contributors, is particularly rancid and reckless. Such actions are impeachable. Howard Zinn, who was an honorably discharged bombardier in World War II, began thinking about how little is devoted to preventing war and how much blood and treasure are devoted to fighting it on the backs of the GIs who are only ordered but never asked.

Zinn, a historian who taught for many years at Boston University, has chronicled "the betrayal of the very ones sent to kill and die in wars." This year he tells the story of twenty-four-year-old Jeremy Feldbusch, a sergeant in the Army Rangers, who was blinded when a shell exploded 100 feet away near a dam along the Euphrates River in Iraq. His hometown of Blairsville, Pennsylvania, an old coal mining town of 3, 600, gave him a parade. His father, sitting by his bed, said: "Maybe God thought you had seen enough killing." Ruth Aitken lost her son, an Army captain in Iraq a few days after the invasion. Before he disembarked, she called it a war for oil. "He was doing his job," his mother said, "but it makes me mad that this whole war was sold to the

American public and to the soldiers as something it wasn't." Cowboy Bush's "Bring 'em on" bravado in July 2003, from the comforts of the Oval Office, infuriated many of these families. One mother of a soldier in Iraq told a television reporter "Bring 'em on? Expose more of our soldiers? My son may be next."

With one of the largest rotations of troops to and from Iraq underway, there will be many eyewitness accounts conveyed to millions of Americans in millions of conversations. Many of them will no longer be dazzled by the political abuse of patriotic symbols, nor will they respect exhortations about fighting for freedom, democracy, and security in a faraway tortured land that we now know possessed no imminent threat to the United States or its allies. What they may not appreciate at first is that they possess the most powerful assets to end a quagmire that breeds more terrorists and hatred throughout the impoverished Islamic world. Those assets are their sacrifice and their credibility, having been in the sands and streets and alleys of Iraq. The chicken hawks in and around the White House, who have been proven wrong by their own weapons inspectors, emissaries, and "embedded" reporters, may have the formal power. The soldiers and their families have the moral power. Once aroused, this moral power can overwhelm the political manufacturers of this war and the exploitative corporations that feed avariciously on lucrative wartime contracts.

The soldiers and their families can rescue our nation, its young men and women, and its resources that could be applied here at home. They need only to heed the call of their own authentic patriotism and organize, organize, organize. It could come quickly because they will have no problem securing the media's rapt attention. It cannot come quickly enough, however, for the rounds of casualties, horror, pain, irreversible anguish for both the American and Iraqi peoples are mounting. It cannot come quickly enough to stop the policy boomerangs or, in the CIA word used by Chalmers Johnson, "blowbacks" against the security and other best interests of our country. Already, in spite of contrary pressures, there are solidarities forming among the parents who lost their children. They are thinking about ways to exercise their freedom to speak their minds and to stand for their country, so grievously betrayed by the arrogance of political rulers in the White House whom a majority of American voters rejected at the polls.

These families, once they take the lead, will be supported by tens of millions of Americans from all backgrounds and counseled by many retired military and diplomatic officials whose dire predictions and warnings before the invasion of Iraq are coming true with appalling consequences. They feared a trap was facing our government in Iraq and a multiple trap of fearsome proportions it has become. Chicken hawks Bush and Cheney sent American soldiers to Iraq, often without key protective equipment and adequate supplies of drinking water. All the while the two bosses were going from one fat-cat multimillion dollar fund raiser to another, selling out our country's political institutions. In the meantime, our soldiers are stuck in a whirlwind of violence, disease, and deprivation in Iraq, with low morale and no exit strategy. A reporter said to a soldier, "What would you ask of your president?" The soldier replied, "I would ask for his resignation."

It takes some doing to turn a world that was demonstrating support for America after 9/11 into a world that is aghast and hostile to the messianic unilateral militarism of George W. Bush and his chronically prevaricating vice president, Dick Cheney—a man who repeatedly expounds on television what is not the case. He does this so often that he is becoming an object of ridicule inside the Beltway. As one civil servant said, "He makes even Republican eyes roll."

The present Bush regime refuses to listen to knowledgeable and experienced people who fought in wars and who believe its current policies are endangering the United States and undermining the struggle against stateless terrorism everywhere. We must ask Mr. Bush, "isn't it time for you to learn what these patriotic Americans and the families of the fallen think by meeting with them? You've dodged them long enough, and since you have been wrong and they have been right, you should adopt some of that humility you promised voters in the campaign of 2000."

George W. Bush ran during the 2000 campaign as the "responsibility" candidate. He said again and again before large audiences that individuals should be held responsible for their public policy actions. His counterterrorism advisor in the White House, Richard Clarke, resigned and later appeared on *60 Minutes* in March 2004, stating that the Bush administration repeatedly gave the impression that Saddam Hussein was involved in the attacks of September 11. Clarke, a highly regarded long-time civil servant under four presidents, uttered these words: "The White House carefully manipulated public opinion, never quite lied, but gave the very strong impression that Iraq did it. They know better. We told them. The CIA told them. The FBI told them. They did know better. And the tragedy here is that Americans went to their death in Iraq thinking they were avenging September 11, when Iraq had nothing to do with September 11. I think for a commander-in-chief and a vice president to allow that to happen is unconscionable." Clarke was speaking for thousands of knowledgeable civil servants and military personnel in the Bush administration who can not speak out.

In his book *Against All Enemies,* Clarke wrote: "Far from addressing the popular appeal of the enemy that attacked us, Bush handed that enemy precisely what it wanted and needed, proof that America was at war with Islam, that we were the new crusaders come to occupy Muslim land."

"Nothing America could have done would have provided al Qaeda and its new generation of cloned groups a better recruitment device than our unprovoked invasion of an oil-rich Arab country. Nothing else could have so well negated all our other positive acts and so closed Muslim eyes and ears to our subsequent calls for reform in their region. It was as if Osama bin Laden, hidden in some high mountain redoubt, were engaging in long-range mind control of George Bush, chanting, 'Invade Iraq, you must invade Iraq.'" So wrote Richard Clarke.

Before the National Commission on the September 11 attack, Clarke testified that "By invading Iraq, the president of the United States has greatly undermined the war on terrorism." Coming from an acknowledged hawk, his words elicited a moment of silence from the panel.

Perhaps it is time for candidate John Kerry to repeat the question that Naval Captain John Kerry put to the Senate Committee in April 1971 when he returned from combat duty in Vietnam: "How do you ask a man to be the last man to die for a mistake?"

The horrors of wars have prompted some of our most celebrated generals to construct broader frames of reference after retirement. Consider the newly elected President Dwight D. Eisenhower's famous "cross of iron" address in April 1953 to the American Society of Newspaper Editors. The context for his remarks was the eight years of tension with the nuclear-armed Soviet Union and its policy of dominating its neighbors. Eisenhower was searching for a peaceful world beyond what he called "the worst to be feared and the best to be expected." He portrayed the confines of the present world situation this way: "The worst is atomic war. The best would be this: a life of perpetual fear and tension; a burden of arms draining the wealth and the labor of all peoples; a wasting of strength that defies the American system or the Soviet system or any system to achieve true abundance and happiness for the peoples of this earth." Then, he provided a contrast which is rarely drawn by our political leaders today, much less the voracious military weapons corporations for which no military budget is ever large enough. Eisenhower's understanding of consequences invites careful attention to his prescient statement a half century ago:

Every gun that is made, every warship launched, every rocket fired signifies, in the final sense, a theft from those who hunger and are not fed, those who are cold and are not clothed. This world in arms is not spending money alone. It is spending the sweat of its laborers, the genius of its scientists, the hopes of its children. The cost of one modern heavy bomber is this: a modern brick school in more than 30 cities. It is two electric power plants, each serving a town of 60,000 population. It is two fine, fully equipped hospitals. It is some 50 miles of concrete highway. We pay for a single fighter with a half million bushels of wheat. We pay for a single destroyer with new homes that could have housed more than 8,000 people. This, I repeat is the best way of life to be found on the road the world has been taking. Under the cloud of threatening war, it is humanity hanging from a cross of iron. Is there no other way the world may live?

It behooves us to listen more to the post-World War II assessments of some of our leading generals, such as George C. Marshall who advanced the uplifting of living standards in Europe to forestall another monstrous dictatorship. Or Douglas MacArthur, who in 1957 warned Americans about the exaggerations of threats by the U.S. government and its defense industries in order to increase military budgets.

Generals, after they have engaged in bloody battles, sometimes acquire a wisdom not within the reach of chicken hawks who let others fight the wars they supported. Remember Vietnam. What would Eisenhower say today about the massive number of world-destroying weapons in our government stockpile, enough to blow up the planet three hundred times and make the rubble bounce? What would he say about the world's $3 billion a day on military budgets, nearly half by the United States alone, while 50,000 infants and small children die each day in the world from entirely preventable or easily curable diseases?

Unlike revolution, the relentless erosion of peoples' standards of living and of fairness does not proceed with sirens or clarion calls.

The very nature of an eroding democratic culture is its insidiousness, its exclusion from the visible indicators of the governing and oligarchic rulers. It comes like Carl Sandburg's fog "on little cat feet":

I'd like to remind George W. Bush about Gandhi's "seven deadly social sins:"

- Politics without principle
- Wealth without work
- Commerce without morality
- Pleasure without conscience
- Education without character
- Science without humanity
- Worship without sacrifice

I would add two more:

- Belief without thought
- Respect without self-respect

"We are ready," Eisenhower concluded, "to dedicate our strength to serving the needs, rather than the fears, of the world."

It is time to define patriotism as a stand for justice, recalling the ringing final words of the pledge of allegiance: "with liberty and justice for all."

Appendix

THE CONSCIOUS VOTER

Most politicians use the mass media to obfuscate. Let's face it. Voters who don't do their homework, who don't study records of the politicians, and who can't separate the words from the deeds will easily fall into traps laid by wily politicians.

In the year 2002, Connecticut Governor John Rowland was running for re-election against his Democratic opponent, William Curry. Again and again, the outspent Curry informed the media and the voters about the corruption inside and around the governor's office. At the time, the governor's close associates and ex-associates were under investigation by the U.S. attorney. But to the public, Rowland was all smiles, flooding the television stations with self-serving, manipulative images and slogans. He won handily in November. Within weeks, the U.S. attorney's investigation intensified as they probed the charges Curry had raised. Rowland's approval rating dropped to record lows, and impeachment initiatives are now underway with many demands for his resignation. Curry has gained favor in the public eye, but the election is long past. Enough voters had been flattered, fooled, and flummoxed to cost him the race.

Tom Frank, a Kansas author, recently wrote: "The poorest county in America isn't in Appalachia or the Deep South. It is on the Great Plains, a region of struggling ranchers and dying farm towns, and in the election of 2000, George W. Bush carried it by a majority of greater than 75 percent." Inattentive voters are vulnerable to voting against their own interests. They are vulnerable to voting for politicians who support big business and ignore their interests as farmers, workers, consumers, patients, and small taxpayers.

Big Business will not spur change in a political system that gives them every advantage. Change must come from the voters, and here's how friends can avoid the three Fs:

- **A liberation ritual.** Rid yourself of all preconceived, hereditary, ideological, and political straitjackets. Replace with two general yardsticks for candidates for elective office: Are they playing fair and are they doing right?
- **Stay open-minded.** Avoid jumping to conclusions about a candidate based solely on their stance on your one or two primary issues. Don't disregard where they fall on twenty-five other realities that affect you and your family very deeply and seriously. If you judge them broadly rather than narrowly, you increase your influence by increasing your demands and expectation levels for their performance. There are numerous evaluations of their votes (see Citizen.org or Commoncause.org for progressive perspectives) and positions to get you behind sly slogans like "Clear Skies Initiative" or "Leave No Child Behind."
- **Know where you stand.** A handy way to contrast your views with those of the incumbents and challengers is to make your own checklist of twenty issues, explain where you stand and then send your list to the candidates. See how their list—or their actual record—matches up to your own.
- **Ask the tough questions.** These are the questions that politicians like to avoid. They include whether they are willing to debate their opponents and how often, why they avoid talking about and doing something about corporate power and its expanding

controls over people's lives, or how they plan to shift power from these global corporate supremacists to the people. Ask them to speak of solutions to the major problems confronting our country. Politicians often avoid defining solutions that upset their commercial financiers (this includes a range of issues, such as energy efficiency, lower drug prices, reducing sprawl, safer food, and clean elections). Ask members of Congress to explain why they keep giving themselves annual salary increases and generous benefits, and yet turn cold at doing the same for the minimum wage, health insurance, or pension protections.

All in all, it takes a little work and some time to become a supervoter, impervious to manipulation by politicians who intend to flatter, fool, and flummox. But I dare suggest that this education can also be fun, that the pursuit of justice can offer great benefits to the pursuit of happiness, and that such civic engagement will help Americans today become better ancestors for tomorrow's descendants.

BIBLIOGRAPHY

Alinsky, Saul D. *Rules for Radicals: A Practical Primer for Realistic Radicals.* New York: Random House, 1971.

Alterman, Eric and Mark J. Green. *The Book on Bush: How George W. (Mis)leads America.* New York: Viking, 2004.

Amar, Akhil R. and Allan Hirsh. *For the People: What the Constitution Really Says About Your Rights.* New York: Free Press, 1998.

Bakan, Joel. *The Corporation: The Pathological Pursuit of Profit and Power.* New York: Free Press, 2004.

Baker, Dean and Mark Weisbrot. *Social Security: The Phony Crisis.* Chicago: University of Chicago Press, 1999.

Berman, Daniel M. and John T. O'Connor. *Who Owns the Sun?: People, Politics, and the Struggle for a Solar Economy.* White River Junction, VT: Chelsea Green, 1996.

Birnbaum, Norman. *The Radical Renewal: The Politics and Ideas in Modern America.* New York: Pantheon, 1998.

Black, Charles L. Jr. *A New Birth of Freedom: Human Rights, Named and Unnamed.* New York: Grosset/Putnam, 1997.

Blum, William. *Killing Hope: U.S. Military and CIA Interventions Since World War II.* Monroe, ME: Common Courage, 1995.

Bogus, Carl T. *Why Lawsuits Are Good for America: Disciplined Democracy, Big Business, and the Common Law.* New York: New York University Press, 2001.

Bollier, David and Joan Claybrook. *Freedom from Harm: The Civilizing Influence of Health, Safety and Environmental Regulation.* Washington, D.C.: Public Citizen Democracy Project, 1986.

Bonifaz, John C. *Warrior-King: The Case for Impeaching George W. Bush.* New York: Nation Books, 2004.

Brown, Lester. *State of the World 2001*. New York: Worldwatch Institute Books/ Norton, 2001. Also published in thirty other languages.

Bryce, Robert. *Pipe Dreams: Greed, Ego and the Death of Enron*. New York: Public Affairs, 2002.

Bullard, Robert D. *Unequal Protection: Environmental Justice and Communities of Color*. San Francisco: Sierra Club Books, 1994.

Burnham, David. *Above the Law: Secret Deals, Political Fixes and Other Misadventures of the U.S. Department of Justice*. New York: Scribner, 1996.

Cahn, Edgar S. *No More Throw-Away People: The Co-Production Imperative*. Warner, NH: Essential Books, 2000.

Carnoy, Martin and Derek Shearer. *Economic Democracy: The Challenge of the 1980s*. Armonk, NY: M.E. Sharpe, 1980.

Caro, Robert A. *The Path to Power (The Years of Lyndon Johnson, Volume 1)*. New York: Knopf, 1982.

Chang, Nancy. *Silencing Political Dissent: How Post-September 11 Anti-Terrorism Measures Threaten Our Civil Liberties*. New York: Seven Stories Press, 2002.

Chomsky, Noam. *Necessary Illusions: Thought Control in Democratic Societies*. Cambridge, MA: Southend Press, 1989

Chomsky, Noam. *Hegemony or Survival: America's Quest for Global Dominance*. New York: Metropolitan Books, 2003.

Clarke, Richard A. *Against All Enemies: Inside America's War on Terror*. New York: Free Press, 2004.

Commoner, Barry. *Making Peace with the Planet*. New York: Pantheon, 1990.

Corn, David. *The Lies of George W. Bush: Mastering the Politics of Deception*. New York: Crown, 2003.

Court, Jamie. *Corporateering: How Corporate Power Steals Your Personal Freedom . . . And What You Can Do About It*. New York: Putnam, 2003.

Derber, Charles. *Corporation Nation: How Corporations Are Taking over Our Lives and What We Can Do About It*. New York: Griffin, 2000.

Derber, Charles. *People Before Profit: The New Globalization in an Age of Terror, Big Money, and Economic Crisis*. New York: St. Martin's, 2002.

Derickson, Alan. *Black Lung: Anatomy of a Public Health Disaster.* Ithaca, NY: Cornell University Press, 1998.

Doyle, Jack. *Taken for a Ride: Detroit's Big Three and the Politics of Pollution.* New York: Four Walls Eight Windows, 2000.

Drew, Elizabeth. *The Corruption of American Politics: What Went Wrong and Why.* New York: Overlook Press, 2000.

Drutman, Lee and Charlie Cray. *The People's Business Controlling Corporations and Restoring Democracy.* San Francisco: Berrett-Koehler, 1996.

Durnil, Gordon K. *The Making of a Conservative Environmentalist.* Bloomington, IN: Indiana University Press, (1995)

Edelman, Peter. *Searching for America's Heart: RFK and the Renewal of Hope.* New York: Houghton Mifflin, 2001.

Ehrenreich, Barbara. *Nickel and Dimed: On (Not) Getting By in America.* New York: Metropolitan Books, 2001.

Estes, Ralph W. *Tyranny of the Bottom Line: Why Corporations Make Good People Do Bad Things.* San Francisco: Berrett-Koehler, 1996.

Farah, George. *No Debate: How the Two Major Parties Secretly Ruin the Presidential Debates.* New York: Seven Stories Press, 2004.

Farnsworth, Stephen J. and S. Robert Lichter. *The Nightly News Nightmare: Network Television's Coverage of U.S. Presidential Elections, 1988–2000.* Lanham, MD: Rowman & Littlefield, 2002.

Finkelstein, Norman G. *Image and Reality of the Israel-Palestine Conflict.* New York: Verso, 2001.

Frank, Thomas. *One Market Under God.* New York: Doubleday, 2000.

Friere, Paulo. *Pedagogy of the Oppressed.* New York: Penguin, 1970.

Gardner, John W. *On Leadership.* New York: Free Press, 1993.

Garfinkel, Simson and Deborah Russell. *Database Nation: The Death of Privacy in the 21st Century.* O'Reilly & Associates, 2001.

Garland, Anne White. *Woman Activists: Challenging the Abuse of Power.* New York: City University of New York Press, 1988.

Gates, Jr., Henry Louis. *America Behind the Color Line: Dialogues with African Americans.* New York: Warner Books, 2004.

Gates, Jeff. *Democracy at Risk: Rescuing Main Street from Wall Street.* New York: Perseus Press, 2000.

Geoghegan, Thomas. *Which Side Are You On? Trying to Be for Labor When It's Flat on Its Back.* New York: Plume, 1992

Goodwyn, Lawrence. *The Populist Moment: A Short History of Agrarian Revolt in America,* New York: Oxford University Press, 1978.

Green, Mark, Michael Calabrese, et al. Introduction by Ralph Nader. *Who Runs Congress?* New York: Viking Press, 1979.

Green, Mark and Robert Massie. *The Big Business Reader: Essays on Corporate America.* Cleveland, OH: Pilgram Press, 1983.

Greider, Katharine. *The Big Fix: How the Pharmaceutical Industry Rips off American Consumers.* New York: Public Affairs, 2003.

Greider, William. *The Soul of Capitalism: Opening Paths to a Moral Economy.* New York: Simon & Schuster, 2003.

Greider, William. *Who Will Tell the People: The Betrayal of American Democracy.* New York: Touchstone, 1993.

Harrington, Michael. *The Other America: Poverty in the United States.* New York: Macmillan, 1997.

Hartung, William D. *How Much Are You Making on the War, Daddy? A Quick and Dirty Guide to War Profiteering in the Bush Administration.* New York: Nation Books, 2004.

Hawken, Paul, Amory Lovins, and Hunter L. Lovins. *Natural Capitalism: Creating the Next Industrial Revolution.* Boston: Back Bay Books, 2000.

Helvarg, David. *The War Against the Greens: The "Wise Use" Movement, the New Right and Anti-Environmental Violence.* San Francisco: Sierra Club Books, 1997.

Helvarg, David. *Blue Frontier: Saving America's Living Seas.* New York: W. H. Freeman, 2001.

Hentoff, Nat. *The War on the Bill of Rights and the Gathering Resistance.* New York: Seven Stories Press, 2003.

Herman, Edward. *Corporate Control, Corporate Power.* Cambridge, England: Cambridge University Press, 1981.

Hertsgaard, Mark. *Earth Odyssey: Around the World in Search of Our Environmental Future.* New York: Broadway, 1999.

Hertz, Noreena. *The Silent Takeover: Global Capitalism and the Death of Democracy.* New York: Free Press, 2001.

Heymann, Philip B. *Terrorism, Freedom, and Security: Winning Without War.* Cambridge, MA: MIT Press, 2003.

Hightower, Jim. *Thieves in High Places: They've Stolen Our Country and It's Time to Take It Back.* New York: Viking, 2003.

Hillsman, Bill. *Run the Other Way: Fixing the Two-Party System, One Campaign at a Time.* New York: Free Press, 2004.

Hochschild, Arlie Russell. *The Commercialization of Intimate Life: Notes from Home and Work.* Berkeley: University of California Press, 2003.

Hock, Dee. *The Chaordic Organization.* San Francisco: Berrett-Koehler, 2000.

Huffington, Arianna. *Pigs at the Trough: How Corporate Greed and Political Corruption Are Undermining America.* New York: Crown, 2003.

Isaac, Katherine. *Civics for Democracy: A Journey for Teachers and Students.* Warner, NH: Essential Books, 1992.

Ivins, Molly and Lou Dubose. *Bushwhacked: Life in George W. Bush's America.* New York: Random House, 2003.

Jacobson, Michael F. *Marketing Madness: A Survival Guide for a Consumer Society.* Boulder, CO: Westview Press, 1995.

Johnson, Chalmers. *The Sorrows of Empire: Militarism, Secrecy and the End of the Republic.* New York: Metropolitan Books, 2004.

Johnston, David Cay. *Perfectly Legal: The Covert Campaign to Rig Our Tax System to Benefit the Super Rich—and Cheat Everybody Else.* New York: Portfolio, 2003.

Kim, Jim, et al. *Dying for Growth: Global Inequality and the Health of the Poor.* Monroe, ME: Common Courage Press, 2000.

King, Martin Luther, Jr. *Why We Can't Wait.* New York: Harper & Row, 1963.

Klare, Michael T. *Resource Wars: The New Landscape of Global Conflict.* New York: Metropolitan Books, 2001.

Klein, Naomi. *No Logo: Taking Aim at the Brand Bullies.* New York: Picador, 2000.

Korten, David C. *When Corporations Rule the World.* Bloomfield, CT: Kumarian Press, 2001.

Kotz, Mary L. and Nick Koltz. *A Passion for Equality.* New York: W.W. Norton, 1977.

Kozlowski, Mark. *The Myth of the Imperial Judiciary: Why the Right Is Wrong About the Courts.* New York: New York University Press, 2003.

Kwitny, Jonathan. *The Crimes of Patriots.* New York: Simon & Schuster, 1988.

Laduke, Winona. *All Our Relations*. Cambridge, MA: South End Press, 1999.

Lappe, Frances Moore. *World Hunger: Twelve Myths*. New York: Grove Atlantic, 1986.

Lekachman, Robert. *Greed Is Not Enough*. New York: Pantheon, 1982.

Lessig, Lawrence. *The Future of Ideas: The Fate of the Commons in a Connected World*. New York: Vintage, 2002.

Lessig, Lawrence. *Free Culture: How Big Media Uses Technology and the Law to Lock Down Culture and Control Creativity*. New York: Penguin Press, 2004.

Levitt, Arthur. *Take on the Street: What Wall Street and Corporate America Don't Want You to Know*. New York: Pantheon Books, 2002.

Levy, Jacques E. *Cesar Chavez: Autobiography of La Causa*. New York: W.W. Norton, 1975.

Lewis, Charles. *The Buying of the Congress: How Special Interests Have Stolen Your Right to Life, Liberty, and the Pursuit of Happiness*. New York: Avon Books, 1998.

Lewis, Charles. *The Buying of the President 2004: Who's Really Bankrolling Bush and His Democratic Challengers—and What They Expect in Return*. New York: Perennial, 2004.

Lindblom, Charles. *Politics and Markets: The World's Political-Economic System*. New York: Basic Books, 1980.

Loeb, Paul R. *Soul of a Citizen: Living With Conviction in a Cynical Time*. New York: St. Martin's, 1999.

Lynd, Alice and Staughton Lynd. *Rank and File: Personal Histories by Working Class Organizers*. New York: Monthly Review Press, 1989.

Marable, Manning. *The Great Wells of Democracy: The Meaning of Race in American Life*. New York: Basic Books, 2002.

McChesney, Robert. *Rich Media, Poor Democracy: Communication Politics in Dubious Times*. New York: New Press, 2000.

McChesney, Robert W. *The Problem of the Media: U.S. Communications Politics in the 21st Century*. New York: Monthly Review Press, 2004.

Mills, C. Wright. *The Power Elite*. New York: Oxford University Press, 2000.

Mintz, Morton. *Power, Inc.: Public and Private Rulers and How to Make Them Accountable*. New York: Viking, 1976.

Mishel, Lawrence, et al. *The State of Working America 2000–2001.* Ithaca, NY: Cornell University Press, 2001.

Mokhiber, Russell. *Corporate Crime and Violence: Big Business Power and the Abuse of Public Trust.* San Francisco: Sierra Club Books, 1988.

Mokhiber, Russell and Robert Weissman. *Corporate Predators: The Hunt for Mega-Profits and the Attack on Democracy.* Monroe, ME: Common Courage, 1999.

Monks, Robert A.G. *The New Global Investors: How Shareowners Can Unlock Sustainable Prosperity Worldwide.* Mankato, MN: Capstone, 2001.

Nace, Ted. *Gangs of America: The Rise of Corporate Power and the Disabling of Democracy.* San Francisco: Berrett-Koehler, 2003.

Nader, Ralph and William Taylor. *The Big Boys.* New York: Pantheon Books, 1986.

Nader, Ralph. *The Consumer and Corporate Accountability.* New York: Harcourt, Brace, Jovanovich, 1973.

Nader, Ralph, Mark Green, and Joel Seligman. *Taming the Giant Corporation.* New York: Norton, 1976.

Nader, Ralph. *Unsafe at Any Speed,* 25th Anniversary Updated Edition. New York: Knightsbridge, 1991.

Newman, Nell and Joseph D'Agnese. *Newman's Own Organic Guide to a Good Life: Simple Measures that Benefit You and the Place You Live.* New York: Villard, 2003.

Noble, David. *America by Design: Science, Technology and the Rise of Corporate Capitalism.* New York: Oxford University Press, 1977.

Phillips, Kevin. *The Politics of the Rich and the Poor: Wealth and the American Electorate in the Reagan Administration.* New York: Random House, 1990.

Phillips, Kevin. *American Dynasty: Aristocracy, Fortune and the Politics of Deceit in the House of Bush.* New York: Viking, 2004.

Phillips, Peter. *Censored 2004: 25 Years of Censored News and the Top Censored Stories of the Year.* New York: Seven Stories Press, 2004.

Piven, Frances and Richard A. Cloward. *Poor People's Movements: Why They Succeed, How They Fail.* New York: Random House, 1977.

Pollin, Robert. *Contours of Descent: U.S. Economic Fractures and the Landscape of Global Austerity.* New York: Verso, 2003.

Pollin, Robert. *The Living Wage: Building a Fair Economy.* New York: New Press, 2000.

Power, Samantha. *A Problem from Hell: America and the Age of Genocide.* New York: HarperCollins, 2003.

Rampton, Sheldon. Stauber, John. *Mad Cow USA: Could the Nightmare Happen Here?* Monroe, ME: Common Courage Press, 1997.

Rampton, Sheldon and John Stauber. *Trust Us, We're Experts! How Industry Manipulates Science and Gambles with Your Future.* New York: Putnam, 2001.

Rasor, Dina. *The Pentagon Underground.* New York: Times Books, 1985.

Reed, Jr., Adolph, Editor. *Without Justice for All: The New Liberalism and Our Retreat from Racial Equality.* Boulder, CO: Westview Press, 1999.

Rensenbrink, John. *Against All Odds: The Green Transformation of American Politics.* Raymond, ME: Leopold Press, 1999.

Ritz, Dean. *Defying Corporations, Defying Democracy: A Book of History and Strategy* (Program on Corporations, Law and Democracy). Muscat, Sultanate of Oman: Apex Press, 2001.

Robinson, Randall N. *The Debt: What America Owes to Blacks.* New York: Plume, 2001.

Rosoff, Stephen M., Robert Tillman, and Henry Pontell. *Profit Without Honor: White Collar Crime and the Looting of America.* New York: Prentice Hall, 1997.

Rustad, Michael L. and Thomas H. Koenig. *In Defense of Tort Law.* New York: New York University Press, 2001.

Schlosser, Eric. *Fast Food Nation.* New York: Houghton Mifflin, 2001.

Schmidt, David. *Citizen Lawmakers: The Ballot Initiative Resolution.* Philadelphia, PA: Temple University Press, 1989.

Schumacher, E.F. *Small Is Beautiful: Economics As If People Mattered.* New York: HarperCollins, 1991.

Shaw, Randy. *Reclaiming America: Nike, Clean Air and the New National Activism.* Berkeley: University of California Press, 1999.

Shipler, David K. *The Working Poor: Invisible in America.* New York: Knopf, 2004.

Singer, Peter W. *Corporate Warriors: The Rise of the Privatized Military Industry.* Ithaca, NY: Cornell University Press, 2003.

Soros, George. *The Crisis of Global Capitalism: Open Society Endangered.* New York: Public Affairs, 1998.

Sparrow, Malcolm K. *License to Steal: How Fraud Bleeds America's Health Care System.* Boulder, CO: Westview Press, 2000.

Stauber, John and Sheldon Rampton. *Toxic Sludge Is Good for You!: Lies, Damn Lies and the Public Relations Industry.* Monroe, ME: Common Courage Press, 1995.

Stiglitz, Joseph. *Globalization and Its Discontents.* New York: W. W. Norton, 2002.

Teitel, Martin. *Genetically Engineered Food: Changing the Nature of Nature.* Rochester, VT: Inner Traditions, 2001.

Terkel, Studs. *Hard Times: An Oral History of the Great Depression.* New York: Pantheon, 1970.

Thornton, Joe. *Pandora's Poison: Chlorine, Health and a New Environmental Strategy.* Cambridge, MA: MIT Press, 2001.

Wachsman, Harvey F. and Steven Alschuler. *Lethal Medicine: The Epidemic of Medical Malpractice in America.* New York: Henry Holt, 1993.

Wallach, Lori. *Whose Trade Organization?: Corporate Globalization and the Erosion of Democracy.* New York: Public Citizen, 1999.

Wasserman, Harvey. *The Last Energy War: The Battle over Utility Deregulation.* Monroe, ME: Common Courage Press, 1999.

West, Cornel. *Race Matters.* New York: Vintage Books, 1994.

Whittelsey, Frances Cerra and Marcia Carroll. *Women Pay More: And How to Stop It.* New York: The New Press, 1993.

Wolfe, Sidney M. *Worst Pills, Best Pills: A Consumer's Guide to Avoiding Drug-Induced Death or Illness.* New York: Pocket Books, 1999.

Wolff, Edward and Richard C. Leone. *Top Heavy: The Increasing Inequality of Wealth in America and What Can Be Done About It.* New York: New Press, 1996.

Woodward, Bob. *Bush at War.* New York: Simon & Schuster, 2002.

Woolhandler, Steffie, Ida Hellander, and David Himmelstein, M.D. *Bleeding the Patient: The Consequences of Corporate Healthcare.* Monroe, ME: Common Courage Press, 2001.

Wylie, Jeanie. *Poletown: Community Betrayed.* Champaign, IL: University of Illinois Press, 1989.

Zinn, Howard. *A People's History of the United States.* New York: HarperCollins, 1995.

A variety of worthwhile information can be found on the following web site:

www.citizen.org
www.citizenworks.org
www.csrl.org
www.cptech.org
www.commercialalert.org
www.essential.org
www.opendebates.org
www.nader.org
www.multinationalmonitor.org

Recommended magazines and other publications:

The Amicus Journal
Boston Review
Consumer Reports
Harper's Magazine
In These Times
Mother Jones
Multinational Monitor
The Nation
The Progressive
Rachel's Environmental & Health News
The Washington Monthly
The Workbook

The following two publications regularly have numerous feature articles on corporate abuses:

Business Week
Wall Street Journal

INDEX